THE POLITICS OF PROTECTION

*Lord Derby and
the Protectionist Party
1841–1852*

ROBERT STEWART

CAMBRIDGE
At the University Press
1971

Published by the Syndics of the Cambridge University Press
Bentley House, 200 Euston Road, London NW1 2DB
American Branch: 32 East 57th Street, New York, N.Y.10022

Library of Congress Catalogue Card Number: 77–152628

ISBN: 0 521 08109 2

Printed in Great Britain by
W & J Mackay & Co Ltd, Chatham, Kent

CONTENTS

ACKNOWLEDGEMENTS

IN THE MAKING of this book I have received help from many people. For two years the Canada Council provided me with money while I was working on the thesis out of which this book has grown. The officials of the British Museum and the Bodleian library carried out their duties with unfailing speed, accuracy, and courtesy. I should like especially to thank the staff of the National Trust at Hughenden for putting up with my company and for making me many cups of tea. Thanks are due also to the Nottingham University library, the Institute of Historical Research, the Public Record Office, the Surrey County Record Office and to the National Portrait Gallery for permission to reproduce the portraits of Lord George Bentinck and the 14th earl of Derby.

I cannot here adequately express my gratitude to Robert Blake for his unobtrusive assistance and kind encouragement as the supervisor of the thesis while I was at Christ Church. I am glad of the opportunity to thank Michael Brock and John Prest, examiners of the thesis, for their notes and comments. For their careful reading of the manuscript of this book and their wise suggestions (some of which I have wilfully ignored), I am indebted to Hilda Neatby and James Conacher. To Mr Conacher's splendid seminar at the University of Toronto I owe my special interest in Victorian England, and I am deeply appreciative of his unselfish interest in my work since then.

Finally, to my mother and father I owe, among so many other things, my love of English words and sentences, and to them this book is lovingly dedicated.

PREFACE

IN A TALK on BBC radio in 1964 the historian, W.G. Hoskins, remarked that most English historians are snobs who write about 'top people'. This book is about very top people, the Anglican landed gentry who, in the nineteenth century, fought a long, losing battle to preserve their traditional social and political pre-eminence in England. That pre-eminence owed much to the privileges which landed parliaments had for two centuries and more granted to the Anglican church and the wheat-growing gentry. Between 1815 and 1846 those privileges were slowly whittled away, above all by the Catholic Emancipation Act of 1829, the Reform Act of 1832, and the repeal of the Corn Laws in 1846. That religious exclusiveness and landed wealth ceased to provide a broad enough basis for political power the failure of the Protectionist party in the years after 1846 clearly demonstrates. At the same time, the strength of the Protectionist party is a reminder that Victorian politics changed very slowly. The age may have been one of 'progress' or 'improvement'; but many Victorians used the word 'progress' only in the neutral sense of 'change'. Underneath the waves of mid-Victorian optimism ran a deep current of fear and despair, emotions which are only in rare circumstances conducive to lasting political success and which undermined the growth of the Conservative party in the mid-nineteenth century. This book is the study of a political tradition in its death throes. History need not always be a success story.

There is another reason why one more study of top people may be offered to the public. Despite the fact that Lord Derby was the leader of the Conservative party for twenty-two years, little is known about him, partly because his papers were for so long inaccessible. The Derby papers are a very large and very valuable collection of documents for the history of Victorian politics. Apart from Robert Blake, who used them for his recent biography of Disraeli, I believe that I am the first person to use any part of

vii

them systematically. They have given me many hours of enjoyment. Whether they have yielded profit in my hands is a question for others to answer.

ROBERT STEWART

Fulham
April 1971

1

HEADS AND TAILS

IN THE LONG WAR which was fought on many fronts against the governing elite in Great Britain in the nineteenth century, no campaign was more bitterly drawn out than the one against the Corn Laws. And on the political front no battle was more important than that which ended in victory for the free traders in 1846. No spectacle can be more demoralising to an army than the defection of its leaders to the enemy camp. Few legal systems permit a lenient attitude towards treason. In 1846 Peel was unable to persuade the majority of his rank-and-file followers that in repealing the Corn Laws he was not deserting them. They found him guilty and the result was a split in the Conservative party of unparalleled proportions. Forty years later the other great question of nineteenth-century British politics, Ireland, ruined Gladstone's great Liberal party. In 1886 the majority of the Liberal party stood by Gladstone and Irish Home Rule. In 1846 more than two-thirds of the Conservative party refused to follow Peel into free trade. In other ways the two episodes were markedly similar. Each split was destined to remain permanent and was therefore the beginning of a substantial re-alignment of party loyalties. And in each instance, although the dispute over a single issue was the occasion of the rupture, the rot had set in some years before.[1] Certainly this is true of the Conservative party in the years before 1846. The agricultural backbenchers' aversion to free trade may, on its own, be a sufficient explanation of the size of the Tory disaffection in 1846. It is clear, however, that widespread dissatisfaction with Peel's leadership, accumulated over the previous four years, had already brought the

---

[1] There is also the interesting parallel between the roles of Disraeli and Chamberlain. Both were underrated by their leaders and both felt ill-used, Disraeli because he was not given office, and Chamberlain because he was not given the Irish secretaryship.

1

Conservative party to a precarious state when Peel announced his conversion to free trade.

The Tories in the 1840s, especially the backbenchers, bore three main grievances against Peel. They objected to the liberal direction of Peel's social, religious, and economic policies. Resentment at these was aggravated by the feeling that, in adopting a liberal policy towards Irish Catholicism and a policy of free trade in corn, Peel was subverting the constitution by falsifying the trust of those who had placed him in office in 1841. The third complaint was that Peel's transition to liberal Conservatism was carried out by tyrannical methods of leadership which left the backbenchers unconsulted and their opinions ignored.

What gave special virulence to the outraged cries of the Tories against Peel in 1846 was the feeling that they and the Conservative electors of 1841 had been betrayed. They believed that the Conservative government had taken office in 1841 pledged to maintain the Corn Laws and to resist concessions to Irish Catholicism. This view has been discredited by historians who argue that the Conservative success at the elections in 1841 derived principally from the confidence which the electorate placed in Peel's administrative ability. Specific issues are held to have counted for little. And it is further pointed out that in the Tamworth manifesto of 1835 Peel addressed himself to 'that class which is much less interested in the contentions of party than in the maintenance of order and the cause of good government',[1] and that thereafter, in his speeches, Peel laid down as Conservative principles the upholding of the just prerogatives of the Crown, the defence of the constitutional integrity of both Houses of parliament, and the maintenance of the Established Church, without making specific reference to either agricultural protection or anti-Irish prejudice.[2] This interpretation accepts the *Annual Register*'s analysis of the Conservative victory.

[1] The Tamworth manifesto is printed in Earl Stanhope and E. Cardwell (ed.), *Memoirs by the Right Honourable Sir Robert Peel* (London, 1858), ii, 58–67.

[2] See, in particular, N. Gash, *Reaction and Reconstruction in English Politics, 1832–1852* (Oxford, 1965), 131–3. Professor Gash thus questions the notion that Peel betrayed his party in 1846. For the best statement of the view that Peel himself dominated the election, see B. Kemp, 'The General Election of 1841', *History* (June 1952), 146–7.

The Conservatives...although they did oppose the ministerial propositions of a fixed duty on corn, and of a reduction of the duty on foreign
sugar...yet openly declared that these were not the grounds on which
they sought to deprive the Government of power. They maintained
that the issue which the country had to try was not whether these
propositions might or might not be beneficial, but whether the Whig
ministry did or did not, by the whole history of its past conduct, deserve
the present confidence of the people.[1]

John Croker, the Tory gossip who wrote the political articles for
the *Quarterly Review*, found the curiosity of the elections to be
that 'all turns on the name of Sir Robert Peel...every Conservative candidate professed himself in plain words to be Sir Robert
Peel's man, and on that ground was elected'.[2] Peel was, of
course, happy to endorse this view of the elections since it left
him considerable freedom to choose his policies in office. He told
his constituents after his election that the Conservatives owed
their victory to the country's disgust with the Whigs' remaining
in office after the Bedchamber Crisis of 1839 and with their
decision to dissolve, not resign, after their defeat on the no-
confidence motion in June.[3]

There can be little doubt that six years of legislative deadlock
and financial deficits under Lord Melbourne swung voters over
to Peel and the Conservatives. Nor is there any disputing Peel's
shrewd exploiting of the prevailing fear of radicalism by identifying Conservatism with the defence of the constitution in Church
and State. But as the *Annual Register* remarked of the opening
of the 1841 session of parliament, 'the hopes or apprehensions of
the public were no longer excited by the prospect of any further

---

[1] *Annual Register*, 1841, 145.

[2] Croker to Peel, 20 July 1841. C.S. Parker, *Sir Robert Peel from his Private
Papers* (London, 1899), ii, 475.

[3] R. Peel, *Speech of the Right Honourable Sir Robert Peel at Tamworth, July 28, 1841*
(London, 1841), 11. Peel called the Whigs' conduct 'an insult to the representative
principle'. He refused to take office in 1839, after Lord Melbourne had resigned,
when the Queen would not consent to remove from her Household certain ladies of
Whig connexion. See also Peel's speech of 27 August 1841, in which he stated that
the Whigs' defeat was the result of their having stayed in power 'in defiance of the
important constitutional principle which declares that any ministry which undertakes
to administer the affairs of this country must possess the confidence of the House of
Commons' (*Hansard*, 3rd Series, lix, 426).

extension of political rights; the outcry for the ballot, or an enlargement of the suffrage, had almost ceased. The established church seemed to be reposing in tranquility after the storm excited by the assaults of the dissenters'.[1] A new set of political issues had come to the fore. Having failed to achieve institutional reform, the Radical member, Molesworth, observed, 'we have fallen back on the inquiry, what can be done to improve the material condition of the people – the answer is in the application of the principles of free trade'.[2]

There, right from the outset, lurked a danger to the newly elected Conservative government. The decline of parliamentary radicalism after its setbacks at the 1837 elections had greatly diminished the relevance of the Tamworth manifesto. By 1841 the fears of the mid-thirties had been replaced by new ones: the Anti-Corn Law League and Irish nationalism were now the major sources of alarm. One of the reasons why the Whigs were judged unfit to hold office was that they were maintained there by the votes of the Irish radicals. Peel acknowledged that the Whigs' uneasy alliance with O'Connell and their attacks on the property of the Irish Church were major contributions to their defeat in 1841.[3] When, moreover, he talked of preserving the constitution, his followers naturally understood him to mean the landed constitution. Professor Gash has described the Conservative party under Peel as 'a constitutional and religious, not a social and economic party',[4] but that description gives too little weight to the fact that the constitution and religion (or Church) which the party was defending were to a great extent based on the social and economic preponderance of the landed class. The Tory protectionists believed that the Corn Laws were necessary to perpetuate that preponderance and that to undermine the agriculturalists' economic position was to endanger the constitution in Church and State.

Judged by Peel's statements (although he was a consistent defender of the Corn Laws in the House of Commons in the

[1] *Annual Register*, 1842, 1–2.

[2] Molesworth to Gladstone, 4 June 1841. Gladstone Mss, Add. Mss 44777, ff. 77–81.

[3] *Speech at Tamworth, July 28, 1841*, 10.

[4] *Reaction and Reconstruction*, 131.

1830s)[1] the free-trade issue might appear to have played an insignificant part in the 1841 elections. Even Peel, however, told his constituents that he deprecated a struggle over the Corn Laws and asked for their votes 'with this frank and explicit declaration of my opinions'.[2] Gladstone assured the farmers at Newark that they could rely on the Conservatives to give them adequate protection.[3] Lord George Bentinck, who was to be Peel's great adversary in 1846, interpreted the election results as a vindication of the Corn Laws. 'First let me congratulate you [he wrote to Lord Lincoln] *that the Country has refused to be cajoled by the latest fabrication from the Workshop of Whig Trickery and delusion.* The cry of Cheap Bread is scouted from one end of England to the other.'[4] The first week's debate in the new parliament made it clear that free trade was the most important issue in many constituencies. Lord Morpeth, the defeated Whig candidate for the West Riding, said at Leeds that the elections were being contested between a free-trade and a protectionist party.[5] When the Whig government met the new parliament in August, Lord Ripon said that the Lords must decide whether they could give their confidence to a government which was bent on the abolition of the Corn Laws.[6] Underlying the debate on the Address in both Houses was the assumption that the Whigs were now a free-trade party and that the country had rejected free trade. When Peel denied that free trade had been at stake at the elections, he did so on the ground that both parties were protectionist.[7] Even Peel's claim that it was not fear of free trade which had prompted

---

[1] See, for example, his speech of 27 August 1841. *Hansard*, 3rd Series, lix, 400–29

[2] *Annual Register*, 1842, 61–2. I do not share Miss Kemp's view that this was an equivocal statement ('The General Election of 1841', 151). At any rate, Peel's constituents were bound to take it in one way, that the Corn Laws were to be left alone.

[3] W. F. Monypenny and G. E. Buckle, *The Life of Benjamin Disraeli, Earl of Beaconsfield* (London, 1910–20), ii, 123. See also J. Morley, *The Life of William Ewart Gladstone* (London, 1903), i, 238.

[4] Bentinck to Lincoln, 6 July 1841 (draft). Portland Mss, PWH/204.

[5] W. Ferrand, 14 February 1842. *Hansard*, 3rd Series, lx, 421. Edward Baines considered free trade to have been the major issue at Leeds (E. Baines, *The Life of Edward Baines* (London, 1851), 273–6).

[6] 24 August 1841. *Hansard*, 3rd Series, lix, 46–7.

[7] 27 August 1841. *ibid.* 415–16.

towns to return Conservatives was perhaps not entirely accurate. At a joint meeting with the Agricultural Association, the Colonial Society, and a West Indian body, the General Ship-Owners Society of Liverpool pledged itself to the defence of agricultural protection, although it was 'not unaware that there are Ship-Owners who look to the extension of the carrying trade by the free introduction of Foreign Corn'.[1]

However tied the Conservative party was to the Corn Laws, it is clear that the party derived enormous benefit in the late 1830s from being the 'Anglican' party, not so much because it fought the Dissenters' attack on the Established Church as because it exploited fears of Irish Catholicism, fears which had greatly increased since the appearance of a nationalist Irish party at Westminster after the Catholic Emancipation Act of 1829.[2] When the Whigs and the Irish parliamentary party made the so-called 'Lichfield Compact' in March 1835, *The Times* took up the party cry of Protestantism against Lord Melbourne.[3] Most of the Protestant landowners in Ireland were Tory, but there was more to the anti-Irish prejudice than religious bigotry. There was the Empire at stake, and *The Times'* most violent outbursts were directed at O'Connell's campaign for the repeal of the Union. *The Times* pointed out that Anglicanism and imperial unity were inextricably linked.

Everything Protestant in Ireland is English – it rests on Great Britain, and clings to her, and constitutes the only bond of union between these islands. Everything Popish is anti-English – it rests on animosity towards Great Britain, clings to the hope of separation from her, and constitutes the only vulnerable spot in the British Empire, the sole element of weakness and of ruin.[4]

[1] *Report of the Committee of the General Ship-Owners Society for the Year 1840* (London, 1841), 10.

[2] The cardinal importance of the anti-Irish sentiment for the Conservative party is discussed by G. A. Cahill, 'Irish Catholicism and English Toryism', *Review of Politics* (January 1957), 62–76. He argues that the Irish issue was used as a wedge to be driven between the alliance of Liberalism and Dissent. For the English reaction to Irish working-class immigration, see A. Redford, *Labour Migration in England, 1800–50* (London, 1926), 141–35.

[3] The Office of *The Times*, see *The History of 'The Times'* (London, 1935), i, 356–63.

[4] *The Times*, 26 February 1836. The *Quarterly Review* for June 1841, ended an article attacking the Whig budget with these words: 'And finally, *every lover of*

Most Conservatives, instead of looking for ways of improving Anglo-Irish relations, were content simply to denounce the evils of Popery. In 1839, during the struggle over the bill to reform the Protestant-controlled Irish municipal corporations, Lord Ashley urged Peel to 'cast aside all other views and...get the Government out on a Protestant point. We shall combine the truths of religion (God be praised for it) with the feelings of the country'. The country must either resist the advance of Irish Catholic nationalism or face the 'disgraceful and perilous submission to the Progress of Popery'.[1] A Conservative pamphleteer wrote in 1841 that 'no sincere Christian can deny that, whatever differences may exist between him and Sir Robert Peel, they are trivial in comparison with the difference which exists between the supporters of a Protestant faith and the Administration of Lord Melbourne'.[2] By far the most virulent campaign against Popery was waged in the pages of the *Quarterly Review*, the intellectual organ of orthodox Conservatism. Croker's articles in 1840 and 1841 were almost exclusively given over to this question. Croker attributed all the social ills of Ireland to the Catholic faith, which had 'soured into superstition'. It was religious error, not, as the Poor Law Commissioners would have it, the system of land tenure, which caused political unrest in Ireland: 'political excitement is in Ireland religious excitement, and religion, or rather superstition, is the very atmosphere of the Irish population'.[3]

Peel and the rest of the Conservative leaders did not contribute to the outpouring of Tory anti-Catholic propaganda; but they were wise enough not to dissociate themselves from it. As a result, the split in the party between the leaders and the backbenchers was papered over.

---

his country, every heart that feels for the safety, honour, and integrity of the British Empire will exert his voice and his influence against the allies – the patrons or more truly the clients and *protégés* – of the Irish Repealers' (280).

[1] *History of 'The Times'*, i, 375.

[2] Anon., *What Have the Whigs Done?* (London, 1841), 8.

[3] 'Romanism in Ireland', *Quarterly Review* (December 1840), 120–3. In fact, clerical interference in Irish politics in the 1830s was rare (J.H. Whyte, 'The Influence of the Catholic Clergy on Elections in Nineteenth-Century Ireland', *English Historical Review* (April 1960), 241–2).

The Tory case, then, in 1841 was a nationalist one. The Tory party, intolerant and fearful of a subject ethnic and religious minority, and hostile to the arguments for an international free trade, represented the socially and politically dominant group in Great Britain: the Anglican, English, landed gentry. And the Tory victory in 1841 was a narrow-based nationalist victory. Of the 40 seats gained by the Conservatives at the elections, 29 were in the counties. Peel took office at the head of a party which represented 136 of the 159 English and Welsh county seats; and all but 5 of those were in the corn district south of the Humber. The opposition held 13 more English and Welsh borough seats than the government. In Scotland and Ireland the government was in a minority of 28.[1] The Tory *Standard* wrote that 'the people have shown that they are willing learners, tired of being led blindfold by the dogmas of political economists...They see that the policy which has made England what she is – the *insular* policy – is the only one by which the national greatness can be preserved'.[2] So long as by 'people' was meant the English county voters, that was a reasonable analysis.

From the start, then, the Tory party in the House of Commons was dangerously unbalanced, and was almost bound to hamper a government intent on serving the interests, not merely of a privileged class, but of the whole nation. Peel had learned from his experience at the Home Office in the 1820s that no government in the nineteenth century could afford to be guided solely by the opinions and prejudices of the squirearchy. Governments, in order to survive, had to adapt themselves to changing circumstances. When Peel came into power in 1841, the circumstances were ominous: a deficit of £234,000, a commercial and manufacturing depression, and the threat to civil order and

---

[1] The five southern county seats won by the Whigs were Middlesex (where Byng had been returned for fifty years), Surrey (where the Whig was a millionaire protectionist), Hampshire (the speaker's seat), the Cavendish-controlled seat in Derbyshire North, and one seat in Staffordshire South. In Scotland the Conservatives seem to have suffered from the refusal of Peel and Wellington to pledge themselves to the Duke of Argyll's bill to reform the system of lay patronage in the Scottish Church (Parker, *Peel*, ii, 467–75; The Dowager Duchess of Argyll (ed.), *George Douglas, Eighth Duke of Argyll, Autobiography and Memoirs* (London, 1906), i, 164–78).

[2] *Standard*, 3 July 1841.

political stability posed by the Anti-Corn Law League, the Chartist organisation, and the Irish repeal movement. Peel had a large majority in the House of Commons[1] and he meant to use that majority to grapple with the great difficulties ahead of him in his own way. In the House of Commons he instructed his followers in the terms on which he consented to be prime minister: 'no considerations of mere political support should induce me to hold such an office as that which I fill by a servile tenure, which would compel me to be the instrument of carrying other men's opinions into effect'.[2] That remark was, of course, as much a jeering allusion to the Whigs' dependence on the Irish as a warning to the Conservatives. Conservative leaders were wont to contrast their homogeneous party with the Whig–Radical amalgam which had supported Melbourne. Peel brushed aside talk of jealousies and differences of opinion within his party. The country, he said, could depend upon it

that that party which has paid me the compliment of taking my advice, and following my counsel, are a united and compact party, among which there does not exist the slightest difference of opinion in respect to the principles they support, and the course which they may desire to pursue.[3]

There were others who foresaw that Peel's great difficulty would be to keep his party together. 'But how are they to manage the taxes and the Corn Laws?' asked Lord John Russell. 'The blockheads of their party will make their insurrection, as Canning said was periodical.'[4]

It was widely believed that the Reform Act of 1832 had made government on Tory principles obsolete. It was this assurance which led the Whig, Lord Lyttleton, to support the motion of

---

[1] According to the tables of returns in the *Annual Register* (1841, 147) the majority was 76. On the vote on the amendment to the reply to the speech from the throne, the vote which defeated the Whig government, the Conservatives had a majority of 91.

[2] 17 September 1841. *Hansard*, 3rd Series, lix, 555.

[3] *Tamworth Election. Speech of Sir Robert Peel, June 28, 1841* (London, 1841), 4–5.

[4] Russell to Lady Holland, 27 October 1841. G. P. Gooch (ed.), *The Later Correspondence of Lord John Russell, 1840–1878* (London, 1925), i, 49.

no-confidence in Melbourne's government in 1841.[1] Another Whig, Lord Spencer, predicted that a Tory government in 1841, supported by a reformed House of Commons, would be a great improvement over Tory governments of pre-Reform days.[2] Certainly Peel's government bore a more liberal aspect than previous Tory governments. The inclusion in the cabinet of men like Sir James Graham and Lord Stanley, both renegade Whigs, seemed to foretell disappointment for 'those who think that no Government ought to stand unless it includes Sir Robert Inglis, Sir Richard Vyvyan and the Duke of Newcastle etc. etc.'[3] and who were dissatisfied with the minor posts given to the Duke of Buckingham, Lord Ellenborough, and the eccentric ultra-Tory, Sir Edward Knatchbull.[4] Stanley's liberal reputation was blurred by his savage treatment of O'Connell when he was Irish Secretary in Lord Grey's government, but he told an Irish friend in the first week of Peel's new administration that Protestant ascendancy in Ireland was 'exploded' and that 'the Catholic in Ireland, who ranges himself on the side of law and order, has an even higher claim on the Executive [for patronage] than a Protest-

---

[1] 'I believe', Lyttleton said in the Lords on 24 August 1841, 'that whatever Government is in office, the principles of liberal policy will be pursued; that this is the real, permanent result of the Reform Bill.' *Hansard*, 3rd Series, lix, 65.

[2] Spencer to Russell, 2 May 1841. S. Walpole, *The Life of Lord John Russell* (London, 1889), i, 373.

[3] Ripon to Graham, 27 July 1841. Peel Mss, Add. Mss 40446, ff. 5–8.

[4] Inglis, member for Oxford University since 1829, was the head of the Church party in the House of Commons. Newcastle and Vyvyan were venerable leaders of the ultra-agriculturalists who for two decades had been advocating the reform of the currency, that is the abandonment of cash payments, or the repeal of the malt tax to relieve the landed class. Buckingham was given the Privy Seal, Ellenborough was made President of the Board of Control, and Knatchbull became Treasurer of the Navy and Paymaster-General of the Forces. The Conservative M.P., J. W. Freshfield, wrote to Peel on 28 August 1841: 'I wish to convey to you what I feel to be a very strong feeling with the most thinking part of the public, that an Administration formed of any considerable portion of Gentlemen who have been long before the public as members of Tory Governments will soon fall into unpopularity...I scarcely need say that the Duke, Lord Aberdeen, Lord Stanley, Sir James Graham, Sir Henry Hardinge, stand deservedly well with the public.' Parker, *Peel*, ii, 482–3. Halévy's comment that 'with a few unimportant changes' Peel's cabinet was 'identical with that of 1834' ignores the prestige of Graham and Stanley and the fact that they were given major posts, the Home Office and the Colonial Office (E. Halévy, *A History of the English People in the Nineteenth Century* (Benn edition, London, 1962), iv, 5).

'ant'.[1] The significance of Stanley's and Graham's joining Peel was not so much that they had become more conservative (in their eyes the Whigs had moved, under Russell and Melbourne, closer to Radicalism) but that they recognised the dominance of Peel, in whose cautious liberalism they had always placed their confidence, over the right wing of his party.[2]

The first job facing the government was to balance the budget. In retrospect the tariff reductions and the income tax of 1842 mark the first step towards the free-trade liberal budgets of the 1850s and 1860s, but Peel's primary motive in making these changes was to eliminate the deficit. He hoped that the reduction in the tariff wall would in time bring so great a rise in imports that the loss of customs revenue would be more than made up. In the meantime, the temporary expedient of the income tax would fill the gap. Peel had not even read the free-trade recommendations of the 1840 Committee on Import Duties before the financial measures of 1842 were drafted.[3] The 1828 sliding scale had placed a maximum duty of 50s. 8d. on wheat when the home price fell to 36s. or less. Peel's revised scale of 1842 began with a duty of 20s. when the home price was 50s. or less. Peel originally showed the cabinet a scale drawn up by John McGregor, joint secretary to the Board of Trade, in which the maximum duty was 16s. According to Cobden only Lord Ripon, president of the Board of Trade, accepted it, and the higher scale was adopted.[4]

Peel was confident, despite the resignation from the cabinet of the Duke of Buckingham and expressions of alarm from several counties,[5] that his proposals would pass by a large majority. He

---

[1] H. Lambert to Stanley, 20 September 1841. Derby Mss, 125/11.

[2] Their chief reason for not joining Peel in 1834 was that his cabinet was dominated by high Tories (see Derby Mss, 131/13, *passim*). For Graham's position, in particular, see D. W. Johnson, 'Sir James Graham and the Derby Dilly', *University of Birmingham Historical Journal* (January 1953), 66–80.

[3] Peel to Goulburn, 18 December 1841. Goulburn Mss, II/18. Gladstone wrote many years later of his beginning at the Board of Trade in 1841: 'I was totally ignorant both of political economy and of the commerce of the country... my mind was in regard to all those matters a "sheet of white paper", except that it was coloured by a traditional prejudice of protection, which had then quite recently become a distinctive mark of Conservatism' (Morley, *Gladstone*, i, 244).

[4] J. Morley, *The Life of Richard Cobden* (London, 1908), i, 233–4.

[5] The effect of Buckingham's resignation was diminished by his reputation for

told Prince Albert that the measures would not lose him any support among his followers, and he was right.[1] The new scale passed easily through both Houses. William Blackstone was the only Protectionist of the future to oppose it in the Commons, where it received a majority of 108 on second reading. Sir Richard Vyvyan's attempt to enlist Disraeli's wit against the bill, after Disraeli had attacked the government's Indian policy, was unsuccessful, and Vyvyan kept silent during the debates.[2] Only two Tories remained faithful to their party's tradition by voting against the income tax. Yet the Tory backbenchers had received Peel's opening statement in silence,[3] and Peel himself believed that in the interest of party unity he would better have made no changes.[4] He kept the Tory votes, because his followers were not prepared to forfeit their newly won power to let the Whigs back in. That was almost certain to mean free trade. It was this fear of the Whigs among his followers which was Peel's strongest political weapon for the next three years. The only organised agriculturalist opposition to Peel in 1842 was over the reduction of the cattle duty, which 80 Conservatives felt safe to vote against because, unlike the sliding scale and the income tax, it was supported by the Whigs.[5]

The agriculturalists had little to fear from a House of Commons which rejected Villiers' annual motion for total repeal by

---

prickly stubbornness. On 23 February, the Buckinghamshire Agricultural Association held a meeting to protest against the new scale. A meeting of farmers opposed to the new tariff was held at Chelmsford on 19 April 1842 (*John Bull*, 28 February and 23 April 1842). See also the *Annual Register*, 1842, 54, and the speeches in parliament reflecting the alarm in the countryside: Heathcote, 18 February 1842 (*Hansard*, 3rd Series, lx, 692), Blackstone, 9 March 1842 (*ibid*. lxi, 310), and Lord Beaumont, 18 April 1842 (*ibid*. lxii, 699).

[1] Peel to Prince Albert, 15 February 1842. A.C. Benson and Viscount Esher (ed.), *The Letters of Queen Victoria* (London, 1907), i, 479–80.

[2] Disraeli to his wife, [13 March] 1842 and 15 March 1842. Monypenny and Buckle, ii, 130, 131.

[3] Palmerston, 16 February 1842. *Hansard*, 3rd Series, lx, 610.

[4] Peel, 16 February 1842. *ibid*. 610.

[5] A Tory peer expressed the helplessness of the high Tories' position to Sidney Herbert: 'If a highwayman stops me on the road and robs me, I have him apprehended, tried, and hanged, and at least I have my revenge to make amends for my loss; but here I am robbed by Peel of far more than the highwayman would take from me, and I have no redress' (Palmerston to W. Temple, 30 September 1842. Lord Dalling, *The Life of Henry John Temple, Viscount Palmerston* (London, 1874), iii, 111–12).

393 votes to 90, and Cobden's for a committee to inquire into the Corn Laws by 156 to 64. But although Peel had kept their votes, he had loosened their attachment to him. In October, Charles Arbuthnot told him that 'many of our Ultra friends are dissatisfied with the measures of last session'.[1] There were disturbing qualifications to Peel's protectionism. The agriculturalists did not accept his statement 'that on the general principle of free trade there is now no great difference of opinion, and that all agree in the general rule that we should purchase in the cheapest market and sell in the dearest'.[2] England was in the midst of an industrial depression and Peel wanted to make the country one in which it was possible to live cheaply. Stanley was already beginning to feel uneasy. He told Gladstone that 'Peel laid that down a great deal too broadly'.[3] Peel described his revised scale as an experiment deserving a fair trial; the agriculturalists regarded it as a final settlement of the question. Peel's openmindedness conflicted with Tory principle. He had told the House of Commons that he was prepared to repeal the Corn Laws if he could 'convince his mind' that they were at the bottom of the industrial distress.[4] The Tories' confidence in Peel was further shaken by the evident pride with which he declared that he had devised his schemes without caring whether they would receive the support of his backbenchers. He would risk his government and for reward be satisfied with 'the consciousness that we have acted on the principles which we believe to be right'.[5] In reply, Lord Stanhope reminded Conservatives that their duty did not consist in merely registering ministerial edicts.[6]

A few Conservatives, including Lord Malmesbury, Lord Lowther, and the Duke of Buckingham, foresaw repeal,[7] but

[1] Arbuthnot to Peel, 30 October 1842. Parker, *Peel*, ii, 532–3.
[2] 10 May 1842. *Hansard*, 3rd Series, lxiii, 382.
[3] Morley, *Gladstone*, i, 263.
[4] 27 August 1841. *Hansard*, 3rd Series, lix, 421–2.
[5] 16 February 1842. *ibid*. lx, 610.
[6] 18 April 1842. *ibid*. lxii, 599.
[7] The Earl of Malmesbury, *Memoirs of an Ex-Minister* (London, 1884), i, 139; Lord Broughton, *Recollections of a Long Life* (London, 1911), vi, 51–3. According to Hobhouse, Richmond agreed with Buckingham but was startled by Hobhouse's prediction that repeal was only four to six years away. Hobhouse reminded Richmond of this conversation in May 1846, and Richmond said wistfully, 'Aye, you knew him better than we did' (*ibid*. vi, 170).

Disraeli's attitude was more characteristic of the whole party. He told his constituents that they ought not to desert Peel 'because you think he will do a certain act which I think he will not'.[1] Croker, assured by Sir James Graham that Peel was absolutely opposed to the Anti-Corn Law League, gave Peel his unqualified support in the *Quarterly Review*.[2] Sir Richard Vyvyan's letter to his constituents, which was an attack both on Peel's policy and on the stern, aloof authority which he exercised over the party, was ridiculed by the Tory press,[3] and his protests were dismissed as the whinings of an ignored office-seeker.[4] Lord Stanhope's Society for the Protection of British Industry, formed in February 1843, to campaign for the repeal of the 1842 tariff, was unenthusiastically received and unsupported by subscriptions.[5] In March 1842, Greville correctly described the condition of the Conservative party.

> It is really remarkable to see the attitude Peel has taken in this Parliament, his complete mastery over both his friends and his foes. His own party, *nolentes aut volentes,* have surrendered at discretion, and he has got them as well-disciplined and as obedient as the crew of a man-of-war...there is every possibility of Peel's being Minister for as many years as his health and vigour may endure.[6]

Peel achieved this mastery over the party by concealing his private doubts that the protective system could stand much longer. In the House of Commons he used the language of a firm protectionist. But to his closest colleagues he confided that he believed the day of repeal not to be far off.[7] The agriculturalists'

---

[1] Speech at Shrewsbury, 9 May 1842. Monypenny and Buckle, ii, 141.

[2] Graham to Croker, 5 December 1842. L. J. Jennings (ed.), *The Correspondence and Diaries of the Late Right Honourable John Wilson Croker* (London, 1885), ii, 85.

[3] *A Letter from Sir Richard Vyvyan to his Constituents Upon the Commercial and Financial Policy of Sir Robert Peel's Administration* (London, 1842). *John Bull* dismissed Vyvyan as a 'queer Conservative' (18 June 1842). See also the *Standard*, 25 October 1842.

[4] For example, by Croker to Gladstone, 7 September 1842. Gladstone Mss, Add. Mss 44359, ff. 181–2.

[5] Anon., *Things As They Are and Things As They Ought to Be* (London, 1843).

[6] C. C. F. Greville (ed. H. Reeve), *A Journal of the Reign of Queen Victoria from 1837 to 1852* (London, 1885), ii, 88.

[7] Peel told Croker that the great difficulty would be to prove that he had gone far enough in relaxing duties. 'Something effectual must be done to revive the languishing commerce and manufacturing industry of this country. Look at the congregation of manufacturing masses, the amount of our debt, the rapid increase of

failure to see where events were leading, the result partly of Peel's reticence and detachment, partly of their own short-sightedness, was fatal to the Conservative party. Their indignation at Peel's turn-about in 1846 was partly conditioned by their being put off guard in 1842. Clearer symptoms of discontent in 1842 might have forced Peel's private reservations into the open, thereby starting a fruitful debate on the subject of the Corn Laws within the party. There was something to the exaggerated judgement of one despairing Conservative, that in 1842 the Conservative party committed a *'felo de se* in a fit of duplicity'.[1]

From 1842 to 1845, Peel's public position on the Corn Laws remained unchanged. He continued to deny that the Corn Laws contributed to urban distress, while promising to repeal them if the national interest required it. In the meantime the 1842 scale deserved a fair trial. Blackstone protested against this equivocation in 1843,[2] but Peel continued to re-assure his party by refusing to vote for committees of inquiry into the Corn Laws or into the burdens on land. Not until Peel's conversion in December 1845 were the Corn Laws again the subject of extensive debate within the Conservative party. And the revival of trade and industry in 1843–4 diminished the attention paid to them in the country. At agricultural meetings the issue was no longer discussed in 1844. A few ultra-Tories continued to grumble,[3] but at the beginning of the 1844 session of parliament, Viscount Hardinge wrote to Lord Ellenborough in India that he knew 'of

poor rates within the last four years...and then judge whether we can with safety retrograde in manufactures' (Peel to Croker, 27 July 1842. Parker, *Peel*, ii, 528–30). Four days after Disraeli assured the farmers at Shrewsbury that Peel was a firm adherent to protection, Peel told Gladstone that 'in future he questioned whether he could undertake the defence of the Corn Laws on principle' (Morley, *Gladstone*, i, 260). Graham wrote to Peel on 30 December 1842: 'It is a question of *time*. The next change in the Corn Laws must be to an open trade' (Parker, *Peel*, ii, 551).

[1] Anon., *Guilty or Not Guilty? Being an Inquest on the Conservative Parliament and Ministry* (London, 1842). (Quoted in the *Quarterly Review* (September 1842), 502.)

[2] 10 May 1843. *Hansard*, 3rd Series, lxix, 167–71.

[3] At the end of April 1844, Thomas Raikes recorded that 'nothing is heard in England except a snarl from the ultra-Tories about corn and tariff...the joke at White's is that the Tories are like old walnuts, because they are *hard to peel*' (T. Raikes, *A Portion of the Journal Kept by Thomas Raikes, Esq., from 1831 to 1847* (London, 1857), iv, 257–8).

no vital question on which the Government need dread any want of its former support'.[1] Nevertheless, it was in 1844 that the Conservative backbenchers, over the government's factory and sugar legislation, mounted their first challenge to Peel's leadership by deserting him in large numbers in divisions of the House of Commons.[2]

In February, Lord Ashley, the evangelical leader of early Victorian humanitarian reform movements, introduced an amendment to the government's factory bill to reduce the working day of women and young persons from twelve hours to ten. The amendment was passed with the support of 90 Conservatives, but four nights later, under threat of resignation by Peel, the House of Commons rescinded its vote and accepted a twelve-hour day. In June the government's sugar bill received almost identical treatment. All foreign-grown sugar was charged with an import duty of 63s. per hundredweight. The government's new proposal was to leave that duty on slave-grown sugar only, reducing the duty on free-grown sugar to 34s. The duty on colonial sugar was to remain at the existing rate of 24s. The structure of imperial preference was thus weakened and Philip Miles, the Conservative member for Bristol, a port with a large stake in the colonial trade, moved an amendment to lower the duty on colonial sugar to 20s. From a protectionist point of view it would have made more sense to raise the duty on free-grown foreign sugar, but Miles was eager to get Whig and Radical support for the amendment. Enough Conservatives voted against the government for Miles' amendment to pass by 20 votes. Again Peel threatened to resign and again the Commons reversed its decision, accepting the government tariff schedule three nights later.

Peel's control over the House of Commons and his party had been put to the test, and for the moment he had survived. But the government's assault on the legislative sovereignty of the House of Commons, which Melbourne not quite accurately des-

[1] Hardinge to Ellenborough, 5 January 1844. Ellenborough Mss, PRO 30, 12/21/7.
[2] For a lengthier discussion of these crises than that given here, see R. Stewart, 'The Ten Hours and Sugar Crises of 1844: Government and the House of Commons in the Age of Reform', *Historical Journal*, XII, 1 (1969), 35–57.

cribed as 'an entire novelty, quite new and unprecedented',[1] brought into question the severe methods of Peel's leadership under which the Tory backbenchers had been chafing. The Tories objected to the measures themselves. They suspected the manufacturers who supported the Anti-Corn Law League of wanting cheaper food in order to reduce workers' wages and they were pleased to have the Ten-Hours stick with which to beat their urban rivals. The sugar bill, too, aroused the concern of those Tories who were opposed to any weakening of the Empire. And in both measures they detected a government desire to woo the Nonconformist voters in the towns, thus weaning the Tory party away from its narrow Anglican base. Of the 90 rebels on the factory bill in 1844, 45 voted against the extended grant to Maynooth College in 1845. Only 11 of the 90 voted for the grant. The differences over policy, however, were not nearly so important as the resentment felt by the backbenchers at Peel's tyrannical hold over the House of Commons. Peel had coerced the House of Commons more successfully than his own party. In March he was able to force 30 Conservatives who had originally supported Ashley's amendment to change their votes. Gladstone believed that a similar switch took place in June on the sugar bill after an eloquent appeal by Stanley to the Conservatives' feelings of loyalty. But the Tories were upset by Peel's readiness to compromise an important article of the Tory creed without consulting them and Stanley's speech had little effect.[2] The government's

[1] Melbourne to Queen Victoria, 19 June 1844. Benson and Esher, ii, 21. Melbourne's memory may have failed him. In 1833, an almost analogous incident took place. On 25 April, the Commons voted by a majority of 10 to reduce the malt tax by one-half. A few days later the chancellor of exchequer, Lord Althorp, introduced a resolution which said that the malt tax could not be reduced without resort to an income tax, which was inexpedient. The resolution passed by a majority of 198 and the malt tax went unchanged.

[2] Gladstone wrote of Stanley's speech, which followed one by Lord Howick in which the narrow ground at hand had been abandoned in favour of a general attack on the government: 'The clouds of the earlier evening hours dispersed, and the Government were victorious. Two speeches, one negatively and the other positively, reversed the prevailing current and saved the Admistration. I have never known a parallel case. The whole honour of the fray, in the ministerial sense, redounded to Lord Stanley. His career in the earlier hours of the Reformed Parliament had been one of particular brilliancy. But I doubt whether in the 26 years of his after life he ever struck such a blow as this' (Gladstone memorandum of 1897. Gladstone Mss, Add. Mss 44791, ff. 86–8). For Stanley's speech, see *Hansard*, 3rd Series, lxxv, 1057–67.

majority of 22 on the second division was the result of 11 Radical free traders' coming to its support and a strong government whip. Thirty-five Conservatives who were absent for the vote on Miles' amendment voted with the government three nights later. Only 5 of those who had supported Miles changed their vote. Had it not been for Russell's unwillingness to defeat the government, Peel would not have survived.[1]

Peel's hold over a large section of his party was at an end, destroyed by his own methods. By the end of the 1844 session there were a number of Conservatives ready to throw him over. Blackstone went to a meeting of the party at the Carlton Club, called by Peel after the division on Miles' amendment to bring the rebels into line, in order to 'announce his intention of blowing up the whole affair in the House this evening',[2] and a fragment among the Peel Papers records that 'Blackstone and Ferrand are exulting and declare that they voted against Peel for the express purpose of throwing him out'.[3] Peel left the meeting muttering that it was the worst he had ever attended and wrote to the Queen that he expected to be beaten.[4] Miles had not hesitated to collaborate with the Whig opposition in drafting his amendment,[5] and Disraeli sounded out the Whigs, at a dinner party given by Baron Lionel de Rothschild, on the possibility of an alliance between the Whigs and the discontented Tories. Hobhouse made the obvious objection that the Whigs could not command the support of the Commons on any major issue of the day, to which Disraeli replied that 'Peel had completely failed to hold together his party, and must *go*, if not now, at least very speedily'.[6]

The Tory backbenchers were embittered by Peel's contempt for their opinions, and by his unwillingness to enter into relations

[1] Russell did not see Melbourne during the crisis, nor did he summon any of the party to make plans for the second vote. Broughton, vi, 116. Thomas Raikes wrote that 'the Whigs [were] just as much or more afraid of Peel's resigning than the Tories themselves' (Raikes, iv, 405).

[2] Lord John Manners to Disraeli, 17 June 1844. Hughenden Mss, B/XX/M/2.

[3] Peel Mss, Add. Mss 40547, f. 7.

[4] Peel to Queen Victoria, 17 June 1844. Peel Mss, Add. Mss 40435, ff. 302–3; Gladstone memorandum, Gladstone Mss, Add. Mss 44791, ff. 86–8.

[5] Buckingham to Bonham, 16 June 1844. Peel Mss, Add. Mss 40547, f. 4.

[6] Broughton, vi, 146.

of mutual confidence with them. *Fraser's Magazine* wrote that 'whether it be from pride, or shyness, or an excess of caution, the minister takes no pains whatever to win the personal love and affection of his supporters. As a party, they are never admitted into his confidences'.[1] During the two parliamentary crises of 1844, Peel made no attempt to conciliate or persuade the malcontents. The meeting which he called after the government's defeat on Miles' amendment was merely to inform them that he would resign if beaten again. In the Commons he was brusque and defiant. Backbenchers were not pleased to be lectured in public on the 'occasions when it is the duty of a Government to overcome the temptation of obtaining party support and of conciliating party favour by acquiescing in a proposition which it conscientiously believes to be injurious to the permanent interests of the country'.[2] Peel seemed not to distinguish between consulting his followers and currying to them. His attitude towards them was unduly arrogant. 'As heads see', he wrote to Hardinge, 'and tails are blind, I think heads are the best judges as to the course to be taken.'[3] Peel assumed that, since the cabinet had more information than the House of Commons, the cabinet's decisions should be automatically accepted.[4] A Tory complained to Hobhouse at the end of the 1843 session that those who resented this system were called *frondeurs*, but that there were many such. 'Peel thinks he can govern by Fremantle [the whip] and a little clique, but it will not do.'[5] In the middle of the sugar crisis, Monckton Milnes registered a severe verdict against Peel.

Peel is absolutely indefensible; he is asking from his party all the blind confidence the country gentleman placed in Mr. Pitt, all the affectionate devotion Mr. Canning won from his friends, and all the adherence Lord

[1] *Fraser's Magazine* (September 1843), 376.
[2] 18 March 1844. *Hansard*, 3rd Series, lxxiii, 1241.
[3] Peel to Hardinge, 24 September 1846. Parker, *Peel*, iii, 74.
[4] 'There has grown of late a very bad habit of canvassing for votes on public questions. The popular side is taken and a hundred men are committed by promises given in private to vote for that which is popular before the argument against is heard. Who is to give way? The government which is responsible and which, when the case comes to be stated, has reason and argument on its side... ?' (Peel to Lady de Grey, 21 June 1844. Peel Mss. Add. Mss 40547, ff. 130–5.)
[5] Morley, *Gladstone*, i, 266.

John and the Whigs get from their 'family compact' without himself fulfilling any of the engagements on his side.[1]

Peel had received the full support of the party for his revised corn duty, for his income tax, and for the Canada Corn bill of 1843, without doing anything to satisfy those who wanted the Poor Law radically amended and a scheme of Church education established.

Ever since the days of Pitt, the alliance between the 'men of business' on the front benches and the country squires behind them had placed a great strain on the unity of the Tory party. The country gentlemen needed Peel in the 1840s, just as their predecessors had needed Pitt and Canning. The difference in the 1840s was that the decline of royal power since Pitt's day and the new importance which the 1832 Reform Act had given to constituency opinion made Peel much more dependent on his party than earlier Tory prime ministers had been. In the 1780s Pitt had been able to withstand major defeats because he had the support of the Crown to fall back on. As Professor Gash has written, Peel understood that regular party support had replaced the Crown as the rock on which ministries had to stand.[2] But in the eighteenth century the functions of a government were primarily administrative. By the 1840s governments were handling an immense load of controversial legislation every year, a development which made habitual consultation between the leaders and the rank-and-file essential. The primitive state of party organisation in the 1840s made the management of a parliamentary party extremely difficult. In the absence of a national party programme and a national party conference, candidates at the elections were free to adopt widely divergent positions on major issues. At the elections of 1841 Peel had demonstrated his lack of sympathy with the Ten Hours movement, but many Conservatives, especially in the North and Midlands, had pledged their support to it. The party leaders had few means of influencing a constituency's choice of candidate. William Black-

---

[1] Milnes to his father, 21 June 1844. T. W. Reid, *The Life, Letters, and Friendships of Richard Monckton Milnes, First Lord Houghton* (London, 1862), i, 331.

[2] N. Gash, 'Peel and the Party System, 1830–50', *Transactions of the Royal Historical Society*, 5th Series (1950), 54.

stone's independence in parliament reflected the autonomous position which he held in the constituency of Wallingford, which returned him unopposed from 1835 to 1847. Management within the Commons was just as difficult. The office of the chief whip, who was still called the patronage secretary, was in its infancy, and private members often knew only by rumour what legislation the government was preparing.

In the mid-nineteenth century, private members were increasingly jealous of their independence because it was so obviously being whittled away, as Gladstone noted in an article for the *Quarterly Review* in 1856, in which he argued that the decline in parliamentary efficiency was caused by the greatly increased control which governments exercised over private members. Cabinet ministers were coming to dominate the debates. Even Stanley, the colonial secretary, whom Peel called his 'right arm',[1] asked to be removed to the House of Lords at the end of the 1844 session on the ground that speeches were not wanted in the Commons and therefore a seat in the Lords would bring him more into the general administration of the government.[2]

Peel's position was intelligent and far-seeing. He knew that in the circumstances of the 1840s governments could carry on the country's affairs only if they were assured of regular support in the lobbies. During the sugar crisis both Lady de Grey and Viscount Sandon urged Peel to give way on a minor matter and reminded him that the party would support him if he tried its attachment 'by any real test'.[3] Peel's compelling defence of his attitude was that declarations of general confidence were no compensation for the loss of authority sustained by a government if it were unable to carry the practical measures of legislation which it had daily to submit to the House of Commons.[4] That was Peel's answer to the question which had perplexed politicians since the Reform Act; how was a government to carry on when 'influence' had been so drastically cut down? Peel did not deny

[1] Peel to Stanley, 30 July 1844. Derby Mss, 129/4.
[2] Stanley to Peel, 27 July 1844 (copy). *ibid.*
[3] Lady de Grey to Peel, 19 June 1844. Peel Mss, Add. Mss 40547, ff. 130–5; Sandon to Peel, 15 June 1844. *ibid.* 40546, ff. 386–92.
[4] Peel to Sandon, 17 June 1844. *ibid.* 40546, ff. 393–4; Peel to Lady de Grey, 21 June 1844. *ibid.* 40547, ff. 136–9.

the right of members to consort with the opposition whenever they so chose, but he insisted that when they defeated the government in this way they must expect the government to conclude that it had lost the confidence of the House.[1] For many backbenchers that was too new and too harsh a doctrine. Greville recorded the prevalent belief that the events of 1844 had badly weakened the government's authority and predicted that the next subject of disagreement in the Conservative party would bring the government down.[2] Sir James Graham, an habitual Jeremiah, came to the rueful conclusion that 'our friends have at last succeeded in rendering our future progress next to impossible'.[3] In the late 1830s and early 1840s the various shades of opinion within the Conservative party had been held together because there was a common bond of respect for, and a common recognition of the necessity of, Peel's leadership. By the end of 1844 that bond was gone. Just as important, Peel was as exasperated with his followers as they were with him. Greville has left a lively description of Peel's state of mind at the end of 1844.

Here is the devil to pay. Peel has not resigned, but he is so disgusted at the conduct of his followers, at their temporary coalition with the Whigs on this question of sugar, and at their insulting and injurious tone towards him personally, so often evinced before, that he is very unwilling to go on...he is so infernally disgusted with the *animus* displayed towards him personally, and the language which his *soi-disant* supporters hold, and he thinks he has so little real dependable influence over them, that he wants to throw the whole thing up.[4]

Predictions of Peel's early fall were premature. His government survived one more major crisis before the repeal of the Corn Laws, the furor raised by Peel's decision to increase and make permanent the parliamentary grant which for the previous fifty years had been voted annually to the Roman Catholic seminary at Maynooth, in county Kildare. The college was founded by the Irish parliament in 1795 and the grant of £9,000 then established

[1] See his speech of 17 June 1844. *Hansard*, 3rd Series, lxxv, 1002.

[2] Greville, ii, 246–9.

[3] Graham to Lyndhurst, 15 June 1844. Lyndhurst Mss, f. 131.

[4] Greville to Raikes, 17 June 1844. H.Raikes (ed.), *Private Correspondence of Thomas Raikes with the Duke of Wellington and Other Distinguished Contemporaries* (London, 1861), 369–71.

had continued to be voted at Westminster after the Union. On two occasions, in fact, the amount had been increased.[1] Yet not since the great reform struggle had a measure so excited the public and parliament as Peel's proposals in 1845. The House of Commons received more than three thousand petitions protesting against the proposed changes, most of them presented by members of the Conservative party.[2] Peel was not surprised by the outcry which his proposals provoked. From 1837 to 1844, 125 Conservatives with seats in the 1845 House of Commons had at one time voted against *any* grant to Maynooth.[3] Peel knew that his bill might destroy the government and had therefore given a year's warning of his intentions in order to avoid the charge that he hoped to catch the country unawares.[4] In the event, the government survived by majorities of 146 and 133 on second and third readings of the bill, because the Whigs supported it. But 147 Conservatives voted against the second reading and 149 against the third, one more, indeed, than voted for it.[5]

Since anti-Catholicism was to be a nerve centre of the Protectionist party, the Conservative opposition to the 1845 bill bears some investigation. The existing grant of £9,000 was clearly inadequate to meet the costs of the college. Students and faculty were living in conditions of near-poverty. The original enactment had relaxed the Statute of Mortmain specially in favour of the college to allow its trustees to acquire land to the value of £1,000 annually. But in the absence of a charter of incorporation the trustees had been unable to do so. Peel proposed, as a remedy, to incorporate the trustees with the power to take and hold land

[1] In 1807 by £7,000 and in 1813 by £4,000 (Peel, 3 April 1845. *Hansard*, 3rd Series, lxxix, 29–30).

[2] Before Peel introduced the Maynooth Bill 'the speaker called on those who were entrusted with petitions against an increase of the amount of the Maynooth grant to present them. Instantly the occupants of the ministerial benches rose *en masse*, while the opposition retained their seats, and roared with laughter' (N. W. Molesworth, *The History of England from the Year 1830* (London, 1871–2), ii, 219–20).

[3] J. Young to Peel, 25 March 1845. Peel Mss, Add. Mss 40563, ff. 275–80.

[4] Peel told Gladstone that the Maynooth issue would 'very probably be fatal to the Government' (Gladstone memorandum, 14 January 1845. Gladstone Mss, Add. Mss 44777, ff. 212–15).

[5] *Illustrated London News*, 24 May 1845. These were also the figures of the Liberal whip (Gash, *Reaction and Reconstruction*, 151).

to the value of £3,000 annually and personal property in an unlimited amount. The grant itself was increased to £26,360 and £30,000 was given for one year only for new building. By making the grant permanent, Peel intended to remove an annual opportunity for the expression of religious animosities.[1]

The state of the Established Church in 1845 made such generosity towards the Catholics particularly galling to Protestants. In Ireland the days of Protestant ascendancy were over. The Whig reforms of the 1830s had transferred the burden of tithe payment from the Catholic occupier to the Protestant landowner and had given Catholics control of the hitherto Protestant strongholds, the municipal corporations. Most hateful of all was the Irish Poor Law. Its guardians were elected annually by a rate-paying suffrage which was nearly universal, with the result that the landowners had seen their control of the elections pass to the priests. The boards of guardians nearly always had a majority of Catholic tenants.[2] The ownership of land no longer carried the absolute power which it had previously done. The Duke of Wellington knew, although Peel made capital fun out of the sentiment, that Protestant landlords in Ireland 'felt themselves to be not only not the favoured class of society, but in fact a persecuted class' and was not surprised to find them flirting with O'Connell's short-lived scheme of Federalism in 1844.[3]

---

[1] Peel, 3 April 1845. *Hansard*, 3rd Series, lxxix, 18–38.

[2] George Cornewall Lewis, a Poor Law commissioner, wrote that 'as a measure tending to strengthen and consolidate the power of the Catholic or popular party in Ireland, it [the Poor Law] certainly ranks next after Catholic Emancipation, the Reform Bill, and the Municipal Bill, to say the least of it. Upon the management of rural affairs, it has a more direct and searching influence than any of these measures' (Lewis to G. Grote, G. F. Lewis (ed.), *Letters of the Right Honourable Sir George Cornewall Lewis, Bart., to Various Friends* (London, 1870), 127–30).

[3] Wellington to Graham, 11 October 1844. C. S. Parker, *The Life and Letters of Sir James Graham* (London, 1907), i, 418–19. Henry Lambert wrote to Stanley that the Orange party were as exclusively in power as sixty years before, but were sulking 'because they are not permitted to abuse it as they did then' (Lambert to Stanley, 24 December 1842. Derby Mss, 125/11). Peel wrote to Lord Lifford on 25 August 1845: 'When one calmly reflects on what the Protestants possess, on their share of the good things which Government has to bestow, the proportion in which they hold office, judicial, legal, fiscal, civil, in addition necessarily to the whole of the appointments connected with the Church, it is impossible not to smile at the lamentations over the abject and degraded condition of the Protestant interest' (Parker, *Peel*, iii, 187). For the question of Federalism, see K. B. Nowlan, *The Politics of Repeal* (London, 1965), 73–9.

In England, the Established Church was reluctant to adapt itself to new conditions. The withdrawal of the education clauses from the government's 1843 factory bill in deference to the Dissenters' protests that they gave the Established Church control over primary education aroused Anglican fury.[1] The political power of Disent also blocked schemes for parliamentary aid to Church extension. Not since 1824 had parliament voted money for that purpose. In 1840, the Conservative front bench supported Robert Inglis' unsuccessful effort to get a grant for Church extension, but since Peel had come to power the government had made no mention of the subject. In 1844, the Church party suffered two defeats, on Lord Powis' motion to spare a condemned Welsh bishopric and on the Bishop of Exeter's bill to provide chaplains for union workhouses. In April 1845, two Conservative members who were secretaries of the lay committee of the Society for the Propagation of the Gospel, appealed unsuccessfully to Peel to restore the grant of £16,000 to their society which the Whigs had discontinued in the 1830s.[2] The Church's strength as an Establishment was clearly declining when it could no longer command, as of right, specific financial aid from the state. It was thus appalling, in the eyes of the Church party, that the Catholic Church in Ireland should be the beneficiary of English taxes.

Protestant Tories were also upset by and dissatisfied with Peel's handling of the Irish repeal movement. The Arms Bill of 1843, a renewal of the 1838 act, merely required that all firearms be registered. *Fraser's Magazine* called it 'the merest drivelling ...to talk of a measure like that as strengthening the hands of the government',[3] and Lord Malmsebury noted that many Conservatives, who wanted the Protestant yeomanry of Ireland called out and the O'Connell 'rent' declared illegal, resented Peel's truckling to the Radicals and throwing over his friends.[4] The huge

---

[1] 'The withdrawal by Sir James Graham of the educational clauses from his Factory Regulation Bill has gone to the hearts of the whole Conservative party. They perceive in it something like the commencement of that miserable system of half-measures, which, even more than their gross offences, brought the Whigs into contempt' (*Fraser's Magazine* (July 1843), 122).

[2] Peel Mss, Add. Mss 40564, ff. 29–30.

[3] *Fraser's Magazine* (July 1843), 124.

[4] Malmesbury, *Memoirs*, i, 145. Greville found the debates on the third reading

repeal meetings of the summer of 1843 finally forced Peel's hand. On 8 October O'Connell was arrested for inciting treason. He was convicted by a packed jury, but acquitted on appeal to the House of Lords. Disraeli wrote that 'as regards his Irish policy, Sir Robert Peel never recovered from this blow'. He abandoned his 'bold and prudent' policy of simultaneously repressing disorder and investigating its causes – a policy symbolised by the O'Connell prosecution and the Devon commission of inquiry into the system of land tenure in Ireland – and instead resolved to 'outbid' the Liberals by sending to Ireland 'messages of peace', the Charitable Bequests Act of 1844 and the increased Maynooth grant'.[1] The Charitable Bequests Act, which replaced the existing Protestant body in charge of Irish charities by a crown-appointed board with equal Protestant and Catholic representation, and which relaxed the Statute of Mortmain to permit gifts to the Catholic Church of real or personal property, received little Conservative opposition. And at the same time, it revealed the dissensions within the forces of Irish nationalism. O'Connell denounced it from prison and John McHale, Archbishop of Tuam, led the clerical attack on the bill.[2] The Vatican and the Irish parliamentary party, however, supported the bill. Peel and Graham were encouraged by these rivalries to continue the policy of conciliation. Peel believed that events had brought about 'a very general Impression throughout the Country that the recent policy of the Government towards Ireland has been a wise one – at any rate that it has been entirely justified by the Result, and that there is no alternative but cautious perseverence in it'.[3]

The Protestant right wing of the Conservative party saw

---

of the Arms Bill remarkable for 'the bitterness and insolence of his [Peel's] *soidisant* friends and the civility of his adversaries' (Greville, ii, 194).

[1] B. Disraeli, *Lord George Bentinck: A Political Biography* (London, 1852), 133–4.

[2] See Nowlan, *Politics of Repeal*, 67–77 and C.G. Duffy, *Young Ireland: A Fragment of Irish History* (London, 1880), 684–729. Clerical opposition may have stemmed from the clergy's desire to be dependent on their flock for support, since this bound them to the people. See, in this connexion, J.A. Murphy, 'The Support of the Catholic Clergy in Ireland, 1750–1850', *Historical Studies V* (London, 1964), 103–19.

[3] Peel to Gladstone, 20 January 1845. Peel Mss, Add. Mss 40470, ff. 284–5.

much more than that in the Maynooth bill. On one level, it represented latitudinarianism carried almost to the point of irreligion. 'The policy of our leaders', ranted the *Statesman*, an Orange paper published in Dublin, 'is to declare decided war against our Lord Jesus Christ. We have long learned to expect nothing else at the hands of Sir Robert Peel, into whose policy the devil has entered.'[1] The Tories in the House of Commons were seldom so strident in their opposition. They were not happy to subsidise what they considered to be religious error, but their repeated objections to the bill lay elsewhere. Sir Robert Inglis, the leader of the Church party in the House of Commons, complained that, since the government had turned down the Irish Church's request for a grant for educational purposes and had withdrawn financial aid to the Kildare Place Society, the Catholic Church was being given special treatment. Much more important, he argued that by making the grant permanent and incorporating the trustees, the government was taking the first step down the road which led, by way of Roman Catholic Establishment and Anglican disestablishment, to the repeal of the Union. J. C. Colquhon reminded the government that for fifty years Maynooth had formed the social character of a priesthood which had participated in two great agitations against the British connexion. He invited the arch-opponents of the Irish Church, Henry Ward and Joseph Hume, to join the government side of the House. 'Are they fearful of the name Conservative? There is, I assure them, nothing in it. It is a mere name, a name too without a notion.'[2]

For some time now the Tory Protestants had struggled in vain to prevent the erosion of the ancient Anglican constitution under which they had been born and which they had steadfastly loved and revered. They had been brought to believe, and still did believe, in the civilising influence of the Irish Church. To purchase a temporary peace now, in their eyes, was to store up calamity for the future. For men like these, men like Robert Inglis, who had represented Oxford University ever since the

[1] J. Irving, *Annals of Our Time* (London, 1869), 81.
[2] Inglis, 3 April 1845. *Hansard*, 3rd Series, lxxix, 38–52; Colquhon, 11 April 1845. *ibid*. 501–12.

day in 1829 when that refuge of English Toryism had thrown out Peel for his apostasy over Catholic Emancipation, it was impossible to stand by and watch Peel throw away Anglicanism and the Union with a piece of short-sighted legislation.

> In proportion as we contribute to the multiplication of Roman Catholic ministers in any part of the kingdom, we were providing for the destruction of our own Church. He would not consent, then, in the name of God, to teach, or pay any other man for teaching, that which he believed contrary to the word and truth of God... All our legislation was founded – he was not ashamed to avow it – on the Protestant Christianity of the country. For the last three centuries, that had been the distinguishing character and essence of the Constitution. Little by little, we had seen the distinguishing marks of the Protestant constitution shattered in the warfare of the last few years. The meteor flag, to which we had so long looked with admiration, had been shattered and torn, but the Protestant colours were still at the masthead; and so long as a single shred of that old flag lasted, he for one would endeavour to nail it to the mast, and he would fight as unflinchingly for it and under it as when, in brighter days, it waved entire and untorn over the empire.[1]

The fears of the anti-Maynooth Conservatives were not entirely unfounded. In their eyes the Irish Church was the link joining Ireland to England, and in February 1844, Peel had made a speech on Irish affairs which was interpreted as signifying his opinion that the Irish Church must be dealt with sooner or later, even though he had made it plain that he could himself have no hand in disestablishment.[2] Gladstone spoke of the Maynooth Bill as the beginning of a new religious policy towards Ireland, and by 1846 he was in a frame of mind to accept disestablishment when the circumstances should arise.[3]

In 1886, T. E. Kebbel wrote that the Maynooth Bill, judged simply on its own merits, was 'one of the most pitiful incidents

---

[1] *Ibid.* 51–2.

[2] Greville, ii, 232–4.

[3] Gladstone, 11 April 1845. *ibid.* 520–54. Gladstone wrote to Lincoln in March 1846 that he could no longer 'pledge to maintain the Ecclesiastical property of Ireland in its present form of appropriation...if my judgment matures itself in its present sense, the declaration of it will probably break me down and extinguish my public life' (Gladstone to Lincoln, 28 March 1846. J. Martineau, *The Life of Henry Pelham, Fifth Duke of Newcastle* (London, 1908), 77–9.

in the whole history of Toryism', outraging Protestant opinion without doing any real good to Ireland.[1] Protestants found it difficult to understand why the bill was introduced, since Gladstone said that he was prepared 'in opposition to what I believe to be the prevailing opinion of the people of England and Scotland, in opposition to the judgment of my own constituents, from whom I greatly regret to differ, and in opposition to my own deeply cherished predilections, to give a deliberate and even an anxious support to the measure'.[2] In one of the finest speeches of his career, Disraeli came out into the open against Peel and besought the House of Commons to defeat the bill on constitutional grounds.

This bill brings affairs to a crisis; the question is not to be decided on its merits; it is to be decided on the fact – who are the men who bring it forward? If you are to have a popular Government, if you are to have a Parliamentary Administration, the conditions antecedent are, that you have a Government which declares the principles upon which its policy is founded, and then you can have on them the wholesome check of a constitutional Opposition. What have we got instead? Something has risen up in this country as fatal in the political world as it has been in the landed world of Ireland – we have a great Parliamentary middleman. It is well known what a middleman is; he is a man who bamboozles one party, and plunders the other, till, having obtained a position to which he is not entitled, he cries out, 'Let us have no party questions, but fixity of tenure.' I want to have a Commission issued to inquire into the tenure by which Downing-Street is held. I want to know whether the conditions of entry have been complied with, and whether there are not some covenants in the lease which are already forfeited…the system is to be brought to a test tonight…whatever may be the various motives which animate…different sections of opinion, there is at least one common ground for co-operation – there is one animating principle which may inspire us all. Let us in this House re-echo that which I believe to be the sovereign sentiment of this country; let us tell persons in high places that cunning is not caution, and that habitual perfidy is not high policy of state. On that ground we may all join. Let us bring back to this House that which it has for so long a time past been without – the legitimate influence and

[1] T.E. Kebbel, *History of Toryism from 1783 to 1881* (London, 1886), 289.
[2] 11 April 1845. *Hansard*, 3rd Series, lxxix, 522.

salutary check of a constitutional opposition. That is what the country requires, what the country looks for. Let us do it at once in the only way in which it can be done, by dethroning this dynasty of deception, by putting to an end the intolerable yoke of official despotism and Parliamentary imposture.[1]

Had the Whigs been united and prepared to take office with the promise of a dissolution, the appeal might have succeeded, although it is improbable that Russell would have chosen an anti-Irish issue to get back to power. By themselves the ultra-Tories were lamentably weak. As the Earl of Arundel and Surrey remarked, Gladstone's decision to go along with the government gave Peel the support of 'every man who was worthy of the name of statesman'.[2]

In Victorian England, nothing revealed more clearly where an English politician stood than his attitude towards the Established Church. Gladstone loved the Anglican Church just as dearly as any ultra-Tory, but he had a wider vision than most of them. He had resigned from the cabinet when the Maynooth Bill was introduced in order to avoid the charge that he had changed his opinions to keep place. Inglis tried in vain to persuade him to lead the opposition to the bill. Inglis reminded Gladstone of the mistake made in 1829 of not sending the Duke of Cumberland, the Orange leader, into Ireland with thirty thousand troops. That only made Gladstone's blood run cold and helped him 'onwards in the path before me'.[3] Gladstone's decision to vote for Maynooth was of tremendous importance for the future of English politics. In 1841 he had told Peel that he shared his view that it was possible 'to adjust the ancient and noble institutions of this country to the wants and necessities of this unquiet time'. But at that time he had made the Church and religious questions in general an exception.[4] Faced with the test in 1845, he supported Peel, and the great obstacle to his becoming a liberal in politics was removed.

[1] 11 April 1845. *ibid.* 565–9.
[2] *Ibid.* 554.
[3] Autobiographical note of 16 July 1892. Gladstone Mss, Add. Mss 44790, f. 60.
[4] Gladstone to Peel, 17 October 1841. Parker, *Peel*, ii, 514–15.

Without Gladstone the Tories were leaderless. Disraeli's bitter sarcasm offended the country gentlemen who, according to *John Bull*, considered him to be an unprincipled office-seeker, a 'weathercock open to all parties, and trusted by none'.[1] The weakness of the Tories in the House of Commons was not made up by support in the country. The energetic campaign waged against the Maynooth grant by the Central Anti-Maynooth Committee, a union of Anglican and Nonconformist opponents of the bill, was ignored by Peel, who knew that the most vociferous opposition came from the Dissenters.[2] The union of Dissenters who opposed the bill from voluntarist principles and Anglicans who opposed it for quite other reasons was a temporary one, unlikely to be of electoral significance in the future.

The Maynooth dispute permanently alienated a large Protestant wing of the Conservative party from Peel. On 17 June 1845, that section withdrew from the Carlton Club and, under the Earl of Winchilsea's leadership, formed the National Club 'in support of the Protestant principles of the Constitution'.[3] Eighteen members of its committee sat in the House of Commons.[4] The National Club began immediately to hold meetings throughout the country denouncing the Maynooth grant and declaring Protestantism to be the only important issue at the next elections. The Protestant Alliance, under its chairman, Lord Ashley, began publishing a series of monthly tracts urging the repeal of the grant. And in Ireland, the Orange Lodge, proscribed by the Whigs in 1836, resumed its various forms of propaganda under a new name after ten years' silence.[5] The religious issue had destroyed the Conservative party in 1829, and it was working its poison again. After the second reading of the bill, Graham wrote in despair to Viscount Hardinge in India.

We are in the midst of a struggle here not unlike the conflict you remember on the passing of the Relief Act in 1829. It is impossible to

[1] *John Bull*, 5 April 1845.
[2] Peel to Croker, 22 April 1845. Peel Mss, Add. Mss 40565, ff. 9–10.
[3] *The Times*, 23 June 1845.
[4] G. A. Cahill, 'The Protestant Association and the Anti-Maynooth Agitation of 1845', *Catholic Historical Review* (October 1957), 273–308.
[5] Fremantle to Graham, 8 September 1845 and Graham to Fremantle, 9 and 10 September 1845 (copies). Graham Mss, microfilm, 148/23.

foresee the exact result; but my anticipation is that the event will be similar. The bill will pass and the Government will ultimately be overthrown in consequence. Our party is shivered and angry and we have lost the slight hold which we ever possessed over the hearts and kind feelings of our followers.[1]

Greville recorded in his diary that everyone knew that the Tory party had ceased to exist,[2] and Thomas Raikes, seeing that the Tories had so eagerly seized the first opportunity to stick their teeth in Peel's flanks, concluded that 'the next opportunity may prove decidedly fatal'.[3]

[1] Graham to Hardinge, 23 April 1845 (copy). *ibid.* 120/88.
[2] Greville, ii, 280.
[3] Raikes, iv, 423–4.

2

THE GOOD OLD CAUSE

GOVERNMENTS, like most people, live from day to day. They deal with issues as they arise, seldom knowing quite what they do. Of those great issues which are the product of a slow growth and the subject of a prolonged discussion the consequences are perhaps more clearly seen than of others. But all political decisions, though they may not be leaps, are at least stumbles in the dark. No one could foresee precisely the consequences of repealing the Corn Laws in 1846. Peel's decision was based mainly on two considerations: that England must become a cheaper place in which to live for the mass of the people, and that a source of class division and antagonism in English society must be removed. In 1846 the economics of the case were strongly on his side. But political habits and political traditions rarely bend easily or quickly before economic 'facts'. Governments have more information than their backbenchers. They are daily made aware of the need to change policies according to changing circumstances. But to be successful in changing policy a government must have the trust of its followers, and by 1846 Peel had used up whatever loyalty and trust his backbenchers had been prepared to place in him in 1841.

The break-up of the Tory party over the repeal of the Corn Laws was the final example of the strain which the alliance between the official 'men of business' and the country gentlemen had, ever since the days of the younger Pitt, placed on the unity of the Conservative party. By the end of October 1845, it was evident that, owing to the potato failure, Ireland was to have a famine year. In the first week of November Peel called four meetings of the cabinet to consider his proposal to suspend and ultimately repeal the Corn Laws. At the end of the week only Graham, the Earl of Aberdeen, and Sidney Herbert approved his suggestion. As home secretary, Graham had daily come into contact both with the 'condition of England' question and the Irish distemper. Since 1842 Aberdeen had, as foreign secretary, been directly involved in the negotiations for reciprocal trading agreements with Prussia, Russia, Brazil, and Portugal. Graham and Aberdeen were not in the tradition of the 'men of business', but their political opinions were deeply coloured by extensive official experience. Experience at the board of trade, rather than the dogmas of political economy, converted Gladstone, who was not in the cabinet, to free trade.[1] Peel's official experience, of course, beginning with his appointment as under-secretary for war and the colonies in 1810, was rivalled only by Palmerston's. The combination of practical experience and a pragmatic temperament, which had gained Peel his reputation as a model administrator, had blunted his Toryism. In the late 1830s Peel had turned his back on those Tories who wished to block all Liberal reforms indiscriminately in the House of Lords. He had remained immune to the agriculturalists' agitation for the repeal of the malt tax and to the ultra-Protestant pressure for the preservation of the self-elected Orange municipal corporations in Ireland. Office forced on Peel's attention the facts of economic and social change which the country gentlemen on the back benches were happy to ignore. He told Croker that 'if you had to constitute new societies, you might on moral and social grounds prefer cornfields to cotton factories, an agricultural to a manufacturing population. But our lot is cast and we cannot recede.'[2]

Peel's decision to repeal the Corn Laws did not mean, however, that he had decided to represent the middle-class view in politics against the landed interest. Repeal was to save the aristocracy and the constitution. In 1841 Peel had been concerned about the effects of superfluous protection in view of 'the present temper of the public mind'.[3] By 1845 he feared that a return to the high food prices and unemployment of 1841–2 might result

[1] 'Even when the Corn Laws were about to be repealed', Lord Farrer wrote, 'he Gladstone did not, I think, take the broad views of Cobden and the Free Traders...he did not insist on the expediency of giving people cheap bread or of opening the foreign markets to our manufactures, so much as on the great evils in the form of speculation and disastrous ups and downs of prices caused by the sliding scale' (F. W. Hirst, *Gladstone as Financier and Economist* (London, 1931), 98).

[2] Peel to Croker, 27 July 1842. Parker, *Peel*, ii, 529.

[3] Stanhope and Cardwell, *Peel Memoirs*, ii, 330–1.

in massive civil disturbances and perhaps bloodshed.[1] 'The worst ground on which we can *now* fight the battle for institutions – for the just privileges of Monarchy and Landed Aristocracy – is on a question of food.'[2] Repeal, Peel told his followers in his opening speech of the 1846 session of parliament, was a conservative measure.

I have thought it consistent with true Conservative policy to promote so much of happiness and contentment among the people that the voice of disaffection should be no longer heard, and that thought of the dissolution of our institutions should be forgotten in the midst of physical enjoyment.[3]

That was precisely the kind of reasoning with which the Whigs had defended their reform bill in 1832. Peel had then argued that by yielding to agitation the Whigs were providing a dangerous precedent for parliament when it should come 'to deal with the Corn Laws, or other questions calculated to excite the feelings and inflame the passions of the people'.[4] The right argument in opposition is often the wrong one in power. After fourteen years' experience of the reformed House of Commons Peel had taken to heart Croker's dictum that 'no minister *ever* stood, or could stand, against public opinion'.[5] Repeal now would prevent 'the humiliation of constituted authorities forced to yield after a disgraceful struggle' and so preserve the independence of parliament.[6] It was for that reason that Peel reacted so quickly to the news of the Irish potato failure. Famine in Ireland might give the Anti-Corn Law League a powerful, if illogical, new argument for the free import of food.

The danger to civil peace was, outwardly at least, far greater in 1831 than in 1845–6, and the protectionists, holding fast to the Tory position during the reform struggle, argued that repeal, by acknowledging the power of the Anti-Corn Law League,

---

[1] Prince Albert memorandum of 7 December 1845. Benson and Esher, ii, 48–51.
[2] Peel to B. Denison, 7 January 1846. Peel Mss, Add. Mss 40532, ff. 89–90.
[3] *Hansard*, 3rd Series, lxxxiii, 95.
[4] 5 June 1832. *ibid*. lxiii, 426.
[5] *Quarterly Review*, February 1835, 263.
[6] Peel to Hardinge, 24 September 1846. Parker, *Peel*, iii, 473. Aberdeen thought it wise not to have been '*forced* to yield what has been granted as a boon' (Queen Victoria to the King of the Belgians, 7 July 1846. Benson and Esher, ii, 103).

would 'encourage, increase, and render irresistible, democratic agitation'.[1] Peel's timid example would make it almost impossible for future governments to withstand the assault on the Irish Church, the Union, and the Monarchy. Croker, who had been surpassed by his pupil, feared that 'the next most probable transition will be a federal Republic after the American fashion',[2] and a Tory pamphleteer declared that 'if the deliberations of the senate are henceforth to be controlled by the party who shall be most successful in sowing discontent and sedition among the people, then is the crown of these realms not worth twelve months purchase'.[3] Not only was Peel vindicating the methods of the Anti-Corn Law League, he was also splitting the landed class, which the Tories believed to be the only class capable of resisting democratic republicanism.[4] The League was more than a pressure group for free trade. In the Duke of Richmond's judgement it was the embodiment of the middle and working classes' democratic aims.

I will ask you, if the Anti-Corn Law League succeed in ruining the Agricultural interest – I will ask you whether they will stop there. Did you ever know success produce moderation upon any political party? It is the first step; they feel that it is the yeomanry of England and the agricultural interest of the Empire that stand between them and the democratic principles which they wish to carry out.[5]

The only way in which Peel could preserve the Conservative party was to persuade the agriculturalists that the economic necessity of free trade overrode all other considerations. He had the evidence to build a strong case. The steadily increasing population of the country needed more imported food and, owing to the

---

[1] Croker to Graham, 3 April 1846. Jennings, *Croker*, iii, 65.

[2] Croker to Brougham, 4 February 1846. *ibid*. iii, 62.

[3] J. Almack, *Character, Motives, and Proceedings of the Anti-Corn Law Leaguers* (London, 1843), 93.

[4] See, for example, Croker to Brougham, 8 February 1846. Jennings, *Croker*, iii, 65. Edward Knatchbull believed that 'the policy of the Government, in addition to the ruin and confusion which in any quarter it must make, will, and possibly is intended to, relinquish the means of governing through the aristocracy and the Church' (Knatchbull to Herries, 2 February 1846. Herries Mss, NRA/34).

[5] Speech at the annual meeting of the Agricultural Protection Society, 12 January 1846. *Morning Herald*, 13 January 1846.

appearance of a collective deficiency in European bread grains, England was likely in the future to be dependent on the distant sources of Russia and America for her wheat.[1] The sliding scale discouraged imports from these sources. Even when conditions were favourable for exporting grain to England, merchants were deterred from doing so by the length of the journey from the Black Sea or America. The wheat might not arrive until after a fall in home prices had brought a large duty into operation again. Peel was aware that the growth in population meant that the Corn Laws, no longer required to protect the farmers from the post-war glut in northern European grains, threatened England with a food shortage by keeping out Russian and American wheat. He had scored in the margin reports of deficiency in Poland which came to him in the summer of 1845.[2]

Yet in a long and tedious speech of 27 January 1846, in which Peel outlined his tariff legislation, he failed to stress what may be called the 'official' case for repeal.[3] The growth in population was not alluded to and the paramount need to exploit new sources of wheat was mentioned almost as an after-thought to a House wearied by endless statistics about tallow, textiles, metals, cattle, and seed. Peel's chief arguments were three: that high farming was a surer protection to the farmer than the Corn Laws, that the success of his reduced tariff scale of 1842 justified advancing to complete free trade, and that the impending famine in Ireland made free trade urgent.

Peel sought to persuade his party that his over-all scheme was for the benefit of all classes. He invited the agriculturalists to

[1] Between 1815 and 1826 Britain imported little wheat and flour, and between 1828 and 1838, considerably less than 1,000,000 quarters annually. But in the years 1839–42, admittedly years of poor harvests, imports rose to 2,500,000 quarters annually, and for the first time a large proportion of these imports were from America (C.R.Fay, *The Corn Laws and Social England*, Cambridge, 1932, 113–17). The population of Great Britain increased by 2,000,000 between the 1831 census and the 1841 census to 26,856,028. The reason for the deficiency in European wheat appears to have been that under the impact of industrialism, other crops such as sugar beet, flax, tobacco, sheep, and cattle were taking precedence over bread grains (A.Fairlie, 'The Nineteenth-Century Corn Law Reconsidered', *Economic History Review* (December 1965), 562–73).

[2] *Ibid.* 572.

[3] For Peel's speech, see *Hansard*, 3rd Series, lxxxiii, 239–85. I do not share Mr Fairlie's view that Peel 'elaborated' on the theme of Russia and America in this speech (*op. cit.* 572).

place their hopes for prosperity in the increased productivity of the soil which would be the result of agricultural improvements. He included in his legislation a scheme for government provision of loans to farmers who undertook to drain their lands. The loans were to be a first charge on landed estates, taking precedence over existing mortgages, and they were to be available even to owners of settled estates. The agricultural politicians, however, had never been convinced by the argument that improvements, particularly drainage, increased productivity, kept rents up, and so enhanced the value of their estates, and they remained sceptical despite the evidence gathered by the 1845 select committee on drainage chaired by the Duke of Richmond. The Central Agricultural Protection Society was deeply hostile to the Central Agricultural Association, a non-political organisation founded to advance the cause of scientific, or improved, farming. The advocates of improved farming claimed that the Corn Laws, by holding out a false promise of high prices, encouraged the farmers to ignore new methods of agriculture, and that that negligence was the true cause of the low prices of which the farmers complained.[1] The protectionists' reply was that the farmers could afford to undertake improvements only if they were assured of high prices by the Corn Laws, and that repeal would ruin those farmers who had made improvements, and become heavily mortgaged, in the expectation of continuing high prices under the Corn Laws.[2] High farming was not an alternative to protection but its handmaiden. The continuation of the policy of national security under the Corn Laws was the condition of increased productivity.

The agriculturalists' argument that the Corn Laws *had* kept prices high was unsound. In the years 1815 to 1846 corn prices were seldom influenced by the tariff. But it is a remarkable fact that in the late 1840s, for the first time, the Corn Laws *would have* affected prices because imports were so high. From Peel's point of view, that food must be cheap, the repeal of the Corn

[1] D.C.Moore, 'The Corn Laws and High Farming', *Economic History Review* (December 1965), 546.
[2] For example, H.Liddell, 27 January 1846. *Hansard*, 3rd Series, lxxxiii, 290–4 and J.Walsh, 9 February 1846. *ibid.* lxxxiii, 587.

Laws came just at the right time. Had the Corn Laws been in effect in September 1848, for example, the price of wheat would have been about 73s. instead of 56s. 10d.[1] For the agriculturalists there was early evidence that high prices and the Corn Laws went together.

Whether the Corn Laws were a prerequisite of high farming was, at any rate, a question of secondary importance. For social and political reasons there was a deep-seated repugnance to improvement among large landowners. Limited in capital, their only means of effecting improvements was to mortgage or sell parts of their estates. And that was to weaken their efforts to build up and perpetuate their estates, perhaps, as Dr Kitson Clark has suggested, the most important objective of the great landowners.

Even though the agriculture to which the great estates contributed was in many ways efficient and scientific, it would be a misunderstanding of the part it played in the making of Victorian England to think of it as an industry organised like any other industry – primarily for the purpose of efficient production. It was...rather organised to secure the survival intact of a caste. The proprietors of the great estates were not just very rich men whose capital happened to be invested in land, they were rather the life tenants of very considerable positions which it was their first duty to leave intact to their successors. In a way, it was the estate that mattered and not the holder of the estate.[2]

That aristocratic attitude, which is so large a part of the explanation of the agriculturalists' opposition to Peel in 1846, was embodied in stringent laws. Owners in fee might mortgage land as they wished, but it has been estimated that in 1847 two-thirds of English land was controlled by testamentary settlement. Such land could be mortgaged only by the lengthy and costly procedure of a private act of parliament or, since 1833, by judgement in chancery.[3] High farming, moreover, would almost certainly mean the granting of increased powers to tenants for improvement. The traditional hierarchical structure of English rural society would be subverted by a new system of long leases or by

[1] This is the estimate of Tooke and Newmarch, *History of Prices*, v, 57.
[2] G. Kitson Clark, *The Making of Victorian England* (London, 1962), 218.
[3] D. C. Moore, *op. cit.* 551.

tenant right; one practical result would be the weakening of landlord control over the votes of the tenant farmers.

Peel's advocacy of high farming as an alternative to protection failed to sway the agriculturalists. He was no more successful in persuading them that the success of the 1842 scale was an argument for complete free trade. That he so believed there is no doubt. The Irish potato failure caused him to repeal when he did, but he was slowly converted to free trade, not by the arguments of the Radicals, but by the operation of the reduced tariffs of 1842. Wages had risen. Livestock farmers had received no shock from the reduced duties on imported meat. Cheaper foodstuffs and material plenty had produced a quieter populace and a larger demand for labour than in the years 1839 to 1842. Finally, despite the tariff reductions, the revenue of the country had increased.[1] By those considerations Peel was brought to free trade, and on the basis of them he asked the House of Commons whether it doubted that even greater benefits would follow the adoption of complete free trade.

The protectionists were unmoved by his arguments and by his statistics. In 1842 they had heard Peel say that distress was not caused by the Corn Laws; in 1846 they were disturbed and angered to hear him say that tariff reductions had ushered in prosperity.[2] Philip Miles attributed the prosperity to the stimulus given to employment by the railway boom, to the termination of war in India, and to three good harvests in succession. Peel had achieved his stated objective, when introducing the 1842 scale, of stabilising the price of corn at about 54s. to 58s., and Miles found it strange reasoning for a man to repeal a law which had achieved its purpose.

The measure of 1842 has been admitted by all parties to have worked well so far, as a Corn Law. It has conduced to great steadiness of price, and it has answered the right hon. Baronet's expectations. Under that law he aimed at a price of 56s. as a 'fair price' for the farmer. I should like to ask him what price he considers a 'fair price' for the farmer now.[3]

[1] Stanhope and Cardwell, *Peel Memoirs*, ii, 102–6.
[2] See Liddell, 27 January 1846. *Hansard*, 3rd Series, lxxxiii, 292.
[3] 9 February 1846. *ibid*, lxxxiii, 555.

Peel's claim to have turned a deficit into a surplus by means of reduced duties was obviously false, as Gladstone had demonstrated in a pamphlet written in 1845. The decrease in revenue from articles whose duty had been lowered or removed in 1842 and 1845 was made up by the income tax receipts. And the surplus was supplied by increased revenue from the duties on articles left untouched by Peel.[1]

The Irish potato failure was even less solid ground for Peel to stand on. On 5 December 1845, after failing to convince the cabinet, in particular Stanley and the Duke of Buccleuch, of the necessity of free trade, Peel resigned. On 20 December the Queen sent for him again because Lord John Russell had been unable, or unwilling, to form a Whig government. Gladstone wrote to his wife that day.

If he [Peel] should determine to form a government, and *if* he should send to me, I am totally uncertain whether I can take office – but my principle, by which under God I hope to decide, is that I am not free to take away Corn Laws unless the facts of the Irish case can on examination prove to be so great and special as to put the question altogether beyond ordinary rules.[2]

Peel, Goulburn, and Lincoln were informed of Gladstone's view 'that nothing could have been more base than to propose the law in 1842 for the chance of a run of good harvests and with the intention of withdrawing it upon the first notion, not even the experience, of a bad one'.[3] It was partly that suspicion which inspired the agriculturalists' mistrust of Peel. Lincoln advised Gladstone to keep an open mind and to trust to Peel's ability to show the absolute justification of free trade in the facts of the potato disease.[4] Gladstone assented and replaced Stanley at the colonial office in Peel's new ministry.

Predictions of an impending famine in Ireland were widely discredited at the end of 1845 and the beginning of 1846.

---

[1] W. E. Gladstone, *Remarks Upon Recent Commercial Legislation* (London, 1845), 7–12. The statistics are presented more clearly by Bentinck (20 July 1847, *Hansard*, 3rd Series, xciv, 617–26).

[2] A. T. Bassett (ed.), *Gladstone to his Wife* (London, 1936), 67.

[3] Gladstone memoranda of 6 and 20 December 1845. Gladstone Mss, Add. Mss 44777, ff. 233–6, 237–42.

[4] *Ibid.*

Throughout December and January reports flowed into England that the disease was not nearly so widespread as had at first been feared.[1] The Duke of Buccleuch, who had agreed to serve in the new government, wrote to Aberdeen on 29 December that people in Scotland, enjoying a bountiful harvest, full employment, and high wages, could not understand the cry of famine,[2] and a party of Whig grandees at Woburn on 18 January, including the Irish landowner, Lord Clarendon, agreed that there was no appearance of likelihood of distress in England or Ireland.[3] But even those who accepted the accuracy of the early reports failed to understand the logic of repeal. In November, Stanley was willing to support the suspension of the Corn Laws as an emergency relief measure for Ireland, not because he believed that free imports would help Ireland, but because he was eager to prevent the break-up of the government. Stanley did not share Peel's opinion that the country would not tolerate the restoration of the Corn Law after a period of suspension and that there was therefore no alternative to total repeal.[4] Suspension of the Corn Laws for a limited time might have kept the party together. In February, Lord John Manners advised Peel to suspend the Corn Laws and then 'leave it to the good sense of the English people to decide' whether the ports should be closed again.[5] What angered the agriculturalists above all else was that Peel had enthusiastically embraced free trade as a wise policy in itself.

Peel expected the Anti-Corn Law League and the Irish repeal movement to be the beneficiaries of government inaction in the face of a food shortage. On a political level there may have been a logical connexion between famine and repeal. But the Irish argument gained Peel no support from the protectionists. Repeal could help Ireland only if there were a general food shortage in Ireland and a population with sufficient purchasing power to buy imported food. Neither condition prevailed. The only shortage was in potatoes. Ireland exported large quantities of wheat,

---

[1] See the *Illustrated London News*, 13 December 1845.
[2] Buccleuch to Aberdeen, 29 December 1845. Aberdeen Mss, Add. Mss 43201, ff. 29–32.
[3] Broughton, *Recollections*, vi, 157–8.
[4] Stanley to Croker, 20 July 1847 (copy). Derby Mss, 177/2.
[5] 17 February 1846. *Hansard*, 3rd Series, lxxxiii, 1092.

barley, and oats to England every year, and continued to do so in 1846.[1] The Irish peasant lived solely on the potatoes grown on his own tiny plot of land. When they failed, he had no money with which to buy other food. In addition, the food and provisions trade in Ireland was developed only in the relatively prosperous districts of manufacturing Ulster and some of the larger southern towns such as Cork. Shops and organisations for selling and distributing food scarcely existed elsewhere.[2]

Croker told Viscount Hardinge, who had remained in the government, that he could not forgive Peel 'this late tergiversation and, above all, the deception of endeavouring to attribute it to the potato failure in Ireland'.[3] The protectionists rightly suspected Peel of having decided, before the news of the potato failure, to introduce free trade.

But the difficulty was to find a practical excuse and opportunity for executing this secret design. The Corn Law scale worked so admirably that prices were low and duties uniform; and if Sir Robert Peel had waited for a high price of corn, he would have had no *locus standi* at all, for the duty would have vanished altogether. The Irish scarcity was therefore in this sense a godsend to him: without raising the price of corn, it raised, or rather provided the opportunity of raising, an alarm of famine; and therefore there was a rate of duty to be removed, which had there been any real scarcity would have removed itself. Nay, prices were falling when this subject was broached, and they continued to fall in spite of all attempts to create alarm.[4]

For five years a war had been fought, in pamphlets, in newspapers, and at meetings throughout the country, between the free traders and their opponents. Peel's failure to demonstrate the economic necessity of free trade or to justify it as a solution to famine in Ireland, meant that the parliamentary debate in 1846 was merely a continuation of that war. Statistics played a major role in only one aspect of the debate, the question of the effect which free trade would have on food prices and therefore on the

---

[1] *Parl. Papers 1849*, 1(588), 405.

[2] C. Woodham-Smith, *The Great Hunger* (London, 1962), 49.

[3] Croker to Hardinge, 24 April 1846. Jennings, *Croker*, iii, 68.

[4] *Quarterly Review* (June 1847), 294–5. Prices fell from 58s. 10d. per quarter of wheat in November 1845, to 51s. 5d. in July 1846.

cost of living. Both sides to the debate became hopelessly entangled in contradictory statements. The free traders attacked the Corn Laws as the agriculturalist monopolists' weapon for artificially raising prices. At the same time they told the tenant farmers, who had the most to fear from reduced prices, since rents might well not follow suit, that the idea of cheap foreign corn was a delusion.[1] The protectionists claimed, with some justification,[2] that the Corn Laws did not keep prices high, while in the same breath insisting that agricultural prosperity depended upon them. The protectionists denied that the Corn Laws were intended to keep up prices when there was an abundant harvest; they were merely meant to protect the home grower by keeping foreign corn out. From 1834 to 1836, during which time England imported only 122,175 quarters of wheat, prices were under 45s., while during the lean harvests from 1838 to 1840, despite the import of 7,858,500 quarters, prices averaged 67s. 2d.[3]

Neither side rested its case on the details of trade and markets. Two views of England's place in the world, and of the world itself, came into conflict. Under the leadership of Cobden and Bright, the free traders held out the promise of a bountiful world at peace, in which commercial interdependence would banish war between nations. If England would only take the lead, all other countries would quickly follow her example and renounce their tariff policies. The people were told that to repeal the Corn Laws was to carry out the will of God,[4] and that their decision would be recorded on high where they would be held to account for it.[5]

[1] George Day, the best of the protectionist pamphleteers, published side by side statements from the *Manchester Guardian* that repeal would reduce rents, prices, and wages and Cobden's statements that it would do none of those things (G. G. Day, *A Letter to Richard Cobden*, London, 1844). In June 1843, Cobden was reported to have said that the cry of cheap bread was never his (*Morning Chronicle*, 30 June 1843).

[2] C. R. Fay's argument that the Corn Laws did not affect prices in the years 1815–46 (*Corn Laws and Social England*, 109–20) has been effectively qualified by Fairlie (*op. cit. passim*).

[3] A Lincolnshire Landowner, *A Reply to the Anti-Corn Law League* (London, 1843), 17–22.

[4] *British Quarterly Review*, i (May 1845), 560: 'Economical trut his not less divine than astronomical truth...All truths of science become, when viewed with reference to their Author, religious truths and draw after them religious duties.'

[5] This was the burden of a tract distributed by the League (Ashworth, *Recollections*, 121–2).

Hearing Cobden, one might have been forgiven for believing that the Garden of Eden was to be restored by an act of parliament.

I have speculated on what the effect of the triumph of this principle may be. I believe that the effect will be to change the face of the world, so as to introduce a system of government entirely distinct from that which now prevails. I believe that the desire and motive for large and mighty empires, for gigantic armies and great navies...will die away ...and I believe that the speculative philosopher of a thousand years hence will date the greatest revolution that ever happened in the world's history from the triumph of the principle which we have met here to advocate.[1]

The free traders appealed to the religious enthusiasm of the nonconformist middle class. The protectionists, supported by the Established clergy, to whom the tithe gave a direct interest in the maintenance of high corn prices, accused the free traders of hypocrisy and unpatriotism, and of a desire to subvert the stability of English society for their own selfish ends.

In every age the tendency of commerce is to destroy patriotism, and to sacrifice everything to the end of gain...See, for example, the way in which the merchants have been poisoning the Chinese, with opium... See again the treatment of the children in the factories.[2]

Only thirty years had passed since England had defeated Napoleon as much by the ploughshare as by the navy. The Tories warned that free trade would imperil the nation's security by making England dependent on foreign powers for her food, by destroying the colonial empire which had been carefully nurtured by a policy of preferential tariffs, and by bringing in its wake the end of the Navigation Laws, which they believed to be the corner-stone of English sea power. Lord Beaumont did not deny that universal free trade might be a beautiful theory, but he knew that all nations could not be of one mind, that disputes must occur, and that therefore the principle of protection was one

[1] J. Bright and J. E. Thorold Rogers (ed.), *Speeches on Questions of Public Policy by Richard Cobden* (London, 1870), i, 363.

[2] H. Drummond, *On Government By the Queen and Attempted Government From the People* (London, 1842), 121.

to which all nations must cling in order to establish their independence.[1] The Tories pointed to the erection of new tariffs by six countries since 1841 and to the famous speech of Henry Clay, the aspirant to the American presidency, in which Clay called free trade 'a beautiful vision...practically repudiated by all nations'.[2]

The Tories' objection to free trade was that it was based on an abstraction. 'I do not think it wise', Croker wrote, 'to overthrow and destroy on mere theoretic prospects, a system under which a nation has risen to a state of grandeur, power and happiness unparalleled in the world.'[3] That was, perhaps, the voice of Burke speaking through the Tory party. But it was also the thinner voice of the great Duke, who in 1830 had delivered the famous statement that the English constitution was as perfect a constitution as men could devise. The Tories did not claim that England could grow corn as cheaply as other places, but nor did they deduce from that a theory of the international division of labour which would make England the workshop of the world. They were not willing to have Lyons destroy Coventry so that Manchester could triumph over Rouen. Protection supplied steady prices and constant employment and secured the national safety. Free trade, on the other hand, was a moral evil which severed the ties holding society together and undermined the values of a landed society.

It is in its very essence a mercenary, unsocial, democratising system, opposed to all generous actions, all kindly feelings. Based on selfishness – the most pervading as well as the most powerful of our vicious propensities – it directs that impulse into the lowest of all channels, the mere sordid pursuit of wealth. It teaches competition and isolation, instead of co-operation and brotherhood; it substitutes a vague and impracticable cosmopolitanism for a lofty and ennobling patriotism; it disregards the claims of the poor... Wealth is its end and Mammon its divinity.[4]

The Tories looked about them at the poverty and ugliness of

---

[1] *Meeting for the Establishment of the Yorkshire Protective Society*, 17.

[2] Britannicus, *Corn Laws Defended; or Agriculture Our First Interest* (London, 1844), 13–14.

[3] Croker to Colonel Wood, 3 February 1847. Jennings, *Croker*, iii, 103.

[4] *Quarterly Review* (December 1849), 183.

London and Manchester, recoiled in fear and disgust from the Satanic mills, and strove to keep England a green and pleasant land.

The Tories believed that a landed constitution was essential to political stability and integrity, since the country gentlemen, whose fortunes were already made and were permanently tied to the fortunes of the country, took a broad view of the national interest, whereas the industrialists and small capitalists, whose fortunes were precarious, were selfish in outlook and unreliable in times of national crisis. Toryism looked beyond theory to the experience of the past for its inspiration. It yearned, amid the bitter conflicts of the 1840s, for what it remembered to be the stability of the past, and it naturally found that stability to have rested on the dominant elements in national life, the Church and, more especially, the land. They identified the national interest with the landed interest, and so were able to prophesy doom for all classes and ruin for the country if free trade were adopted. They appealed to England's progress at home and power abroad as evidence of the wisdom of the country's traditional policy. When, in 1846, even the powerful leadership of Lord George Bentinck and Disraeli was unable to persuade an overwhelmingly landed House of Commons that free trade would destroy the country's greatness, it looked as if it were their brand of Toryism which was doomed.

3

THE ORGANISATION OF THE PARTY

F R E E T R A D E was probably sometime inevitable. That it was the work of the 1841 parliament owed less to argument than to political calculation. When Peel resigned on 5 December, almost the whole cabinet disapproved of free trade. Yet when he formed his free-trade government two weeks later, only Lord Stanley refused to come back in. Croker could not understand how the others were able to consent to the triumph of a policy which they had for so long so earnestly denounced. Peel had changed his mind. But why, Croker asked Wellington, should those who had not done so help Peel out of his self-inflicted difficulty? In reply, Wellington reminded Croker that in May 1832, he had failed to form a government because many Tories (including, ironically, Peel) had decided that it was the Whigs' business to carry a reform bill and that the result had been a radical, not a moderate, reform bill. That was, however, a minor consideration. For Wellington, the crucial fact of the matter was that, since Russell's failure to form a government left no alternative to Peel, ministers owed it to the Queen to support him. A strong government was more important to the country than the Corn Laws.[1] Most of the cabinet had spent their political youth in the days when the great test of a politicians' constitutional loyalty was his readiness to support the Crown's ministers, and the Duke's attitude carried great weight in the cabinet. Lord Ellenborough thought that what the Duke believed to be right could not be very wrong,[2] and the Duke of Buccleuch, who was so distressed by events that he wrote three letters to Peel on 22 December before making up his mind, finally decided that it

[1] Croker to Ashburton, 30 December 1845. Jennings, *Croker*, iii, 48–9; Croker to Wellington, 4 January 1846. *ibid*. iii, 51–2; Wellington to Croker, 6 January 1846. *ibid*. iii, 52–5.

[2] Ellenborough to Redesdale, 26 December 1845. Ellenborough Mss, PRO 30, 12/21/9.

was his 'imperative duty to my Sovereign and to my country' to swallow his convictions and support Peel.[1] Lord Lyndhurst abdicated all personal responsibility for judging the issue. He told Peel that he had confidence in whatever course Peel should adopt.[2]

There was also, among certain Conservatives, a feeling of relief that the country had been saved from the Whigs. Despite misgivings about the awkward position in which Peel had placed himself, William Heathcote rejoiced that he had returned, since the mere administration of everyday affairs by the Whigs would inflict lasting mischief on the country.[3] Wellington had the same fear of a Whig government,[4] and Mathew Bell foresaw 'nothing but war abroad and misery and disaffection at home' under Lord John Russell.[5] Lord George Bentinck had foreseen this reaction to Peel's resignation and suspected Peel's motives in resigning.

I am a good deal puzzled about Sir Robert Peel's motives in resigning the Government upon Lord Stanley's and the Duke of Buccleuch's refusing to assent to his measures and afterwards upon Lord John Russell's failure to form a Government consenting to go on without Lord Stanley. I incline however to think it all a trick to make it more easy for him to carry on the Government upon his new principles; he hopes I think by these means in some measure to escape the taunts with which he was attacked in 1829... He thinks I dare say that by resigning the Government of the Country into the hands of the Whigs he will have frightened a great body of the Landed Aristocracy into submission.[6]

In December 1845, the Conservative opponents of free trade separated into two camps: there were those, like Wellington, who believed that they must forego their opinions and do their duty to the Crown by supporting Peel and there were those, like

[1] Buccleuch to Peel, 22 December 1845. Stanhope and Cardwell, *Peel Memoirs*, ii, 254–7.

[2] Lyndhurst to Peel, 2 December 1845. Peel Mss, Add. Mss 40442, ff. 305–6.

[3] Heathcote to Gladstone, 24 December 1845. Gladstone Mss, Add. Mss 42208, ff. 9–10.

[4] Arbuthnot wrote to Peel of Wellington's distress on 26 December 1845: You can have no notion how much he suffered when he thought we were to be cursed with a Whig-Radical government' (Peel Mss, Add. Mss 40484, ff. 244–5).

[5] Bell to Peel, 19 December 1845. *ibid*. 40581, ff. 3–4.

[6] Bentinck to his father, 28 December 1845. Portland Mss, PWH/192.

Bentinck, who thought that to do so destroyed the validity of the party system and thus brought the constitution to ruin. Lord Stanley, in a manner characteristic of his career, attempted to find a middle course. He decided not to impede Peel's efforts to repeal the Corn Laws, but also not to tarnish his own reputation by remaining in the cabinet. Disraeli said afterwards that Stanley broke up Peel's government in the first week of December with the words, 'It is no use arguing the matter. We cannot do this as gentlemen'.[1] Caught between letting down the government or his order, he hoped to be able to do neither.

By 1845, Stanley had gained a reputation for playing at politics, a reputation which was not helped by his seeming inability to form any lasting political affiliation. He entered the House of Commons as a Whig in 1820 and in 1827 went over to Canning with the Lamb section of the Whig party. He held minor office under Canning and Goderich, but resigned when Wellington formed his high Tory government in 1828. Two years later he was made Irish secretary in Lord Grey's reform government. In 1834 he deserted Grey, accompanied by Sir James Graham, Lord Ripon, and the Duke of Richmond, in protest against the policy of appropriating funds of the Irish Church for lay purposes. For the next three years he and Graham made a half-hearted attempt at starting a centre party before joining the Conservatives in 1838.[2] Stanley's restlessness was, of course, partly a reflexion of the fluid party structure in the 1820s and 1830s. Graham had followed Stanley step by step. But Graham had achieved a great reputation for efficiency and hard work at the Admiralty. Stanley had made a far deeper mark in the columns of *Hansard* than in the Blue Books. It is understandable that his resignation in 1845 should have been widely interpreted as a clash of personality between the carefree, flamboyant heir to the Derby fortune and his earnest, socially awkward leader.

Lord Stanley...was antagonistic to his chief in every propensity derived from nature, habits and position. Reckless in his language, aristocratic in his tendencies...above all haughty and domineering in his tendencies, though gay and playful in manner...But what was worst of all

[1] Broughton, *Recollections*, vi, 228–9.
[2] See Johnson, 'Sir James Graham and the Derby Dilly'.

was the eternal habit of quizzing, or, to use the modern word, 'chaffing', which the inconsiderate noble lord indulged in, and which the somewhat prim and stately commoner could not endure. If private stories are to be believed, the Premier, indeed, had determined – at a shooting party early in the autumn [1845] and at which the dignified calm of his countenance had been unwillingly ruffled by a volley of bad jokes which he could neither tolerate nor resent – to take the first occasion of shaking himself free from a colleague whose familiarity had become insupportable to him.[1]

George Denison found great fault with Stanley's levity after the break-up of the cabinet. He reported to Gladstone that Stanley had 'been reading abusive paragraphs against Peel, with roars of laughter, in the railway carriage before Lord George Bentinck and others'.[2] But both Stanley and Peel deeply regretted their separation in 1845,[3] and Stanley was particularly distressed to part with Graham, his closest political ally since their Canningite days and one 'from whom I have never differed on any public question for above twenty years'.[4] It was partly this warm attachment to his colleagues which misled Stanley, in the next few years, to over-estimate the chance of a reunion of Peelites and Protectionists.

It is clear, nevertheless, that Stanley was not reluctant to leave official life. In 1830 a brilliant future had seemed to lie before him. Heir to one of the largest Whig estates in the country and already renowned at an early age as the most compelling, if somewhat old-fashioned, orator in the House of Commons, he awaited the demise of Althorp and Grey to assume the leadership of the Whig party. In 1831, when Stanley became Irish secretary, that office was raised to cabinet rank because Lord Grey wanted the future leader of the party in the cabinet.[5] When Disraeli told Melbourne in 1834 that he wished to become Prime Minister, Melbourne replied that the question was settled.

---

[1] Lord Dalling, *Palmerston*, iii, 183–4.

[2] Gladstone memorandum of 20 December 1845. Gladstone Mss, Add. Mss 44777, ff. 237–42.

[3] See Stanley to Peel, 2 November 1845. Stanhope and Cardwell, *Peel Memoirs*, ii, 160–1.

[4] Stanley memorandum for the cabinet, 3 November 1845. Derby Mss, 27/5.

[5] A. Aspinall, 'The Cabinet Council, 1783–1835', *Proceedings of the British Academy* (1952), 160–2.

Nobody can compete with Stanley. I heard him the other night in the Commons, when the party were all divided and breaking away from their ranks, recall them by the mere force of superior will and eloquence; he rose like a young eagle above them all, and kept hovering over their heads, until they were reduced to abject submission. There is nothing like him . . . You must put these foolish notions out of your head; they won't do at all. Stanley will be the next Prime Minister, you will see.[1]

The most fruitful years of Stanley's career were spent under Lord Grey. At the Irish office he was responsible for the Irish reform bill, the education act, the Irish Board of Works, the Church temporalities bill, and the tithe act. When, in 1833, Althorp and Stanley came to loggerheads over the tithe issue, Stanley was removed to the Colonial Office. Russell believed that had Althorp resigned, as he wanted to do, Stanley's 'infinite skill, readiness and ability' would have earned him the leadership of the Commons as Althorp's successor.[2] At the Colonial Office Stanley guided the bill abolishing slavery through the Commons. That was the last important piece of legislation with which his name is associated with the Reform Act of 1867. His attempt to form a centre party of moderate Whigs and Tories in the mid-1830s was abortive, and his decision to join the Conservatives may be seen, in retrospect, as the termination of the creative or constructive part of his career.

In 1841 he returned to the Colonial Office in Peel's administration, given to him because Peel held by the outdated view that it was more interesting and more important than the Home Office.[3] Education, Ireland, the Poor Law, and factory reform were the leading questions of the day, and Stanley soon slipped into the background while Graham, at the Home Office, became Peel's closest colleague. Stanley was out of sympathy with the kinds of

---

[1] W. M. Torrens (ed.), *Memoirs of Viscount Melbourne* (London, 1890), 275. After Stanley's defence of the Irish Coercion Bill in 1833, Abercromby remarked to Le Marchant that 'had it been the old House, I should have quietly walked home and put on my nightcap under the conviction that Stanley would in a few weeks be Prime Minister and remain so as long as he pleased, and that he would govern us on tory principles' (A. Aspinall (ed.), *Three Early Nineteenth Century Diaries* (London, 1952), 313).

[2] Lord John Russell, *Recollections and Suggestions, 1813-73* (London, 1873), 114.

[3] Peel to Stanley, 30 July 1844. Derby Mss, 127/4.

problems which came to the Colonial Office, especially those concerning Canada, where his vision extended little beyond providing firm government in a situation which required a deeper understanding of the colonists' demands for responsible government.[1] The Colonial Office wearied him by its routine and presented him with few opportunities to shine in debate. In 1844 he asked Peel to transfer him to the Lords, where he could enter more into the general business of the government than was possible in the more tightly-controlled House of Commons. Peel, though reluctant to lose his 'right arm', consented, and in September 1844, Stanley went to the Lords. Henry Goulburn, chancellor of the exchequer, regretted his departure as much as Peel.

I have for some time past been sensible that a re-inforcement of the House of Lords was essentially necessary and I have always been apprehensive that it would be effected by your removal to it. I can truly say that I know no change in the House of Commons that could have been more distasteful to me than that which deprives me of your society during those many wearisome hours of every day...I hope that our less frequent intercourse which must result from our service in different houses of Parliament may not diminish on your part the friendly feeling which you have always evinced towards me and which I assure you I cherish as one of the most substantial advantages which I have derived from my tenure of office.[2]

In the next few years Goulburn was the man most frequently mentioned for the position of leader in the House of Commons of a re-united Conservative party under Stanley.

In the Lords in 1845, Stanley took little interest in politics. After the stormy days of his quarrels with O'Connell his quiescence attracted notice, and *Fraser's Magazine* remarked that it was impossible to 'recognise in the quiet, unobtrusive minister who now sits under the wing of the Duke of Wellington...the fierce, fiery leader who was named the Hotspur of the Conservative forces'.[3] Stanley was better known as the Rupert of debate,

---

[1] See W.P.Morrell, *British Colonial Policy in the Age of Peel and Russell* (Oxford, 1930), 47–81.

[2] Goulburn to Stanley, 30 August 1844. Derby Mss, 125/1.

[3] *Fraser's Magazine* (November 1845), 505–8,

but by 1845 he no longer lived up to the nickname. He was only forty-five years of age, but was already suffering from gout. Leadership had eluded him, and younger men, like Gladstone and Sidney Herbert, appeared to be leaving him in the shade. Excessively fond of country life and, in the family tradition, devoted to the turf, Stanley looked forward to fighting the battle for the constitution against the radicals as an independent peer. Peel returned to power strengthened by Stanley's avowal that he neither desired nor thought it possible to form a protectionist government.[1]

In December 1845, Stanley had no thought of leading a protectionist party. He did not even intend to speak against repeal, but simply to vote against it. He urged Gladstone to join Peel's government, and made no attempt to dissuade the Duke of Buccleuch, with whom he had resigned in the first week of December, from re-entering the cabinet.[2] It is quite clear that Stanley felt marooned. He could not bring himself to vote for free trade, but he had no close ties with the disaffected wing of the Conservative party. On every issue which had driven them away from Peel, Stanley had given the government his full support. He had approved of Peel's tariff reductions of 1842 and 1845, and he had enthusiastically advocated a liberal policy towards Ireland.[3] Indeed, he had introduced the government's stillborn tenants' compensation bill for Ireland in 1845. During the two crises of 1844 no one in the cabinet had shown less sympathy for the rebels.[4] There was thus no place for Stanley to go. The party which began to emerge in January, and which was to become the Protectionist party, was an outgrowth of the earlier opposition to Peel. Of the 152 Conservatives who had voted against the Maynooth grant in 1845, 135 were to vote against

[1] Stanhope and Cardwell. *Peel Memoirs*, ii, 229–32.

[2] Peel to Graham, 21 December 1845. Parker, *Peel*, iii, 286; Stanley to Peel, 22 December 1845. *ibid.* iii, 287; Peel to Prince Albert, 23 December 1845. Benson and Esher, ii, 76.

[3] See, for example, Stanley to Peel, 18 February 1844. Peel Mss, Add. Mss 40468, ff. 132–7.

[4] See Gladstone's memorandum of the cabinet meeting of 25 March 1844. Gladstone Mss, Add. Mss 44777, ff. 155–8. At the meeting Stanley and Graham argued that concessions to the rebels would purchase only a momentary peace, while establishing a precedent for future revolts.

the repeal of the Corn Laws,[1] as were 62 of the 90 Conservatives who had voted for Ten Hours. The formation of a die-hard Tory party seemed to Stanley to be not only a futile, but a dangerous, endeavour, since it would destroy the power of conservative forces in politics to resist radicalism. On 27 January, he explained his position to Lord Ellenborough:

I could not honestly have supported, in my place in Parliament as a minister, measures in which, as an individual peer, I can honestly advise acquiescence. I rejoice that the public is again to have the benefit of your services...I am afraid that you will have a stormy opening of the Session, but I am doing, and shall do, what I can to pour oil on the waves...though it is difficult to foresee the future, my own opinion is that my official life is over, and I am well content that it should be so. The political current seems steadily setting in a direction which leaves me high and dry on the beach.[2]

Stanley's fundamental political objective was to preserve the Conservative party in the state as a force against radicalism. It may be argued that to do so he might better have remained in the government, but it ought not to be forgotten that public life is devalued every time a minister lays himself open to the charge of changing his opinions in order to keep place. Still, to be a middleman in politics, as Falkland and many others had discovered, is a frustrating and impotent experience, and before long Stanley was to be drawn once again into the fray.

In the 1845 session of parliament no leader had emerged from within the Tory opposition to Peel, and in December none appeared to be forthcoming. Peel had previously weathered the unorganised, spasmodic revolts of his right wing and in January

---

[1] Professor Gash cites slightly lower figures, given to him by Professor Aydelotte: 147 Conservatives against the Maynooth Bill and 111 of them against repeal (*Reaction and Reconstruction*, 152). For some reason he has chosen figures for the second reading of the Maynooth Bill and for the third reading of the Corn Bill, despite accepting the higher figure of 149 for the third reading of the Maynooth Bill. My figures are the total number of Conservatives who voted against *either* the second or third reading of *each* bill.

[2] Stanley to Ellenborough, 27 December 1845. Ellenborough Mss, PRO 30, 12/21/9. The *Illustrated London News* wrote of Stanley on 27 December 1845, that 'as he has no party to attach himself to in Opposition, he will not be formidable as an enemy; and thus has a once great and prominent public character been politically extinguished'.

1846, he was guardedly optimistic that, on the tariff issue, he might do so again.[1] His government had suffered only four resignations, and although the Protectionists won six of eight by-elections in January and February,[2] discontent in the agricultural constituencies had gone unreflected in the Commons in 1842 and 1845 and might do so again.

The county protection societies were reluctant to declare themselves against Peel. The first of them had been formed on the initiative of tenant farmers in Essex in April 1843, after which similar organisations were established in Sussex, Lincolnshire, Berkshire, Kent, and Yorkshire by the beginning of 1844.[3] But they were for the most part lifeless bodies, presided over by peers or members of parliament who counselled acquiescence in the government's policies and proclaimed their confidence in Peel.[4] In February 1844, the Central Agricultural Protection Society was formed under the leadership of Richmond and Buckingham, but its constitution forbade the discussion of party politics and interference in elections. The society was little more than a pacifier to stop the tenant farmers from crying. At a meeting of the society on 9 December 1845, after Peel had resigned, a tenant farmer from Warwickshire accused the gentry of forming the society 'in obedience to the voice of the tenant-farmers' and then sitting back to do nothing because they were unwilling to break up a great party.[5] The Conservative gentry

---

[1] Peel to Arbuthnot, 7 January 1846. A. Aspinall (ed.), *The Correspondence of Charles Arbuthnot*, Camden Society, 3rd Series (London, 1941), lxv, 239–40; Peel to C. Hardinge, 5 February 1846. Peel Mss, Add. Mss 40584, ff. 159–60; Gladstone memorandum of 4 October 1851. Morley, *Gladstone*, i, 286.

[2] The Earl of Lincoln, chief secretary for Ireland, was defeated by Thomas Hildyard, who was supported by Lincoln's father, the Duke of Newcastle, at Nottinghamshire South (see the correspondence between Lincoln and Newcastle printed in the *Illustrated London News*, 28 February 1846, and J. Martineau, *Newcastle*, 59–60). Captain Carnegie, a Lord of the Treasury, was beaten by the Protectionist pamphleteer, Sleigh, at Stafford. Gladstone did not contest his Newark seat against J. Stuart. Protectionists were also returned uncontested for Hertfordshire, Sussex East, and Buckingham. The only defeated Protectionist candidate was Captain Rous, beaten by the Radical, de Lacy Evans, at Westminster. The Protectionists did not contest the West Riding, where the Whig, Lord Morpeth, regained the seat which he had lost at the 1841 elections.

[3] *Morning Post*, 11 January 1844.

[4] See, for example, the speeches of Lord Faversham and Lord Beaumont, *Meeting for the Establishment of the Yorkshire Protective Society*, 18–21.

[5] *Standard*, 11 December 1845.

was, of course, not eager to encourage movements of popular opinion whose purpose would be to coerce the House of Commons. Nor were large landowners ready to imitate the Anti-Corn Law League and buy up 40s. freeholds to gain Protectionist votes in the county elections, since once the specific crisis had passed the result would be ultimately in favour of democracy. Up until December 1845, the protection societies were politically powerless.

The ministerial crisis, however, suddenly transformed the situation. In the weeks between Peel's resignation on 5 December and his speech of 27 January containing details of his proposals, meetings of local protection societies were held in every county in England.[1] At a meeting of 9 December the Central Society revised its constitution. Henceforth the battle was to be fought in the registration courts; petitions were to be sent to both Houses of Parliament and memorials to the Queen asking for a dissolution; and pledges against repeal were to be extracted from all members of parliament with the threat that otherwise they would be thrown out at the next elections.[2] 'The Agricultural Constituencies seem to be riding in every direction,' Lord George Bentinck wrote to his father on 2 January, 'and the cry of "No Surrender" seems very general.'[3] At meeting after meeting in January and February, Conservative members pledged themselves to the Corn Laws, a turn of events by which some historians have explained the unexpectedly large opposition which Peel encountered in the House of Commons.[4] The extent to which the agitation in the counties determined anti-Peel votes cannot be gauged, but the decision of the Agricultural Protection Society to interfere in elections helped Thomas Hildyard to defeat the popular Lord Lincoln (who had entered Peel's cabinet in December) in the Nottinghamshire South by-election in

[1] The proceedings and speeches at these meetings are reported daily in the *Standard* and *John Bull*.

[2] *Standard*, 11 December 1845.

[3] Bentinck to his father, 2 January 1846. Portland Mss, PWH/193.

[4] This is the view of G.L.Mosse, 'The Anti-League, 1844–46', *Economic History Review* (December 1947), 134–42, of G.Kitson Clark, 'The Repeal of the Corn Laws and the Politics of the Forties', *ibid*. (August 1951), 1–13, and of M. Lawson-Tancred, 'The Anti-League and the Corn Law Crisis of 1846', *Historical Journal*, III, 2 (1960), 162 83.

February. The society contributed £2,000 and its most experienced agent, Mr Croucher, to Hildyard's campaign.[1]

There were many agriculturalists who continued to believe throughout December and January that Peel would not introduce a total repeal of the Corn Laws, or at least that he would accompany repeal with sufficient compensation in the form of tax relief to counteract the injury which they would sustain from free trade. Such men were unwilling to organise against Peel and were prepared to give the government a fair hearing.[2] Lord George Bentinck was exasperated by this attitude, and by Stanley's advice to ministers and Conservative members who were prepared to vote for repeal not to resign their seats and seek again their constituents' support. Bentinck told Stanley that

it would have been very good and very Constitutional advice to have given them before they got elected, 'to give no pledges' – but having been elected by virtue entirely of specific pledges, it is too late to repent the indiscretion of having given them. Honour – Honesty – and every feeling of a Gentleman dictate in my opinion in such cases the obligation to resign their seats before giving a vote in breach of these pledges.

I think the most damning fact of the whole of this bad business will be the shock that will be given to the mind of the Middle Classes of the English People by such wholesale examples of political lying and pledge-breaking on the part of the more educated and exalted Rank of Men who constitute their Representatives and the Peers of Parliament.[3]

Bentinck's fury was inspired by a high aristocratic ideal, but Stanley took a more practical view of affairs. He discouraged the party from adopting Bentinck's suggestion of moving an amendment to the address.[4] Bentinck hoped that a display of firmness would force Peel to stick by his party, but Stanley knew that

[1] Bentinck to his father, 11 and 13 February 1846. Portland Mss, PWH/203, 205.

[2] The Duke of Buckingham believed that Peel would adhere to the sliding scale, rather than throw himself into the arms of Russell and the Radicals (Buckingham to Disraeli, 7 December 1845. Hughenden Mss, B/XXI/B/1157). Croker shared Buckingham's optimism (Croker to Peel, 16 December 1845. Jennings, *Croker*, iii, 40–1).

[3] Bentinck to Stanley, 20 January 1846. Derby Mss, 132/13.

[4] Bentinck to his father, 28 December 1845. Portland Mss, PWH/198.

nothing could change Peel's mind and that the factious course of asking the Commons for a hasty vote before Peel had produced his proposals would secure a large majority against the protectionists.[1] Bentinck was infuriated by Stanley's reserve, and, taunting him with the question whether he meant 'to act a second edition of Gladstone on Maynooth', drew from Stanley a full statement of his position at the beginning of 1846.

If you ask me what course I mean to take in Parliament, I must answer that my course must be guided by circumstances which I cannot at present at all foresee; and that I shall not be called on to take any course, unless a measure proposed by the Government shall come up to the House of Lords... In such a case I think the Lords ought very well and carefully consider the whole position of parties with reference to such a question before they reject the Bill. I will be no party to any premature declarations of hostility, or to amendments volunteered upon the Address... I think further that the Landed Interest ought not to allow themselves to be influenced by the personal feelings which they may entertain towards those by whom it is introduced; that they ought to consider it as a whole and as a system of Government, not merely as an isolated measure in which the interests of different classes of the community are to be pitted against each other... They should weigh well the consequences of the overthrow of the present Government, and the practicability of forming one, with a chance of permanence, upon any other system, and composed of any other materials. To such a result I confess I do not see my way; and I own I would rather accept from the present Administration a measure of which I did not wholly approve, though I might think it would have come with better grace from others, than run the risk of all the evils which must result from the long interregnum in the formation of an Administration, or from a long struggle on such a subject as the Corn Laws, to be finally decided by an appeal to the excited passions of a General Election. Such are my views at the present time – I am afraid they will not be very satisfactory to you, and I have no great reason to hope that they will be adopted by the bulk of the Agricultural party either in or out of Parliament.[2]

The experience of office and the memory of Peel's kid-gloved opposition to Melbourne's government had left their mark on Stanley. The studied coolness of his letter to Bentinck sprang

[1] Bentinck to his father, 20 January 1846. *ibid.* PWH/200.
[2] Stanley to Bentinck, 14 January 1846 (copy). Derby Mss, 176/2.

from his concern to maintain political stability, to prevent the destruction of the Conservative party, and thus to preserve the aristocratic order. Since he saw no possibility of forming a government on principles different from Peel's, nor any individuals with whom effectively to cooperate – 'I try in vain to picture to myself the idea of a purely Protection cabinet' – Stanley considered it his duty to preserve 'a party to which, notwithstanding many and not unimportant differences of opinion among themselves, I have looked upon as a safeguard against the innovating spirit of the present day in matters even more essential than the maintenance of the Corn Laws'.[1] It is difficult to escape the conclusion that Stanley ought to have remained in the cabinet and have shared in whatever obloquy befell it for the same reasons that Wellington did. On hearing that Wellington had agreed to serve Peel, Stanley remarked that only Wellington could belong to a government of whose measures he disapproved, to which the Duke replied, with more bite, that Stanley was incapable of so doing.[2]

On 12 January, Monckton Milnes told Guizot that the protectionist forces were so slight and so disorganised that the agriculturalists were at Peel's mercy.[3] The *Illustrated London News* predicted that, as on previous occasions, Peel would be able to persuade the Tories that they were better off with him than with Russell and the Whigs.[4] But the government had already used up that argument. The protectionists heard Peel's proposals on 27 January in silent dismay. Instead of abolishing the malt tax, or transferring local rates on land to general taxation, Peel offered as compensation an amendment of the law of settlement, the transfer of the upkeep of the Irish constabulary from Irish landowners to the central government, the consolidation of the highway administration, payment of the Poor Law auditors out of the national purse, and the drainage loan scheme. Malmesbury

[1] Stanley to Colquhon, 17 January 1846 (copy). *ibid.* 176/2.
[2] Stanley to Peel, 1 December 1845. Parker, *Peel*, iii, 236; Wellington to Croker, 29 December 1845. Jennings, *Croker*, ii, 252.
[3] Reid, *Milnes*, i, 368.
[4] *Illustrated London News*, 17 January 1846.

immediately denounced the schemes as 'mere mockery'.[1] In Disraeli's words, 'no degree of rhetorical skill could invest with any substance these shadowy schemes of compensation. A feeling of blank disappointment or renewed indignation seemed to pervade the whole Conservative benches.'[2] George Bankes sounded the protectionist call to arms and asked the House of Commons to repudiate the very notion of compensation. There could be no compensation for the injury which Peel was doing the farmers.[3] But what was the purpose of a fight when, as Philip Pusey remarked, defeat was a foregone conclusion, since any bill introduced by Peel was as if it were an act of parliament?[4] Peel had refused to consider a dissolution, on the sound ground that members were not delegates and that the House of Commons was therefore competent to deal with the Corn Laws as with any other question. On 31 March, agriculturalists from Kent, Surrey, Sussex, and other southern counties met to form a society to agitate for the repeal of the malt tax.[5] That was the sign that the farmers had despaired of the Corn Laws.

By the time that the debate began, Bentinck had abandoned his hopes of defeating the Corn Bill in the Commons, but he was still determined that 'for the sake of Political Morals and the Characters of Public Men...a salutary lesson should in all cases be taught to the delinquent Politicians'.[6] Unlike Stanley, he was prepared to destroy the Conservative party in a losing cause. The formation of a Protectionist party in parliament was quickly begun. Bentinck appeared for the first time at a meeting of the Agricultural Protection Society, held after Peel's speech of 27 January. All his parliamentary life Bentinck had been a silent backbencher. His single contribution to parliamentary activity had been as chairman of the select committee on the Game Laws in 1845. He had refused office in Grey's ministry of 1830,[7] to

---

[1] Malmesbury, *Memoirs*, i, 65.

[2] Disraeli, *Bentinck*, 74–5.

[3] 27 January 1846. *Hansard*, 3rd Series, lxxxiii, 328.

[4] Pusey to T. D. Acland, January 1846. A. H. D. Acland (ed.), *Memoir and Letters of the Right Honourable Sir Thomas Acland* (London, 1902), 134–5.

[5] *Standard*, 1 April 1846.

[6] Bentinck to his father, 10 February 1846. Portland Mss, PWH/202.

[7] *Dictionary of National Biography* (London, 1885), iv, 298.

which, like the rest of the Canningites, he gave his support and from which he withdrew it in 1834 to follow Graham and Stanley into the Conservative party. Unwilling to take time away from his racing life, he again refused office in 1841 under Peel, despite Stanley's attempts to persuade him to accept.[1] Suddenly, in 1846, Peel's betrayal shocked him into political activity, and he began to work towards the creation of a permanent third party of the landed interest. 'I keep horses in three counties,' he told a political opponent, 'and they tell me that I shall save some fifteen hundred a year by free trade. I don't care for that; what I cannot bear is being sold.'[2] At the meeting of the Protection Society he outlined his strategy: to prolong the debate night after night in the Commons while agitating the question in the country, particularly at by-elections, so that the voice of the country could make itself heard before the Corn Bill reached the House of Lords. Debaters were carefully lined up, a committee was appointed to communicate with possible opponents of Peel, and a parliamentary staff was created to secure attendance at the debates.[3]

After the first night of the debate, Lord John Russell described the Protectionists as 'a very strong and compact party, from 220 to 240 in the House of Commons, and no one knows how many in the Lords'.[4] Peel, astounded by the rapid emergence of a Protectionist party, gave up his slight hopes that the Conservative party might survive.[5] The party was well enough organised to keep up a steady flow of Protectionist speeches and draw out the debate on the first reading of the Corn Bill for three weeks. And yet as late as 16 February, the *Standard* was still calling for the formation of a country party.[6] The party was already there; what was wanting was a leader. Bentinck was unwilling to assume the position. Handicapped by a very weak voice, unversed

[1] *Ibid.* iv, 299; W. Harris, *The History of the Radical Party in Parliament* (London, 1885), 366.

[2] Monypenny and Buckle, ii, 360.

[3] Disraeli, *Bentinck*, 80-1.

[4] Russell to his wife, 16 February 1846. D. MacCarthy and A. Russell, *Lady John Russell: A Memoir* (London, 1910), 81.

[5] Peel to Queen Victoria, 11 February 1846. Parker, *Peel*, iii, 339.

[6] *Standard*, 16 February 1846.

in parliamentary debate, and ignorant of economic questions, he did not even, at first, feel up to speaking as a private member.[1] The Duke of Bedford called him 'the most bigoted and violent of Tories',[2] and while his vote for the Maynooth grant and his life-long support of the Jews clear him of the first charge, violence was his watchword in 1846. He considered Peel and his colleagues to be 'no better than Common Cheats' whose punishment in the 'good old days' would have been cropping of the ears and consignment to the pillory.[3] Once aroused against Peel, he threw himself into the subject of the Corn Laws, working long hours getting up statistics, and attending the debates in the Commons with almost fanatical regularity. After his speech winding up the debate on the first reading, he was asked to take the leadership, but he wrote to his father that the party's confidence in him was misplaced.

So conscious was I of how much better a speech might have been made from my matter that till I sat down and to my astonishment received the congratulations not only of my own friends but of my Opponents, I was throughout painfully oppressed with the feeling and conviction that I had signally and disgracefully failed... They now most of them want me to stand forward as their avowed Leader, but I have no thoughts or pretensions to do anything of the kind; one speech upon a subject on which I have devoted so much time and trouble does not qualify a man to be a Leader; on General Subjects I am much too ill-informed and on multitudes of Questions utterly ignorant. I therefore am resolutely determined to keep my place and have no thoughts of listening to any hasty entreaties that I would set up as a Leader.[4]

The party badly needed an acknowledged leader and a formal organisation. It was no easy matter explaining to the country gentlemen the manoeuvres of a sustained parliamentary strategy. 'Pray continue to be at the Carlton about three,' Stafford O'Brien wrote to Disraeli on 23 February. 'The squires cannot in the least comprehend our schemes of voting and there may be some

---

[1] He tried to persuade a lawyer friend to read his speech for him. Disraeli received this information (Martin to Disraeli, 6 October 1851. Hughenden Mss, B/XX/Be/758) and included it in his biography of Bentinck (90).

[2] Walpole, *Russell*, i, 386.

[3] Bentinck to Stanley, 7 January 1846. Derby Mss, 132/13.

[4] Bentinck to his father, 5 March 1846. Portland Mss, PWH/212.

hideous confusion tonight.'[1] O'Brien arranged a meeting for 31 March, at which a committee was formed for 'considering and deciding upon the course to be adopted by the Party in Parliament on all important occasions'.[2] The first meeting of this committee, of which Disraeli was a member, took place at George Bankes' house on 21 April to discuss the party's relations with the Irish members.[3] So did the *ad hoc* organisation formed to fight the Corn Bill become a permanent party. Bentinck yielded to pressure and accepted the leadership, with the qualifications that he be replaced as soon as a more suitable candidate were found and that he be free to act independently on religious questions.[4] Since Bentinck was a thorough believer in religious toleration and equality, it was distinctly ominous for the future of the party that the Protestant bigot, William Beresford, was, without Bentinck's knowledge, elected party whip with Charles Newdegate.[5]

Until Bentinck's installation as leader, the party had been directed by George Bankes, William Miles, and Stafford O'Brien though with great reliance on Disraeli's assistance.[6] Disraeli had attempted at the end of January to persuade J. C. Herries, the chancellor of the exchequer under Goderich in 1828, and one of the most respected financial authorities of the day, to return to parliament at a by-election and take the lead of the Protectionists. Herries was an ardent protectionist, but he advised Disraeli to seek a younger man for the leadership.[7] Disraeli himself was distrusted by the Protectionists, whose sensibilities were offended by his bitter invective against Peel,[8] and so the leadership devolved upon Bentinck.[9]

[1] O'Brien to Disraeli, 23 February 1846. Hughenden Mss, B/XXI/S/449.
[2] O'Brien to Disraeli, 28 March 1846. *ibid*. B/XXI/S/452.
[3] Beresford to Disraeli, 13 April 1846. *ibid*. B/XX/Bd/1.
[4] Disraeli, *Bentinck*, 179.
[5] Greville, ii, 376.
[6] The *Illustrated London News*, 2 May 1846, wrote that Bentinck was 'at present recognised as the head of the Protectionist party, Mr Miles and Mr Stafford O'Brien having apparently fallen into the ranks'.
[7] Herries to Disraeli, 30 January 1846. Hughenden Mss, B/XXI/H/529.
[8] The *Standard*, 26 January 1846, warned the party against associating with Disraeli.
[9] Bankes to Disraeli, 31 December 1850: 'I do not think Lord George ever gave a formal assent to the recognition made of him as leader of his party. It was

Parliamentary strategy was henceforth controlled by Bentinck, which meant an all-out attack on the government. Stafford O'Brien wanted the party to take the ground of a fixed-duty compromise,[1] but Bentinck would have nothing to do with compromise. He continued his unbending assault upon the government, a strategy which had one, albeit dim, prospect of success: that by playing for time the Protectionists might keep the Corn Bill from becoming law before the next general election. The Lords would not receive the bill until well after the Easter recess. The House of Commons was in its fifth year, so that if the bill could be defeated in the Lords, or sent back to the Commons with too many amendments to get through in the remainder of the session, a dissolution would probably take place before the bill could be introduced again. The Protectionists' only hope lay in an election. 'There is no doubt', Bentinck wrote to Stanley on 20 April, 'but that our fight in the Commons has worked with great effect in the Country and that the Country is fast changing its mind.'[2]

Attempts to turn out the government on side issues failed. Whig–Protectionist combinations defeated the government on a Charitable Trusts Bill in the Lords and on a minor question involving the Poor Law in the Commons, but neither was important enough to force Peel's resignation. In the Commons, the government talked out a Ten Hours bill on 13 May, when they were in some danger of being beaten.[3] Peel decided to postpone legislation on the touchy question of the sugar duties, due to expire on 5 July, until the Corn Bill should have safely got through the Lords.[4] For a brief moment in April an Irish–Protectionist alliance against the government had seemed possible. In March

often pressed upon him and at last tacitly acceded to' (Hughenden Mss, B/XXI/B /38); Bentinck to his father, 31 March 1846: 'The language on both sides of the House every day is growing to be that our Party is coming into Power. Should this be the case I see very clearly that I shall be forced whether I will or not to lead the House of Commons for which I feel quite unfitted and quite unequal – but I greatly fear I shall not be able to help myself' (Portland Mss, PWH/216).

[1] O'Brien to Disraeli, 28 March 1846. Hughenden Mss, B/XXI/S/452.
[2] Bentinck to Stanley, 20 April 1846. Derby Mss, 132/13.
[3] Peel had decided that his behaviour in 1844 meant that he would have to resign if beaten (Peel to Hardinge, 23 May 1846. Peel Mss, Add. Mss 40475, ff. 232–4).
[4] Peel to Dalhousie, 16 May 1846. *ibid*. 40592, ff. 24–5.

a coercion bill for Ireland was introduced in the Lords, and on 6 April Bentinck chastised the government for prescribing coercion instead of remedial legislation, for Ireland's ills. Smith O'Brien, the Young Ireland leader, sounded out Bentinck on an arrangement whereby the Irish would vote against the Corn Bill if the Protectionists would support a bill to admit grain duty-free into starving Ireland for three years and vote against the coercion bill. No formal agreement was reached, and when every Irish Protectionist and most of the rest of the party voted for the coercion bill on 2 May, the Irish members no longer had any reason to vote against the Corn Bill. The episode may even have hurt the Protectionist cause. It served as a warning to Peel to postpone the second reading of the coercion bill until the Corn Bill had been passed in the Lords.

Thus the fate of the Corn Bill came to rest with the Lords. By the time that it reached its second reading there, Stanley had become an open opponent of the government and, to all appearances, leader of the Protectionists in the House of Lords. In January and February he held to his original position that he would do nothing until the Corn Bill came to the Lords. On 19 February, Wellington wrote him a long letter, beseeching him to put himself forward as the leader of the Conservative party in the Lords. Wellington explained that since October his chief object had been to preserve Peel's party, but that he now saw that the confidence of the Commons in Peel had vanished. He therefore wanted Stanley to take control of the party so that the country would not be endangered by its disintegration. He himself would not be accepted by the party, and so the way was open for Stanley to persuade the Lords to accept the Commons' decision and then, the food issue out of the way, lead a re-united Conservative party.[1] The proposal must have been attractive to Stanley, but there was one insuperable objection to it: he was still determined to vote against repeal and therefore could not counsel the Lords in the opposite direction. Wellington's letter had no perceptible effect on him. In March, he continued to

---

[1] Wellington to Stanley, 19 February 1846. Derby Mss, 133/2.

abstain from exerting influence on his fellow peers. On 7 March, he explained his position to the Duke of Rutland.

I cannot say that further reflection, or the arguments which I have heard...tend to reconcile me to the measure, or to shake my conviction of its impolicy and of the injury which the Government and the House of Commons have suffered in public estimation for their sudden conversion: and which injury the House of Lords will sustain also, should they reverse their former decisions...The division, I hear, will be very close, but I keep myself as far aloof as I can from conversations on the subject; and from deference to the Duke, shall abstain from taking any more active part than that of recording my vote, and stating my opinion, in opposition to the second reading of the Bill. So much I cannot avoid doing, though I need not say I do it with great reluctance.[1]

Stanley had thus abandoned his intention of not even speaking against the bill. But his position was clearly becoming unintelligible. The reference to the Duke, after the latter's letter of February, was a shield to protect him from making a choice. Though Stanley seems not to have been aware of it, there was, in fact, no choice. The Lords could not throw out the Corn Bill, as he thought they should, without his becoming leader of the Protectionist party.

On 9 March, a group of Protectionist peers met at the house of the Duke of Richmond. Stanley knew nothing of its arrangements and did not attend.![2] But the Earl of Eglinton, unbeknownst to Stanley, read a letter in which Stanley had expressed his views to him and in which he had promised to support the Protectionist party. It was thereupon decided by the peers 'to look upon Stanley as the leader of the party, and to do nothing without consulting him'.[3] Eglinton and Malmesbury were chosen to act as whips. Malmesbury reported Stanley to be 'evidently very much pleased and flattered at the confidence reposed in him'.[4] Stanley was astonished by the strength and ability of the Protectionist party in the Commons, but as late as 19 March he was again considering whether he ought to speak against the

---

[1] Stanley to Rutland, 7 March 1846 (copy). *ibid.* 176/2.
[2] Stanley to Lord Exeter, 7 March 1846 (copy). *ibid.*
[3] Malmesbury, *Memoirs*, i, 169.
[4] *Ibid.*

bill.[1] Finally, on 29 March, he presented some protectionist petitions in the Lords and declared himself to be against the bill. Party connexion he continued to abjure, on the same ground as before, that the formation of a Protectionist party was foolhardy and that the natural, and desirable, outcome of events was the rehabilitation of the Conservative party in opposition to the Whig government which was bound to come into office after the Corn Bill had been passed. He spent the whole of April in the country, enjoying the 'relief from office' and from political discussions.[2]

Bentinck urged Stanley to return to Westminster after the Easter recess in battle dress.

My opinion is very strong that without any division there should be a vigorous debate on the 1st reading of the Bill and that you should take the occasion to exert yourself and make one of your powerful speeches. There is no doubt, I believe, but that our fight in the Commons has worked well in the Country and that the Country is fast changing its mind. If our miserable speeches in the Commons can do anything in the Country, how much more would your handling of the question work its way to the hearts of the Sober thinking. I want to see your speech go forth to the Country to be learnt by the Country, learnt by heart and well digested before the second reading of the bill in the Lords, so I hope you will insist upon a long interval between the first and second readings of the Bill.

My opinion is that unless the Lords 'win or lose' fight an obstinate and fearless battle something like ours in point of duration and superior by far I hope in skill, vigour and ability, they will forever sink into insignificance as an effective Body in the Constitution and will and ought to be looked upon hereafter as a mere cypher in the State, a Chamber of Invalids and fit only to be superannuated and abolished.[3]

The new, flattering, conciliatory tone of Bentinck's correspondence with Stanley is evidence that Bentinck knew that Stanley was coming round. But for the moment Stanley resisted all pressure. He remained silent during the debate on the first reading. On the eve of the second reading, a great meeting of landowners, farmers, and members of parliament, presided over

[1] Stanley to Portland, 19 March 1846 (copy). Derby Mss, 176/2.
[2] Stanley to C. Murray, 26 and 29 April 1846 (copies). *ibid.*
[3] Bentinck to Stanley, 20 April 1846. *ibid.* 132/13.

by Buckingham and Richmond, 'swore eternal hostility to the Corn Bill and...announced [Stanley] the leader of the opposition with great triumph'.[1] Three days later, Stanley delivered a long, impassioned speech against the Corn Bill and then, having done his duty as an independent peer, took no further part in the campaign against the bill. However loudly men might proclaim him as their leader, he persisted in not taking on the job.

Stanley's ambivalent reaction to the Corn Law crisis was the result of his inability to choose between two conflicting considerations both dear to his heart; the desire to prevent a permanent split in the Conservative party and the need to satisfy his personal concern for political consistency. His original intention, resignation without opposition, lost meaning as a method of keeping the party together once a strong Protectionist party had been organised in the Commons. Since abstention from the debate could no longer help to save his party, Stanley was able to speak against the bill and uphold, at least in his own eyes, his reputation for political integrity. And by the time that he spoke, on 25 May, there was little chance of the bill's being defeated, so that he was saved from making a choice between Bentinck's view that the Lords committed suicide if they meekly accepted the Commons' decision, and Wellington's opinion that another collision with the lower House so soon after 1831 would threaten the existence of the House of Lords.[2]

The most notable aspect of Stanley's speech was the absence of any personal rancour against Peel and his colleagues. Stanley wanted to leave the door open for the Protectionists to find their way back into the Conservative fold. His speech was, even so, far more than a face-saving defence of the Corn Laws: it was an eloquent plea for aristocratic government.

If against your own deliberate opinions, you consent to pass this measure, be prepared to abdicate the hitherto high place you have held

---

[1] Broughton, *Recollections*, vi, 172.

[2] On 28 May, Wellington said in the Lords that, the bill having been passed by the Commons and having the known approval of the Crown, 'there is an end of the functions of the House of Lords' (*Hansard*, 3rd Series, lxxxvi, 1404). Disraeli found this opinion 'not easy to distinguish from the vote of the long parliament which openly abrogated those functions' (Disraeli, *Bentinck*, 229).

in the Constitution; if you sacrifice your own opinion to the intimidation of faction, the allurements of power, or the dictation of any Minister on earth, be prepared hereafter to be looked upon as a subordinate branch of the Constitution, to be looked upon only as the registrars of the edicts of the House of Commons, and as the pliant followers of the Minister of the day. My Lords, if I know anything of the constitutional value of this House, it is to impose a salutary obstacle to rash and inconsiderate legislation – it is to protect the people from the consequences of their own imprudence. It has never been the course of this House to resist a continued and deliberately formed public opinion... but it is yours to check hasty legislation, leading to irreparable evils... if, by the blessing of God, your decision on this great question shall arrest the progress of this hasty and inconsiderate measure; if you shall thus give time for the intelligence of the country to act upon the public mind; if, happily, you shall succeed in leading back the country to a wiser course, and in adopting the too much despised wisdom of your ancestors, then you will justly be a 'proud aristocracy'; proud of having faithfully discharged the duty vested in you by the Constitution; proud of having withstood alike the seductions of power, and the threats of popular clamour; proud of having succeeded in saving your country from this great delusion, this hazardous and fearful experiment.[1]

It was a powerful peroration, worthy of the former Rupert of debate. But deep as was Stanley's attachment to the House of Lords, would he have made that speech if he had believed that there was still a chance that the Corn Bill might be thrown out? The speech, whatever else it might have achieved, settled one question. Though Stanley continued to deprecate the formation of a permanent Protectionist party, there was no longer any doubt that, whatever kind of conservative party were to survive the Corn Law crisis, Stanley would be its leader.

While Stanley dithered, an attempt was made to find a meeting house for Protectionist and Whig peers in an amendment substituting a small, fixed duty on corn for the sliding scale. There was some prospect of success, since most of the Whig peers disliked total repeal and were dissatisfied with Peel's meagre compensation to the landed interest.[2] Even among Conservative

[1] 25 May 1846. *Hansard*, 3rd Series, lxxxvi, 1175–6.
[2] Russell to Graham, 18 August 1852: 'I induced my party, much against their will, to agree to support Sir Robert Peel's repeal of the Corn Laws' (Parker,

ministers in the Lords only Aberdeen, and perhaps Dalhousie, favoured the bill itself; the others were voting for it to keep Peel in power.[1] As Lord Brougham put it, unless some compromise were reached, there was 'a measure of great importance about to pass, with 50 Commoners and 20 Peers in its favour'.[2]

Early in the session, Lord and Lady Beaumont had hatched a scheme to place Palmerston at the head of a fixed-duty party, but the plan had not passed beyond the dreams of its authors.[3] Then, after the Easter recess, the project of a fixed-duty alliance was again taken up. In the first week of April, at a party of Whigs and Protectionists, the Duke of Bedford promoted the idea, and in the next few weeks it became evident that the plan had the approval of almost all the Whig peers. In May, Lord Normanby made formal overtures to Stanley through Malmesbury, and it was arranged that the Whigs would vote for a Protectionist amendment, although it was not decided how large the fixed duty should be.[4] Russell, who had pledged his party to total repeal in his famous Edinburgh Letter of 22 November 1845, took alarm and called a meeting of the Whig peers at Lansdowne House on 23 May. There the peers gave way to his threat to resign the party leadership if they combined with the Protectionists. Palmerston later summed up the meeting: 'All unanimous against the Bill, and all unanimous not to oppose it'.[5] The Lansdowne House decision ended the Corn Law struggle, and two nights later Stanley delivered his speech against repeal.

In the Commons, the Corn Bill had received majorities of 97, 88, and 100. On 28 May, it passed the second reading in the

---

Graham, ii, 174). Charles Arbuthnot dined at Lord Ashburton's early in May and found the Whigs there in agreement that nearly every Whig disliked the bill (Arbuthnot to Peel, 6 March 1846. Peel Mss, Add. Mss 40484, ff. 60–3). See also Brougham to J. Murray, February 1846. Brougham Mss, Add. Mss 40687, ff. 45–8.

[1] Brougham to Murray, February 1846. *ibid.*
[2] Brougham to Murray, 28 February 1846. *ibid.* 40687, f. 51.
[3] H. C. F. Bell, *Lord Palmerston* (London, 1936), 363–9.
[4] Malmesbury, *Memoirs*, i, 172.
[5] Broughton, *Recollections*, vi, 173. Lord Ashburton told Croker that 'Melbourne bounced and complained, saying that seeing you are as a party resolved to eat any dirt Peel may make, I will not refuse my mouthful' (Ashburton to Croker, 24 May 1846. Jennings, *Croker*, iii, 71).

Lords by 211 votes to 164. Buckingham's amendment to continue protection after a three-year suspension was lost by 33 votes, as was Winchilsea's amendment for a fixed duty. Had the Lords returned the bill to the Commons with a fixed-duty amendment, Peel might have dissolved parliament and a Protectionist majority might have been returned at the elections. More probably, free trade would simply have been delayed for a year and the Protectionists split into the warring factions of those who accepted the compromise and those, like Bentinck, to whom the very notion of compromise was odious. The failure to achieve a compromise in the Lords gave the Protectionist party a *raison d'être* and left it permanently estranged from Peel.

There remained the question of what to do about Peel. It was intolerable that he should remain in office backed by a party comprising little more than one-sixth of the House of Commons. The Irish Coercion Bill provided the earliest opportunity to turn him out. Disraeli wanted to do so over the sugar duties bill, which the government was bound to introduce before the end of June. As the price for the colonial interest's support for the Corn Bill,[1] Peel would have to maintain the distinction between free-grown and slave-grown sugar. Whig opposition to the bill would therefore be solid, and Disraeli suggested that the Protectionists should also oppose it on the ground that, while in principle they opposed the free import of slave-grown sugar, they were forced to seek compensation in the form of cheap sugar for the loss of agricultural protection. But Bentinck rejected the manoeuvre outright: 'No, we have nothing to sustain us but our principles. We are not privy-councillors, but we may be honest men.'[2]

The Irish Coercion Bill was not a happy instrument with which to depose Peel. Russell was embarrassed by the support given to it by the Whig party in the House of Lords. Even more awkward was the fact that the Protectionists had voted for the first reading of the bill in the Commons. During the Whitsun recess, nevertheless, Bentinck agreed to Disraeli's suggestion that the Protec-

[1] *John Bull*, 18 April 1846, estimated the West Indian interests' strength at 15, of whom only Miles voted against Peel. According to Bentinck the combined strength of the East and West Indian interests was 16, of whom 14 supported the government (Bentinck to his father, 9 June 1846. Portland Mss, PWH/220).

[2] Disraeli, *Bentinck*, 233–4.

tionists oppose the bill on second reading. At the same time, the Whig peers, Bessborough and Clarendon, advised Russell to oppose the bill on the ground that, if coercion were really necessary, its passage ought not to have been delayed for three months.[1]

In March, Peel had come to a tenuous agreement with Bentinck, through his whip, John Young, by which the Protectionists were to vote for the Coercion Bill if it were introduced in the Commons immediately after the Lords were finished with it. In return, Peel was to leave the third reading of the Corn Bill until after Easter. The Coercion Bill came down from the Lords on 15 March, but was not introduced in the Commons. On 26 March, the government announced that it would proceed the next day with its Customs Bill. Bentinck then disclosed in the Commons the substance of his negotiations with Young and asked Peel why the Customs Bill was taking precedence over the Coercion Bill. Peel and Young denied that a binding agreement had been made, and Peel declared himself to be at perfect liberty to postpone the Coercion Bill. Bentinck replied that 'if Her Majesty's Ministers did not in their hearts believe that there was any urgent necessity for passing this measure... if they showed this by their conduct in postponing this to other measures, some of which were not to come into operation for three years, then the case assumed a different complexion, and he could not say that the party with whom he acted in such a case would support Her Majesty's Ministers'.[2]

Not until 1 May did the bill receive its first reading, and another six weeks passed without its being debated, even though there were four nights on which government business other than corn and customs was debated.[3] On 8 June the Protectionists met at George Bankes' house to decide whether to support Russell's amendment that the Coercion Bill be read that day six months. Bentinck knew that there would be great difficulty in persuading the party to oppose the bill, 'unless the vote can be turned into one of confidence'.[4] Stanley was enthusiastically in favour of such

[1] Arbuthnot to Peel, 2 May and 7 June, 1846. Peel Mss, Add. Mss 40484. ff. 311–12, 315–16.

[2] *Hansard*, 3rd Series, lxxxv, 141.

[3] Disraeli, *Bentinck*, 245.

[4] Bentinck to Disraeli, 5 June 1846. Hughenden Mss, B/XX/Be/3.

an arrangement. He had decided that Peel had become more of a radical threat than Russell, and that he would henceforth try to keep power by outbidding Russell for liberal support. Russell, he thought, would remain tied to the old Whigs. The reunion of the Conservative party would therefore have to exclude Peel, and the great immediate object was to get the dissolution out of his hands. 'If he had dissolved the parliament', Bentinck wrote, after discussing the matter with Stanley, 'there would have been a terrible division of the Conservative ranks, which we hope will now in great measure be avoided.'[1] If Russell came into office, it was not to be expected that he would call an election before October, and probable that he would wait until the end of the next session, by which time, Stanley hoped, the Conservative party would be able to present a united front to the electorate.

Two strains in the high Tory mentality came into conflict over the vote on the Coercion Bill. On the one hand, as in 1830 when the ultra Tories took up reform to spite Wellington and Peel, they were willing to form any combination on any issue in order to remove a government which they believed to have betrayed them. On the other hand, they loathed a pragmatic approach to politics: political consistency was the mark of the country gentleman. The Protectionists came to no firm understanding on 8 June. It was not known how they would vote before the division took place. Since Disraeli wrote that 'the party was never better managed than on this division',[2] the future prospects of the Protectionist party must have looked dim on 25 June when the vote was taken. Only 69 Protectionists voted with Bentinck and Disraeli against Peel, while 105 supported the bill and 74 did not vote.[3] The bill was defeated by 292 votes to 219; Peel resigned and the Queen sent for Lord John Russell.

Sir James Graham accused those Protectionists who voted

---

[1] Bentinck to his father, 9 June 1846. Portland Mss, PWH/220.

[2] Disraeli, *Bentinck*, 295.

[3] Graham spoke of the 'seventy-three conservative members of parliament who displaced the late government by a factious vote' (Morley, *Gladstone*, i, 296), but he may have confused the number of Protectionists who voted against with the size of the majority against the bill. Monypenny wrote that 'over seventy' Protectionists voted against the bill (Monypenny and Buckle, ii, 402) but I have trusted to my own calculations.

against their principles of 'vindictive recklessness' in consenting to leave Ireland exposed to bloodshed and anarchy,[1] and Lady Westmorland denounced the vote as 'the basest combination one ever heard of'.[2] But the debate was never a serious discussion of the Irish question. There were never more than forty members in the House at one time while the bill was being debated.[3] The vote was known to be, and accepted as, a vote of confidence. During the debate on the Corn Bill Disraeli had justly accused Peel of destroying the basis of the constitution, the party system.

What I cannot endure is to hear a man come down and say ,'I will rule without respect of party, though I rose by party; and I care not for your judgment, for I look to posterity'. Sir, very few people reach posterity. Who amongst us may arrive at that destination I presume not to vaticinate. Posterity is a most limited assembly...But one thing is quite evident, that while we are appealing to posterity – while we are admitting the principles of relaxed commerce – there is extreme danger of our admitting the principles of relaxed politics. I advise, therefore, that we all, whatever may be our opinions about free trade, oppose the introduction of free politics... Above all, maintain the line of demarcation between parties; for it is only by maintaining the independence of party that you can maintain the integrity of public men, and the power and influence of Parliament itself.[4]

By 1846, disgusted with his followers, Peel had become the symbol of national government, government which overrides mere considerations of party support in the interest of what it conceives to be the national welfare. For this broad and 'unselfish' attitude, Peel has received much praise. Modern historians have agreed with Thomas Raikes' judgement that Peel was 'too good for his party'.[5]

Government by party, however, for all its drawbacks, is the safest guarantee of political liberty to the elector and of political integrity in the elected. In an elective, representative system,

---

[1] Graham to Lord Heytesbury, 11 July 1846. Parker, *Graham*, ii, 41.

[2] Lady Westmorland to Arbuthnot, 7 June 1846. Parker, *Peel*, iii, 351.

[3] C. Woodham-Smith, *The Great Hunger*, Signet edition (Toronto, 1964), 82.

[4] 22 January 1846. *Hansard*, 3rd Series, lxxxiii, 122–3.

[5] Raikes, iv, 407. See A. A. W. Ramsay, *Sir Robert Peel* (London, 1928), 329 and G. Kitson Clark, *Peel and the Conservative Party* (London, 1929), 107–9.

party ought to represent opinion.[1] Peel was apt to think of a party as little more than a number of votes in the division lists. In the eighteenth century there may have been some justification for the view. But in an age when central legislation in almost every field was coming to be accepted as a means of shaping society, the view was inadequate. The question was no longer merely whether, but in what manner, the Queen's government was to be carried on. In 1845, Lord John Manners complained to Gladstone that Peel was using his followers unfairly by saying to the opposition: 'measures, not men', and to his own party: 'men, not measures'.[2] Disraeli was more bitter:

> He is so vain that he wants to figure in history as the settler of all great questions; but a Parliamentary constitution is not favourable to such ambitions: things must be done by parties, not by persons using parties as tools – especially men without imagination or any inspiring qualities, or who, rather, offer you duplicity instead of inspiration.[3]

Peel's defeat was necessary from a purely practical point of view, since he could no longer rely on a majority in the Commons. The sooner he were removed from office the better. The Protectionist opposition to the Coercion Bill required no other justification. Peel recognised the justice of his defeat. 'A Government', he said, on quitting office, 'ought to have a natural support. A Conservative Government should be supported by a Conservative party.'[4]

---

[1] In 1853, Disraeli denounced the mixture of opinion represented in Aberdeen's coalition government. 'The excellence of representative government...is that it should represent opinion. It is this quality which compensates for its inimitable and innate deficiencies...The representative form is not merely a clumsy machine; it has a tendency to be a corrupt one. Five or six hundred individuals invested with legislative functions, and subject to the influences of a powerful executive, are capable of any misconduct. Their very numbers divide the responsibility, and their assumed popular origin diverts and dissipates the odium. Our ancestors discovered in party, or political connection, a remedy for these injurious consequences, and a means of combining efficient and comparatively pure government with popular authority and control. Bodies of men acting in concert, advocating particular tenets, and recognising particular leaders, were animated by the principle of honour as well as by a sense of duty' ('Coalition' in W. Hutcheon (ed.), *Whigs and Whiggism* (London, 1913), 432).

[2] Manners to Gladstone, 6 February 1845. Gladstone Mss. Add. Mss 43362, ff. 68–71.

[3] Disraeli to Manners, 17 December 1845. Monypenny and Buckle, ii, 338–9.

[4] Memorandum for the cabinet of 21 June 1846. Parker, *Peel*, iii, 364.

4

IN THE DOLDRUMS

THE REPEAL of the Corn Laws left three parties in the field, none of which was capable of governing by its own strength. The one political alliance with any chance of permanence which might have been forged out of the chaos of 1846 – that between Whigs and Protectionists – had been killed at birth by Lord John Russell, the new prime minister, at the Lansdowne House meeting in May. There were members of both parties who regretted their failure to act together,[1] but once Peel had been dislodged and a Whig government assured of his support (in order to secure the triumph of free trade) installed, the tactical advantages which junction had offered disappeared. Although a loose engagement to support the new ministry was given by Richmond, Eglinton, Beaufort, Malmesbury, Bentinck, and Stafford O'Brien at a Lansdowne House dinner on 28 June,[2] Russell would not consider formal ties with any section of the Protectionists: 'neither principle nor prudence would permit it'.[3] He was unwilling to rest his government on the support of men whom he considered to be too extreme to assist him in extending the Irish franchise,

[1] Arbuthnot to Peel, 5 April 1846: 'I am sure from the Duke of Bedford's language that the Whigs are ill at ease. They have a hankering after a connection with part of the Protectionists...They have been led, as the Duke of Bedford told me, to look to the Protectionists in consequence of what Lord George Bentinck has said to a Whig friend of his...that a considerable portion of the persons with whom he acted would be glad to see a moderate Whig government formed; and that their demands would be very moderate and easily satisfied' (Peel Mss, Add. Mss 40484, ff. 292–7); Richmond to Stanley, 4 July 1846: 'If the small fry [Peelites] rejoin our ranks one by one all very well. For myself, I should much prefer John Russell and Co. to Graham, Sydney Herbert, and Lincoln...though I must add that I cannot support either' (Derby Mss, 131/13).

[2] Graham to Peel, 29 June 1846. Peel Mss, Add. Mss 40452, ff. 130–1. The Duke of Buccleuch, Graham's source of information, did not know whether Stanley was at the dinner.

[3] Russell, *Recollections and Suggestions*, 242. Russell declined, after a 'long and friendly conference' to grant the Protectionist Duke of Beaufort's request for office.

77

in providing some sort of tenant right for Ireland, and in extending direct taxation in England.[1] Lord Clarendon warned his cabinet colleagues that alliance with the Protectionists was the way to political destruction. The Whig party, 'aristocratical in its opinions, exclusive in its personnel, and guided by past historical reminiscences rather than by present public opinion', owed its newly won power to accident, not support in the country. It was therefore in need of 'the true conservative process of reform', and should look to fusion with the Peelites and some of the extreme free traders in order to enlist the sympathy of the middle class on which future governments would depend. The Whigs must demonstrate that they represented the 'industrial mind and conservative progress of the country'. Compact with the Protectionists would estrange the urban voters from the government.

The country will not stand still: an impetus has been given to men's minds that cannot be checked: wants and hopes have been excited that must be satisfied: commercial, financial and social reforms have been commenced and must be continued. The aristocracy – the party that has already announced its intention to promote a backward agitation, and hopes in two years to acquire strength sufficient to govern the country upon the principle of undoing all that has been done with much difficulty and sacrifice – cannot lend itself to the labours which a Liberal government has on hand. During the last five months this party has shown itself ignorant and regardless of the wants and wishes of the country, and as we are bound to believe its views are incorrect and its predictions of injury are falsified by events, time will diminish its power instead of giving it the strength it expects to gain, and it will consequently become an element of weakness as well as an increasing drag upon the government which looks to it for support. No voluntary aid from the Protectionists should be rejected, but none should be courted by any futile attempt at shaping the policy of the government to meet their objects.[2]

Russell was not convinced that the Whig party needed a large infusion of new blood. Three Radicals accepted non-cabinet posts

---

[1] Russell to Duncannon, 11 April 1846. Walpole, *Russell*, i, 423–4.

[2] Memorandum for the cabinet meeting on 29 June 1846. H. Maxwell, *The Life and Letters of George William Frederick, Fourth Earl of Clarendon* (London 1913), i, 265–7.

in the government, but Cobden, who left for the Continent in July, was not offered a cabinet seat, although Russell expressed a vague desire to find a place for him on his return. Cobden, at any rate, who placed his hopes for the introduction of a thorough system of direct taxation in Peel, had 'not the most distant desire' to mix with the Whig clique.[1] Cobden's exclusion from the cabinet pleased the conservative wing of the Whig party, represented in the cabinet by Lansdowne, Beauvale, and Duncannon, who desired the informal support of the Protectionists. The old party labels were beginning to belie the real division of parliament into liberal (Peelites and Radicals) and conservative (Whigs and Protectionists). Clarendon and Horsman wanted Cobden in the cabinet to detach him from a possible confederation with the Peelites.[2] Had they prevailed, the government might have taken up reform in earnest, leaving the Protectionists a more distinct place in politics and driving the conservative Peelites, like Goulburn and Gladstone, towards them. Russell's conservative policies over the next six years left the Protectionists with little more than protection to distinguish them from the Whigs.

Russell failed to bring any of the Peelites into his government, but the sincerity of his offer to Dalhousie, Lincoln, and Herbert was rendered suspect by his insistence that they agree to join before general policy was discussed.[3] The country was thus once more in the hands of a purely Whig cabinet, a result which gave encouragement to those Protectionists who wanted an early reunion of the Conservative party.

From the time that Smith O'Brien approached Bentinck in April 1846, the Protectionists were always suspected of, and occasionally indulged in, flirtation with the Irish Radicals. But even the few Protectionists who had sided with the Irish in the vote on the Coercion Bill had nothing in common with them. In 1844, O'Connell listed the minimum concessions which would satisfy the Irish: religious equality by concurrent endowment of

---

[1] Cobden to Russell, 4 July 1846. Gooch, *Later Correspondence*, i, 176–8.

[2] Gash, *Reaction and Reconstruction*, 194.

[3] Gladstone memorandum of 12 July 1846. Gladstone Mss, Add. Mss 44777, ff. 252–8.

the Catholic and Protestant Churches, extension of the county franchise, increase in urban representation, a fivefold increase in the income tax upon absentee landlords, and fixity of land tenure.[1] The Protectionists were prepared to grant none of these, and Bentinck's and Disraeli's future attempts to reach an understanding with the Irish came to naught. Neither their followers in parliament nor their supporters in the country would suffer a pact with the Irish, for which Melbourne's government had paid heavily. Even Peel had come to see, on retiring from office, that the Tories' prophecy of the futility of appeasing the Irish had been fulfilled.

There is an Irish party, a determined and not insignificant one, for which British indignation has no terrors. Their wish is to disgust England with Irish business and Irish members, and to induce England through sheer disgust, and the sense of public convenience from the obstruction offered to the progress of all other business in Parliament to listen to a repeal of the Legislative Union.[2]

Peel determined to remain aloof from all parties, and Graham resolved never again to act with the Conservatives who had combined with the Whigs to defeat Peel's government.[3] For the moment, the Peelites were content to prop up the Whig government. Lincoln urged Gladstone, who had been without a seat in the Commons since December 1845, to stand against the cabinet minister, Hobhouse, at the Nottingham by-election, but Gladstone could see no issue on which to oppose him. Members of the government, he said, had 'a perfect title to so much at least of a fair trial that their return to Parliament shall not be obstructed by persons who would find so much difficulty as I should in showing a broad and palpable and fundamental difference of views'.[4] The Peelites' toleration of the government did not imply kinship with it. One of Peel's reasons for resigning rather than

[1] O'Connell to C. Buller, 1844. Walpole, *Russell*, i, 395–6.

[2] Peel memorandum of 21 June 1846. Stanhope and Cardwell, *Peel Memoirs*, ii, 290–1.

[3] Graham told Gladstone that his resentment was not against Russell's government, but 'against the seventy-three conservative members of parliament who displaced the late government by a factious vote...with those gentlemen I can never unite' (Morley, *Gladstone*, i, 296).

[4] Gladstone to Lincoln, 29 June 1846. Gladstone Mss, Add. Mss 44262, ff. 74–6.

dissolving parliament in June was that a dissolution would have led the Peelites into an unnatural and merely temporary electoral combination with the Whigs on the sole issue of the defence of free trade.[1]

In the other direction, the personal animosities which the repeal struggle had engendered were bound to prevent an early reconciliation between the two wings of the Conservative party, especially since the most vicious personal attacks on Peel had been made by Bentinck. Early in July, Bentinck exacerbated the ill feelings by accusing Peel of having harried Canning to his death by withholding support from his government of 1827 despite having been converted to Catholic emancipation two years earlier. Bentinck could not prove his charge to the satisfaction of the Commons, and so damaged his reputation, not only with the Peelites, but with his own party.[2] The Peelites had been equally disappointed, however, by Peel's speech of resignation, in which he lauded Cobden as the man almost singly responsible for the repeal of the Corn Laws. Aberdeen, Herbert, and Gladstone were upset that Peel had told only part of the truth and had overlooked the sad fact that Cobden had held up the landowners to the people of England as knaves and plunderers. Aberdeen thought that the speech was 'for the purpose of making it impossible that he [Peel] should ever again be placed in connexion with the Conservative party as a party'.[3] Graham defended the speech to Gladstone: 'you can have no conception of what the virulence is against Peel and me'.[4] Graham and Peel alone turned their backs for ever on the Protectionists, but for the moment a united opposition against the Whigs was impossible. When asked by Lyndhurst to lead the Conservatives in the Commons, Goulburn replied that immediate organisation would bear a 'factious aspect' and that reunion must await the course of events.[5]

[1] Peel to Wellington, 21 June 1846. Parker, *Graham*, ii, 42; Peel to Wellington, 23 June 1846. Stanhope and Cardwell, *Peel Memoirs*, iii, 305–7.

[2] Arbuthnot to Peel, 10 June 1846: 'The vile and blackguard attack of Lord George Bentinck has done good. Everybody, save the most rabid portions of the Protectionists, is disgusted' (Parker, *Peel*, iii, 361).

[3] Gladstone memorandum of 9 July 1846. Gladstone Mss, Add. Mss 44777, ff. 242–52.

[4] Gladstone memorandum of 12 July 1846. *ibid*. ff. 252–8.

[5] Gladstone memorandum of 24 July 1846. *ibid*. ff. 261–8.

In the Lords, where the repeal debates had been free of personal recriminations, the prospects of reunion were brighter. In June, a group of Conservative peers, headed by the free traders, Ellenborough and Brougham, had tried, albeit unsuccessfully, to persuade Peel and Graham to retire so that the rest of the cabinet could carry on with Protectionist support.[1] Croker observed early in July that a regrouping of the Conservative forces was quickly taking place.

In the Lords there is almost unanimity – that is, they are all rallied under Stanley – Peelites and Protectionists; but in the Commons the reconciliation is more difficult, if it be at all possible... The appearance of the House of Lords on the first night of the new Ministry was striking – the whole of the Opposition side was crowded, so that some could not find places... while there were not fifteen peers – ministers, bishops, and all – at the Ministerial side.[2]

Brougham and Ellenborough took their places beside Buckingham and Richmond as a sign 'that the quarrel was a bygone quarrel – that the animosities attending it ought now to be forgotten'.[3] In the next couple of years Bentinck was to criticise Stanley for not espousing the cause of protection warmly enough, but Stanley, in the Lords, breathed a quite different atmosphere from Bentinck in the Commons.

In the Commons the Protectionists were encouraged by their large numbers to believe that the triumph of free trade could be reversed. The precise size of the party cannot be known: the line between Peelite and Protectionist was not sharply drawn. Peel had been supported by 116 Conservatives,[4] which left 254 to be accounted for. Of these, 221 had voted against repeal. Only one-

[1] Peel to Ellenborough, 30 May 1846. Peel Mss, Add. Mss 40473, ff. 332–3.

[2] Croker to Hardinge, 10 July 1846. Jennings, *Croker*, iii, 72.

[3] Gladstone memorandum of 9 July 1846. Gladstone Mss, Add. Mss 44777, ff. 242–52.

[4] The Peelites have generally been reckoned at 112, since that was the number of Conservatives who voted for the second reading of the Corn Bill. But that figure excludes the tellers (Henry Baring and John Young) and two persons (Viscount Newry and Lord Granville Somerset) who voted for the third reading. Gladstone was not in the Commons in 1846 and so the number would be 117, except that William Baird accepted the Chiltern Hundreds in May, after voting for the second reading in February.

third of the 221 had followed Bentinck and Disraeli into the lobby against the Coercion Bill, but in December 1846, Beresford, the chief whip, numbered the Protectionists at 220.[1]

Although it was numerically powerful in the House of Commons, the Protectionist party suffered from great deficiencies as a national party. The basis of the party was anti-Catholic prejudice and an unaltered faith in the Corn Laws. But no party could claim a monopoly of anti-Irish and anti-Catholic sentiment in early Victorian England, and distrust of Irish Catholicism was, at any rate, too vague and too touchy a subject to serve as the foundation of a party. Free trade might in time be discredited; in July 1846, it was futile to hope to arouse the energies of the country over a dispute at long last settled. Geographically and socially the party was dangerously exclusive. Intellectually, the party was deprived. In 1844 Viscount Sandon had warned Peel that a split over the sugar bill would render the re-appearance of the Conservative party impossible, 'because it would be, at least apparently, a schism between the great party in the country and all its leaders in Parliament'.[2] So it was in 1846. Only Stanley brought official experience and national stature to the Protectionist party. All the front bench, most significantly the young newcomers to office, Gladstone, Herbert, Lincoln, Cardwell, and Dalhousie, had sided with Peel. The Protectionists were largely a collection of silent country gentlemen. Of the 132 representatives of the English counties, 107 were Protectionists. The editor of the *Shropshire Conservative* referred to them as 'good and true independent Tories',[3] and Disraeli applauded them as 'right or wrong...men of honour, breeding and refinement, high and generous character, great weight and station in the country... men of metal and large-acred squires'.[4] But local standing carried less weight in the reformed House of Commons than it had in the eighteenth century. A recent historian of the Whigs has described the Protectionists as 'judges of horses, hounds and cattle' who 'were not remarkable for cultivated intelligence or political

---

[1] Graham to Peel, 15 December 1846. Peel Mss, Add. Mss 40452, ff. 188–91.
[2] Sandon to Peel, 15 June 1844. *ibid*. 40456, ff. 386–92.
[3] T.J.Ousley to Disraeli, 22 March 1845. Hughenden Mss, B/XXI/0/68.
[4] Disraeli, *Bentinck*, 299–300.

sophistication'.[1] He may have had in mind Bagehot's damning portrait of the Tory party in the mid-century.

> The grade of gentry who fill the county seats, and mostly compose the Conservative party in the Commons, are perhaps the least able and valuable part of English society. They have neither the responsibilities nor the culture of great noblemen, and they have never felt the painful need of getting on, which sharpens the middle class. They have a moderate sort of wealth which teaches them little, and a steady sort of mind fit for common things, but they have no flexibility and no ideas. Almost the worst of the class, too, are often sent to Parliament, and the best left out, because a foolish prejudice requires that the member shall have land within the county.[2]

The Conservative party has often stupidly been called the 'stupid party'. It was Disraeli's good fortune (though he knew what he was about) that the split in 1846 left it so for a generation.

Bentinck was the pure representative of the squirearchy, while no man in England, so Eglinton believed, could boast a better descent than Stanley, who could trace his lineage directly back to the fourteenth-century Robert III of Scotland.[3] The Derby family was one of the richest in the country. In 1864, Disraeli placed Derby's annual income at 'considerably more than £100,000',[4] and the fifteenth earl, Derby's son, was reputed to spend £15,000 a year on his aviary and menagerie.[5] Stanley's tastes would not have endeared him to Bagehot. Disraeli was appalled to discover that Knowsley, the family seat near Liverpool, was 'furnished like a second-rate lodging house...not from stinginess, but from sheer want of taste', while the stables, both in town and country, were beautifully kept. 'No one has more splendid horses and equipages than Lord Derby.'[6]

---

[1] D. Southgate, *The Passing of the Whigs, 1832–1886* (London, 1962), 100.

[2] W. Bagehot, 'Why Mr. Disraeli Has Succeeded' in N. St John-Stevas (ed.), *Bagehot's Historical Essays* (New York, 1965), 285–6.

[3] Eglinton to Stanley, 21 July 1851. Derby Mss, 148/2. The First Earl of Derby was created in 1485.

[4] Hughenden Mss, A/X/A/66. By 1883, the Derby estates were valued at the colossal amount of £163,000 annually (R. Blake, 'The Fourteenth Earl of Derby', *History Today* (December 1955), 851). In 1846, however, Greville placed Stanley's wealth at £60,000 annually (Greville, ii, 380–1).

[5] W. Pollard, *The Stanleys of Knowsley* (Liverpool, 1868), 111.

[6] Hughenden Mss, A/X/A/66.

However congenial by style of life Stanley and the Protectionists might have been, Stanley was so deeply conscious of the inadequacies of the Protectionist party that his great political object at the beginning of Lord John Russell's government was to heal the wounds in the Conservative party.

On 4 July 1846, Cobden presided over the dissolution of the Anti-Corn Law League.

I look upon it that the mere boasting and vapouring of a few of the less wise part of the protectionist party may be very well excused by us. It is quite natural that men who felt worsted in an argument and in all the tactics of political action should console themselves with the promises of what they will do in the next seven years. But I hold that you may as soon abolish Magna Charta, or do away with Trial by Jury, or repeal the Test and Corporation Act, or the Catholic Emancipation Act, as ever re-enact protection as a principle again in this country.[1]

In the agricultural constituencies, protectionism remained strong. In August, Bonham was impressed by 'the bitterness of a *select* but most active portion of the Protectionists which extends to many of the Constituencies and renders impossible any concert at the Elections between the different sections of the Opposition'.[2] With the elections not more than a year away, two methods of rebuilding a Conservative majority were open to Stanley. On the assumption that the House of Commons did not represent opinion in the country and that free trade would be quickly discredited, he might lead a forthright protectionist offensive until the appeal to the electorate. Or he could choose to direct his gaze to the House of Commons and attempt, by a gradual retreat from protection, to bring the two sections of the party back together. Stanley was too shrewd to place much confidence in the first course, but the obstacles bestrew the second one. For one thing, neither he nor the Peelites were prepared to defeat Russell, which would be the practical result of reunion. On 27 June, two

---

[1] Bright and Rogers, *Speeches by Cobden*, i, 389.
[2] Bonham to Gladstone, 14 August 1846. Gladstone Mss, Add. Mss 44110, ff. 187–8.

days after Peel's resignation, Stanley told a meeting of Protectionists that he would not hinder Russell's government unless it attacked the Irish Church.[1] On 8 July, he spoke at the annual Conservative dinner given by the Duke of Richmond and, without accepting free trade as a *fait accompli*, asked the Protectionists to end their quarrel with the Peelites. 'I did all I could to promote peace last night,' he wrote to Lyndhurst, 'but there is a good deal of angry feeling still alive, especially among the Commons.'[2]

At the beginning of July, Lyndhurst and Brougham sought to unite the party in opposition to the government's sugar legislation. But although the Peelites had declared as late as June that they could not be party to the abolition of the distinction between free-grown and slave-grown sugar, the merits of the question were overriden by other considerations. 'Having escaped the frying pan of office', Peel wrote to Graham, 'I am little disposed to jump into the Hell-fire of a conciliabule of which Lord Brougham and Lord Londonderry would be leading members... I *cordially* agree with you in keeping aloof from all such combinations.'[3] Stanley, who was in the country, and did not hear of the scheme until after it had been scotched by the Peelites, declared that he 'would not have touched it with the tongs'.[4]

Brougham's plan was to rename the party the 'New Conservatives' and to place Goulburn in the lead in the Commons, but since Herbert and Lincoln were to be excluded, the plan amounted to the engrafting of Goulburn and Gladstone on to the Protectionist party, not the fusion of Peelites and Protectionists.[5] The proposition was thus undeserving of serious consideration, although both Stanley and Gladstone assured Lyndhurst of their sympathy with his object. Gladstone held that the Peelites 'were bound to give a fair trial to the government', but that 'if so much confidence is due to them, how much more is due towards friends from whom we have differed on the single question of free trade'.[6] The sugar bill was supported by 47 Peelites and opposed

---

1 *Illustrated London News*, 28 June 1846.
2 Stanley to Lyndhurst, 9 July 1846 (copy). Derby Mss, 177/1.
3 Peel to Graham, 2 July 1846. Peel Mss, Add. Mss 40452, ff. 140–1.
4 Lord Campbell, *Lives of Lord Lyndhurst and Lord Brougham* (London, 1869), 164.
5 *Ibid.* 163; Bentinck to Stanley, 10 July 1846. Derby Mss, 132/13.
6 Morley, *Gladstone*, i, 294.

by none. The majority of 130 which it received in the Commons paralysed the Lords. Stanley and Richmond had been prepared to throw the bill out if the division in the Commons were narrow.[1]

The sugar issue revealed the course which politics were to take for the remainder of the 1841 parliament's life. Peel justified his vote for the bill on the ground that his first duty was to prevent the Protectionists from coming into office.[2] That meant, as Beresford saw, that nothing more could be done about the tariff issue until the next elections.

> The only remedy is an appeal to the constituencies. If they sanction the votes of those who in 1841 were loud against slavegrown sugar and in 1846 vote for it, then farewell to all consistency and sense of honour among the English Representatives.[3]

In the event, sugar went unnoticed at the 1847 elections and the question passed out of English politics. The lesson of the sugar vote was re-inforced in August. Stanley chose not to oppose the bill empowering colonial legislatures to abolish differential tariffs, since the removal of preferential duties which injured the colonies was a just corollary to the removal of those in their favour. For the second time, the Lords did not divide on a free-trade measure, and it was clear that the government was safe until the dissolution.

The sugar issue exposed the divisions within the Protectionist party. Bentinck had rejected Lyndhurst's scheme for reunion for quite different reasons from Stanley.

> My heart sickens at the thought of any such early reconciliation with those who have been either principals or Aids and Abettors in the Conspiracy against the Constituencies of the Empire – and I feel confident that we shall lose caste in the Country and with that portion especially of the Country in which our strength lies if we do anything of the kind. My inclination is to rouse the Country to make a clean sweep of them from the face of the Earth, and with the exception of Peel alone, I believe that this may be easily done, indeed that it will not be easy to prevent it.[4]

[1] Stanley to Richmond, 12 July 1846 (copy). Derby Mss, 177/1.
[2] 27 July 1846. *Hansard*, 3rd Series, lxxxviii, 95–6.
[3] Beresford to Stanley, 28 July 1846. Derby Mss, 149/1.
[4] Bentinck to Stanley, 10 July 1846. *ibid.* 132/13.

Bentinck's expectations were the projection of his hopes. Stanley, who wanted to save the party from hardening into a minority party of reaction, counselled a more moderate course. He warned Bentinck against building a reputation for personal vindictiveness, and then argued that Bentinck's opinions were misguided.

> Look, as I have done, over the list of the 112 who supported Peel; you will find that a considerable portion of them represent Constituencies which will not be disposed to quarrel with them for their late votes. Where this is the case, there is no use in gratuitously securing their permanent alienation by interfering between them and their constituents, who may be left to settle their own affairs...In the meantime, that is until a general Election, your policy should be, not to invite, but not to repel, their support; to treat them coolly if you will, but not to provoke them by injudicious epithets and reflections on the past. As to any proposition for a junction, I think it would be sufficient to have it clearly understood that the very first object at which we aim is the undoing in another Parliament that which has just been done in this. I do not see how you can refuse the aid of those who tender it on these terms, but I think these terms cannot be accepted by any whom you would wish to exclude. My opinion, therefore, is that separation must continue till a new election shall have decided whether the Corn Laws are to be finally repealed.[1]

To allow free-trade measures to pass while maintaining a theoretical preference for protection, to keep distance from the Peelites while holding out the olive branch, and to await the electorate's final decision at the 1847 elections – these were Stanley's somewhat equivocal directions to the Protectionist party. Firm and adroit leadership was required for such a strategy, but during the sugar debates the party was confused by Stanley's indecision. They had been informed by Bentinck that the bill would be resisted in the Lords, only to discover that when the bill got there Stanley had changed his mind.[2] After the sugar bill passed, Stanley retired to Knowsley where he remained until the end of August, remote from the struggle taking place within the party.

Bentinck seized the opportunity to press his militant anti-Peelite line on the party. Beresford 'failed utterly' to persuade

---

[1] Stanley to Bentinck, 12 July 1846 (copy). *ibid.* 177/1.
[2] Bentinck to Stanley, 10 July 1846. *ibid.* 132/13.

him that fraternisation with the minor Peelites could do no harm and ought to be welcomed.[1] Lord John Manners, who found Stanley indisposed to assert his influence over the party,[2] and who was upset that Bentinck was gaining control and that the battle for the Corn Laws was to be fought all over again, turned to Disraeli to 'prevent such a shipwreck'.[3] But as the summer wore on Bentinck's influence over the party grew, much to the alarm of the moderates. In August Bentinck became embroiled in a bitter dispute with Lyndhurst and Ripon which widened the breach between Peelites and Protectionists. Just before quitting office, Ripon appointed a new chief justice for Bombay. The new appointment left a vacancy in the Liverpool commission of bankruptcy, which was filled by Lyndhurst's private secretary. Although the patronage of the Bombay administration was in Ripon's hands, the new chief justice had been chosen by Lyndhurst. Bentinck's charge that a 'barter of patronage' had occurred was successfully repelled by Lyndhurst, but the really damaging aspect of the affair was that the new justice was not appointed until the day after Peel's government resigned, so that the Whigs were deprived of an appointment which ought to have been theirs. Bentinck declared that 'a more profligate avidity for patronage never was displayed by any Government' and that the transaction was 'one of the most nefarious jobs that he recollected during the eighteen years that he had had a seat in parliament'. Not the least unfortunate aspect of the episode was that Gladstone, the Peelite most friendly to the Protectionists, was implicated in the affair, since, as colonial secretary, he had signed the writ of appointment.[4]

Lyndhurst and Croker were shocked by Bentinck's rash language. Lyndhurst declared that 'if the councils of the party were to be directed by Lord George Bentinck, there would soon be an end to the Conservatives'.[5] Stanley sympathised with Bentinck,

[1] Beresford to Stanley, undated. *ibid.* 149/1.

[2] Manners to Disraeli, 15 August 1846: 'Stanley is here, full of fun and chaff; but he does not give me the idea of a statesman' (Hugherden Mss, B/XX/M/10).

[3] *Ibid.*

[4] The episode may be traced in *Hansard*, 3rd Series, lxxxviii, 893–904.

[5] Lyndhurst to Croker, undated. Jennings, *Croker*, iii, 82. Ashburton made a similar lament to Croker: 'I wish I could see much chance of our great party rallying after its marvellous betrayal; our best hopes lie with Stanley, but we must have

but reproached him for meddling. 'Let me earnestly advise you to abstain so far as possible...from making personal attacks which must multiply the number of your personal enemies and diminish your powers of usefulness.'[1] The episode increased Beresford's doubts about the value of Bentinck's leadership.[2]

It was partly to counteract the ill-effects of Bentinck's behaviour that Croker offered Stanley the services of the *Quarterly Review* for the propagation of moderate Conservatism. The press was as divided as the party; the editors of the *Standard* and the *Morning Herald*, mouthpieces of high Toryism, were personally hostile to Lyndhurst and opposed to accommodation with the Peelites. Croker therefore believed it to be urgent that the *Quarterly* should take a more conciliatory line.[3] The separation of Croker and the *Quarterly* from Peel was almost the sole advantage with which Stanley began his career as leader of the Protectionists. Beginning with 'The Close of Sir Robert Peel's Administration' in September 1846, every political article printed in the journal received Stanley's approval, as previously it had received Peel's. But the *Quarterly* had not nearly the influence of the national dailies, the *Standard* and the *Herald*, whose links with the party were Beresford and Newdegate. Both papers wished to be the official organ of the party, as did the *Morning Post*. The Central Protection Society had maintained close communication with all three. In July 1846, the editorship of the *Herald* fell vacant, and Newdegate hoped that the paper would amalgamate with the *Post* under a new editor and assume the role of party organ.[4] He wanted Phillips, a leader writer for *The Times*, who was embarrassed by that paper's shift to free trade, to fill the vacant chair. The negotiations for amalgamation broke down and Phillips took over the *Herald* as the quasi-official organ of the party. Both the *Standard* and the *Herald* kept up a rabid anti-Catholic tone, and early in August Stanley chided

a commoner...I do not see him through my telescope' (Ashburton to Croker, 20 August 1846. *ibid*. iii, 78–9).

[1] Stanley to Bentinck, 23 August 1846 (copy). Derby Mss, 177/1.
[2] Beresford to Stanley, undated. *ibid*. 149/1.
[3] Croker to Stanley, 21 August 1846. Jennings, *Croker*, iii, 80–2.
[4] Newdegate to Stanley, 13 July 1846. Derby Mss, 148/1.

Phillips for printing two offensive articles on the alleged intention of the government to pay the Irish Catholic clergy.

These articles... are written with the view of exciting the Protestant
feeling of this country against such a proposal. I cannot say that I
approve of such a course; on the contrary, I thought that I had personally explained to you, that as I had supported a proposition in 1825 for
paying the R.C. clergy, so I was still of opinion that if such an arrangement could be effected, it would be in itself most desirable... I neither
entertain myself, nor would aid in keeping up in others, objections to it
on religious grounds.[1]

Although he knew that a large section of the party disagreed
with him, Stanley would not tolerate a 'Protestant' cry on the
hustings. But he found the affairs of the press bewildering and
tedious and did not again try to influence Phillips. There was
little he could have done, since the *Herald* was financially independent of the Protectionist party. Under the sympathetic eye
of Beresford, the Tory press intensified its Protestantism as the
elections approached. Just as important, no clear Protectionist
policy reached the country through the press, as Stanley, without
attempting to improve things, was aware.

I do not know much about the affairs of the press; but it seems to me
that they are all at sixes and sevens. The editor and newly engaged
writer in the *Herald* are not on the best terms, and very jealous of each
other, and that paper and the *Morning Post* do not pull well together,
while I believe the *Standard* takes a line of its own, quite apart from
the others.[2]

Any other state of affairs was not to be expected in view of the
confusion within the party. Stanley's lack of interest in the press
was partly a reflexion of his reluctance to take control of the
party. On 2 August Arbuthnot recorded that Graham '*believes*
that Stanley will put himself in the Lords at the head of the old
Tory party',[3] and as late as January 1847, Lincoln wrote that 'it
appears now quite certain that Lord Stanley has accepted the
Leadership of the Protectionists as a Party'.[4] Stanley preferred

[1] Stanley to Phillips, 8 August 1846 (copy). Derby Mss, 177/1.
[2] Stanley to Bentinck, 14 November 1846 (copy). *ibid*.
[3] Arbuthnot to his son, 2 August 1846. Aspinall, *Correspondence of Arbuthnot*,
240 (my italics).
[4] Lincoln to Peel, 1 January 1847. Peel Mss. Add. Mss 40481, ff. 392–7.

to leave the Protectionists unorganised in order that a Conservative reunion could be more easily effected, although he realised that his policy of playing a waiting game until the country should have returned its verdict on free trade at the next elections placed a strain on the party, and feared that there were 'no leaders in the House of Commons with enough of *sangfroid* to act upon this cautious and, I must admit, difficult line of policy'.[1]

Before the end of the 1846 session, Disraeli and Bentinck began a series of appearances in agricultural constituencies to rally the faithful.[2] Although it was not clear exactly what the Protectionist policy was, whether a return to the 1842 sliding scale, as Disraeli recommended at King's Lynn, or a fixed duty of 8s., which Bentinck offered as a second choice, the general tenor of their speeches was enthusiastically received. In September, Disraeli reported that the Conservative rancour flourished 'in all its primal virulence',[3] and Bentinck found the framers of Essex to be 'in high spirits, not the least alarmed, but incensed beyond all measure against Peel and correspondingly fond of me...They look upon me as their own "Pet" '.[4] The farmers' enthusiasm raised Bentinck's political expectations so high that he sold his stables, hitherto his most prized possession. It was an enormous sacrifice, though Beresford saw him shortly afterwards at Epsom 'in excellent spirits, I think really glad to have got rid of the weight and responsibility of his Stud'.[5]

The immediate outlook for the party was darkened by the prosperity which was the result of the expansion in railway building. Wages for navvies, engineers, bricklayers, miners, iron and machine-factory workers, and others in occupations directly allied to railway construction had risen sharply in the first six

[1] Stanley to Croker, 23 August 1846. Jennings, *Croker*, iii, 77–8.

[2] See Monypenny and Buckle, iii, 4–8.

[3] Disraeli to Lady Londonderry, 1 September 1846 (draft). Hughenden Mss, B/II/7.

[4] Bentinck to Stanley, 28 September 1846. Derby Mss, 132/13. Beresford also gave Stanley an account of the meeting: 'Bentinck made a good impression on them and pleased them uncommonly...Whenever the slightest allusion was made to the probability of Sir Robert Peel's returning to power, their excitement was very great; I think it was a decidedly successful meeting' (Beresford to Stanley, undated. *ibid.* 149/1).

[5] Beresford to Stanley, 20 September 1846. *ibid.*

months of 1846, and this boom, combined with the Irish famine, kept up food prices, a circumstance which Bentinck knew 'the lying, rascally Free Traders will claim to themselves and the foolish Farmers half of them will believe to be such'.[1] On 24 September, Stanley told the Liverpool Agricultural Society that he could not speak to them of the free trade legislation, because its effects could not be gauged for some time. At the same time he reiterated his opinion that the next election must settle the issue.[2] Bentinck was dissatisfied with this illogical position, and continued to tell the farmers that they could at least expect an 8s. duty from the Protectionists.

As the 1847 session drew near, Bentinck felt increasingly uneasy about his position. When Stanley asked him to send out a circular to all the Conservatives who had voted against repeal, Bentinck replied that his support was more widespread among the farmers and squires in the country than among the Protectionists in parliament who had forced the leadership upon him. 'I had served their purpose when the Corn Bill and Tariff had passed. They never meant that I should pursue the Traitor Ministry to its death; but the betrayed County Electors did.' He complained that the anti-Catholic diatribes in the Tory press were as distasteful to him as they were welcomed by the majority of the party and pointed out that he had no influence with the Tory editors. 'Under the circumstances I do not think it desirable and it is repugnant to my own feelings to solicit unwilling troops to follow me.'[3]

Circulars were therefore sent out in Beresford's name on the eve of the 1847 session to 220 Protectionists, but to none of the Peelites. While Peel remained in the Commons, many Peelites were inhibited by feelings of loyalty to him from accepting Stanley's command. Stanley feared that Peel's decision to take a leading part in debate, and to act as the arbiter between the government and the Protectionists, would not only render the reconstruction of the Conservative party 'all but impossible', but would also 'smooth the way for those measures of gradual

---

[1] Bentinck to Stanley, 14 September 1846. *ibid.* 132/13.
[2] *John Bull*, 24 September 1846.
[3] Bentinck to Stanley, 2 January 1847. Derby Mss, 132/13.

downward progress which Lord John Russell must introduce'.[1] Greville noted in 1846 that 'the ultra-Liberals lean rather to Peel than to John Russell'.[2] Peel's temperament gave the lie to his nominal Conservatism. At the beginning of 1846 he had claimed 'the privilege of yielding to the force of argument and conviction, and acting on the result of enlarged experience'.[3] With the Tamworth manifesto, Peel had wriggled out of his high Tory robes. When he broke with his party over the Corn Laws, he threw off the last remnants which had clung to him and stood ready to be outfitted by Cobden. He died too early to be buried in his new clothes, which were eventually discovered to be Gladstone's size. In August 1846, Peel had written an open letter from Ellbing in which he called for an end to direct taxation and hinted at a far-reaching reform of the Church.[4] Credibility was therefore attached to Redesdale's information that most of the Peelites now distrusted Peel and were ready to follow Stanley.[5] Lord Combermere advised Stanley to make overtures to the leading Peelites.

Their confidence in your political integrity and power of intellect would furnish an ample justification of their return to principles which you alone can realise. With the addition of such as you deem most efficient amongst them, you could name your projected government and thus prove to the Country that the Protectionists can form an Administration.[6]

It was the 'shadow cabinet', not the back benches, which needed bolstering. The Peelites would add official experience and ability to the Protectionist numbers. Stanley, however, stuck to his decision that an election must precede reunion, and declined to

[1] Stanley to Croker, 27 September 1846 (copy). *ibid.* 177/1.
[2] Greville, ii, 380. In 1838 Sir Charles Grey was prescient enough to say that 'Russell is a Whig, Stanley is a Tory, Peel is a Radical' (Walpole, *Russell*, i, 304).
[3] 22 January 1846. *Hansard*, 3rd Series, xxxiii, 69.
[4] See the *Quarterly Review* (December 1846), 266–7. Ashburton wrote to Stanley of the Peelites: 'This is the party you will have to watch and, if possible, conciliate, unless they adopt the supposed new visions of Peel in trade, finance and the Church, in which case there is no alternative but to set them all at defiance...from the glimpses we occasionally have of his reformed views, I am more afraid of him than of anybody' (Ashburton to Stanley, 17 January 1847. Derby Mss, 147/15).
[5] Redesdale to Stanley, 20 December 1846. *ibid.* 149/6.
[6] Combermere to Stanley, 27 December 1846. *ibid.* 150/3.

approach the Peelites. He knew that by forcing Bentinck out of the leadership of the Commons he would remove a major obstacle in the way of those Peelites who wanted to follow him, but he also knew that by getting rid of Bentinck he would run the risk of enraging the agricultural constituencies and splitting the party in the Commons.

Bentinck's fury with Peel went so deep that he supported the Tory press when it backed John Bright against Lord Lincoln at a by-election in Manchester, because Lincoln's return 'would be an immense moral triumph for Peel'.[1] Stanley asked Beresford to stop the Tory press from running down Lincoln and building up 'a Blackguard and a Democrat',[2] but Beresford replied that Lincoln was more dangerous than Bright, since he would 'in the end go nearly if not quite so far as the other, and being a Gentleman covers the iniquity better'.[3] The zeal with which Beresford and Bentinck sought Lincoln's defeat was galling to the moderates who looked upon Lincoln as a possible leader of a reunited party in the Commons.[4]

The current was running in the opposite direction. The Peelites were busy throughout December organising themselves into a third party, partly because, as Ellenborough lamented, the conditions of re-entry into the Protectionist party were intolerable.

I think it is due to those who supported the late Government to the last that they should not be thrown adrift and left to find their way individually into the ranks of the Protectionists, to be received there as penitents – they have nothing to repent – they did what was right – and they should evince a consciousness that they did so, and a proper self-respect, while they are willing to co-operate on new ground with those who differed from them last year.[5]

[1] Bentinck to Stanley, 2 January 1847. *ibid.* 132/13.

[2] Stanley to Beresford, 30 December 1846 (copy). *ibid.* 177/1.

[3] Beresford to Stanley, 30 December 1846. *ibid.* 149/1.

[4] High station, wealth, and speaking ability, Lincoln told Ellenborough, were insufficient qualifications for leadership. Personal acceptability to one's followers was also required, and 'no member of the late Government except Sir Robert Peel shares so large a portion of their [the Protectionists] hatred' (Lincoln to Ellenborough, 5 January 1847. Ellenborough Mss, PRO 30, 12/21/3).

[5] Ellenborough to Lincoln, 3 January 1847. *ibid.* When Russell had taken office, Inglis, Redesdale, and a few others were eager to have the Protectionists

Since the Protectionists still stood on the same old ground, the 1847 session of parliament opened with the Conservatives divided into two distinct parties. Graham and Peel persisted in remaining free of party combination; the organisation of the Peelites was undertaken by Lincoln, Cardwell, Goulburn, Dalhousie, Bonham, and John Young, the whip in Peel's government. Their object was to maintain themselves as a party of observation rather than of opposition, as Goulburn put it with characteristic Peelite *hauteur*, as the conscience of the nation. They could not drift into the Whig ranks, but neither could they enlist under Stanley until he renounced protection and rid himself of Bentinck. In the meantime, they would exist as an 'organised body composed of men to whom the Country gave credit for some knowledge of public affairs and calculated therefore to command the public confidence'.[1] Young sent circulars to 240 Conservatives and by the beginning of January had received 90 'cordial' replies.[2]

Stanley agreed to hold a dinner for Protectionists in both Houses before the opening of parliament and prepared to make 'a sort of Protectionist Progress' from Knowsley to London in the second week of January.[3] Graham knew nothing of Stanley's opinions, but believed that he would not pledge himself to the Corn Laws.[4] And yet the party had somehow to distinguish itself from the Liberals, especially since there would be little opportunity to harass the government before the election. The continual topic of debate in parliament would be the relief of Irish distress, a subject which the Protectionists agreed was too important and too difficult to be treated as a party question.[5]

---

replace Peel and his colleagues on the opposition front bench, but Stanley and Beresford thought it wiser to remain where they were below the gangway. Bentinck was pleased thus to avoid close contact with the Peelites, whereas Stanley hoped that the change in seating would come about by the Peelites' moving to join the Protectionists in 'an overt act of submission on their part' which would make it 'quite clear that they came to you and not you to them' (Stanley to Bentinck, 12 July 1846 (copy). Derby Mss, 177/1).

1 Goulburn to Peel, 19 December 1846. Peel Mss, Add. Mss 40445, ff. 386–7.
2 Lincoln to Peel, 1 January 1847. *ibid.* 40481, ff. 392–7.
3 *Ibid.*; Eglinton to Stanley, 1 and 2 December 1846. Derby Mss, 148/2.
4 Graham to Peel, 3 January 1847. Peel Mss, Add. Mss 40452, ff. 199–204.
5 Stanley to Eglinton, 10 October 1846 (copy). Derby Mss, 177/1.

To those Protectionists who were demanding a specific party programme Stanley quoted Tierney's famous doctrine that an opposition should oppose everything and propose nothing. He warned the party against making pledges in opposition which would cause embarrassment later and make it difficult to secure cabinet ministers (Stanley's eyes were on the Peelites) when an administration was being formed.

I do not think the present would be a good opportunity for raising Agricultural Protection questions. My own opinion of the effects of last year's policy remains quite unshaken, but present high prices have blinded the farmers to their danger, and the disappointment of the Manufacturing Operatives has not *yet* reached the point at which it *will*, I think certainly, produce a reaction on the subject of Free Trade.[1]

Stanley and Redesdale were in favour of sitting quietly until either radical legislation or the lack of it should break up the Liberals and bring about a Conservative reunion.[2]

The more passionate doctrinaires in the party chafed under this restraint and urged Bentinck to find a rallying cry for the party. Bentinck decided to take up the traditional Tory grievance, the malt tax. He had first sounded the idea of the repeal of the malt tax at a farmers' meeting at Chelmsford in September. He discovered that the farmers entertained little hope of an early restoration of the Corn Laws and were bent upon the repeal of the malt tax as compensation.[3] Its repeal would deprive the Exchequer of almost £5,000,000 annually, which Bentinck aimed to supply by an 8s. duty on wheat, a 3s. 6d. duty on maize, barley, peas, and oats, and the restoration of the 1842 sliding scale as it applied to timber, cotton, butter, cheese, coffee, wool, and silk. Bentinck estimated that the revenue so derived would be £4,630,000. The scheme ought to appeal to the colonial, agricultural, and beer-drinking interests. 'The *Quart Pot* for *Two Pence* would shout down any day now the already suspected "*Cobden cum Peel*" cry of "*Cheap Bread*" and a "*Big Loaf*".'[4] Bentinck had not divulged the details of his 'budget' before

[1] Stanley to Newdegate, 10 December 1846 (copy). *ibid.*
[2] Redesdale to Stanley, 26 December 1846. *ibid.* 149/6.
[3] Bentinck to Stanley, 1 October 1846. *ibid.* 132/13.
[4] *Ibid.*

Stanley stepped in to chastise him for pledging himself to the repeal of the malt tax and to inform him that he could not be a party to the cry of 'the Quart Pot for Two Pence' as the rallying point of the gentry. He told Bentinck, in a taut sentence indicative of the strained relations between the two leaders, that 'you have not to propound a financial budget in the House of Commons, and I cordially rejoice that you have not, just at present'.[1]

In December, the Duke of Richmond, who was still chairman of the Protection Society, received a petition from Kent farmers asking the Protectionist party to press for the repeal of the malt tax in the coming session.[2] As the anti-malt tax movement gathered force in the country, Stanley's attitude became more guarded. But while he admitted that the party could occupy no more popular ground, he knew that the repeal of the malt tax would incur the resentment of the powerful brewers' interest, without substantially benefiting the consumer or the grower.[3] On 10 December, the committee of the Protection Society resolved unanimously that the party should demand the immediate and total repeal of the malt tax, but they were unsupported by almost every section of the parliamentary party, and when the resolution was placed before the whole society in January, it was defeated. The society decided to await Russells' measures and contented itself with condemning 'the impolicy and injustice of the malt tax'.[4] Stanley was thus the victor in his first specific dispute with Bentinck. 'You will see', Stanley wrote to Ashburton, 'that we have succeeded in putting a stop to the agitation on the subject of the Malt Tax, but I am sorry to say not

[1] Stanley to Bentinck, 2 October 1846 (copy). *ibid*. 177/1.
[2] Richmond to Stanley, 5 December 1846. *ibid*. 131/13.
[3] Stanley to Richmond, 5 December 1846 (copy). *ibid*. 177/1.
[4] *John Bull*, 12 January 1847. It is clear from reports throughout December and January in the Tory press that Bentinck over-estimated the strength of the anti-malt tax feeling in the country. At two party meetings early in January, during his 'Protection Progress', Stanley found that 'every Member of Parliament present, among whom were representatives of the Agricultural interest in several Counties, concurred in deprecating the agitation' (Stanley to Ashburton, 16 January 1847 (copy). Derby Mss, 177/1). The right wing of the party, headed by Salisbury and Vyvyan, considered Bentinck's proposal to be a wicked compromise (Salisbury to Stanley, 7 January 1847. *ibid*. 134/6). See also Brougham to Ellenborough, undated: 'I find Duke of Richmond, Wilton, Forrester, Brownlow – all against G.B. and his malt duty' (Ellenborough Mss, PRO 30, 12/21/8).

without much dissatisfaction on the part of G. Bentinck, who is bent on violent measures and I fear is a good deal annoyed at not carrying the party with him.'[1]

In November, Stanley had felt at a loss for a rallying cry. Having rejected the malt-tax agitation, he found the situation unimproved two months later. The party was in low spirits, and his relations with Bentinck were deteriorating. In the third week of January, Stanley and Bentinck again clashed at a dinner given by Stanley to the parliamentary party. Bentinck interpreted Stanley's advice to the party to forbear from strong language and agricultural agitation as a personal rebuke. Stanley assured Bentinck that his remarks were not so intended, but merely expressed the general sense of 'the strongest and best men of the party'.

If we do not gain we shall lose Adherents. We must make a *pont d'or* for the penitent (and we must not ask them to pass over it in a white sheet) or we must close the Drawbridge; and if we take the latter course, we shall only hem in an unwilling Garrison and keep out useful recruits...Every man present yesterday without exception, and they consisted in most part of your most devoted followers, partook of the pained astonishment with which I learnt the effect of what I had said on your mind...If we are to act together in public, I must on all occasions frankly communicate to you my views. If I am to have an influence over the House of Commons, the language held by the Leader there must be in accordance with my feelings and opinions; but rely upon it that I will never take any indirect modes of gaining that influence...I trust that our friends, who will not be unobservant, will have cause to see that what has passed has not impaired our mutual regard and confidence.[2]

Stanley's soothing words failed to mollify Bentinck, whose reply to Stanley must surely rank as one of the most uncivil in the history of English politics.

I am told that I must answer your letter. I confess the occasion of it is so revolting to my feelings that having shaken hands with you, I could wish to forget the whole subject.

I never imagined you intended '*covertly*' to address yourself to me or at me. My complaint is that you openly denounced that action of

[1] Stanley to Ashburton, 16 January 1847 (copy). Derby Mss, 177/1.
[2] Stanley to Bentinck, 24 January 1847 (copy). *ibid.*

which I am the notorious Representative, that in Publick you joined the Hue and Cry with which Peelite, Roebuck and Anti-Corn Law Leaguers had in vain attempted to run me down. Of the unreserved expression of your disapprobation of my proceedings in the House of Commons communicated to me in private letters or in the presence of familiar friends I have never complained; on the contrary you will admit that I have always listened to your private rebukes with patience, humility and good humour...

So long as any portion of the Gentlemen of the House of Commons are pleased undeservedly to choose me for their Leader, I must insist upon proper consideration being paid in publick at least by the Leader of the Party in the Lords to the dignity of the holder of the corresponding office in the Commons, which if not maintained must necessarily deprive him of all useful influence and authority.

I demand for myself, as long as I remain Leader of the House of Commons, the same personal consideration I have always paid you, which whatever may have been my inward convictions has a hundred times in Society induced me to defend you when in the crisis last year you hung back and sheathed your sword when the general opinion was that you should have thrown away the scabbard. I did not then speak contemptuously of timid and pusillanimous Leaders who lost the day when possibly it might have been saved but for lack of courage and decision in the hour of danger to rush to the front and rally the sinking spirits of a panic-stricken Party. I did not then chime in with your Detractors – quite the contrary on all occasions I scouted the idea that by want of either bravery, resolution, or fidelity you had 'lowered yourself in public opinion' and proved yourself unfit to lead a Party in difficult times...

You tell me that 'if you are to have an influence on the House of Commons the language held there must be in accordance with your feelings and opinions'...I cannot agree that the Leader of a Party, being a Peer, is without previous discussion and amicable arrangement to enunciate, lay down, and dictate to the whole Party the Commercial and Financial Policy which they are to pursue, without first ascertaining that the Leader in that House where such measures can alone be effectively discussed and carried out is prepared to adopt the other's views. It appears to me that the business of no Opposition and of no Party can be carried on upon such Dictatorial principles...

For the rest, having reluctantly recorded my own sentiments to secure myself with you against misconstruction hereafter, I have only to add that true to the pledge I gave last Saturday, I shall never desert the men who have so nobly defended the cause of Independence in the House of Commons; I shall continue, though broken in spirit, to do my best for them, exerting myself to the utmost to encourage and raise up some fitter leader for them, but should the day come when our party is called to power I shall step aside...

I can only conclude with expressing my everlasting regret that any-thing should have occurred to break off the bloom of a friendship which I had hoped our latest days could never have seen withered or fading.[1]

It is an immensely sad letter. There is no record of Stanley's speech. Clearly Bentinck had cause to feel injury, but only an embittered, distraught man, near losing self-control, could have accused Stanley of dictatorial methods. The pathos of it is that Bentinck had never wanted the leadership. He was utterly devoted to a cause, without a trace of the self-seeking in him. Still, for six months Stanley had made his position clear to him, and if he could not accept it, he ought to have resigned. Stanley made an effort to avoid future clashes with Bentinck, but the rela-tions between the two men never recovered from this unfortunate episode, and Bentinck's stock in the party began rapidly to fall.

When the 1847 session began the Protectionists moved to the opposition front benches, alongside Graham and Peel, though not in the spirit of opposition. The Whigs were officially in-formed that Ireland would not be made the battleground of parties.[2] The repeal of the Corn Laws closed an era in English politics. The *Illustrated London News*, commenting on the return of all but two of the new cabinet ministers without a contest, wrote that 'the old stock of political capital is "used up", and a new one has yet to be created'.[3] Politicians of the centre foresaw an age of practical improvements ahead. The great ideological quarrels of the 1830s and early 1840s had subsided. Conservative parties are always at a disadvantage when there is no obvious and great evil to be warded off.

Not only was Stanley unable to devise a coherent conservative programme relevant to the times without permanently alienating

---

[1] Bentinck to Stanley, 29 January 1847. *ibid.* 132/13.
[2] Beresford to Stanley, undated. Derby Mss, 149/1.
[3] *Illustrated London News*, 11 July 1846.

the Peelites, but he felt the want of materials in his party from which to form an efficient administration should the opportunity ever come. Stanley's quarrel with Bentinck was over strategy, not ultimate political ends. Bentinck would rouse the country to place in office a government committed to the restoration of the Corn Laws. Stanley was intellectually a protectionist, but he saw the need to build a party within the House of Commons capable of governing when the country turned the Whigs out. He remembered how carefully Peel had nurtured his party after its destruction in 1830, how discreetly he had abstained from upsetting Melbourne until he had created a powerful and, as he thought, united instrument of power backed by public opinion. As the ultra Tories had fretted under Peel's short lease in the late 1830s, so did Bentinck now under Stanley's. Croker instructed the readers of the *Quarterly Review* in the essential difference between a Whig and a Tory opposition. The latter was seldom, if ever, aggressive, since its interest was the maintenance of order and the undisturbed working of the system of government. 'It is the natural policy and inclination of that [Tory] party to support the Crown in all that is proper, and indeed all that is even tolerable.'[1]

On two occasions, nevertheless, the Protectionists took issue with Russell's Irish policy. At the end of the 1846 session, Russell had introduced a Labour Rate Act for Ireland, by which Irish landlords were forced to pay money out of local rates for a number of unproductive public works projects, which, while they provided employment to a starving population, established nothing of permanent value to the Irish economy. As an alternative to this wasteful policy, Bentinck took up the hitherto ignored recommendation of the royal commissions of 1836 and 1843 that a government-sponsored programme of railway building be undertaken in Ireland.[2] Railway construction would not only provide wages for a famine-struck people, but, by encouraging the growth of Irish industry, would relieve some of the enormous pressure of labour on the land. Bentinck proposed to have the

---

[1] *Quarterly Review* (December 1846), 265.

[2] By the beginning of 1847, only 123 miles of track had been laid in Ireland (Bentinck, 4 February 1847. *Hansard*, 3rd Series, lxxxix, 777).

government lend railway companies up to £16,000,000 at $3\frac{1}{2}$ per cent interest, with the railroads taken as security.[1] Stanley was wary of a project which entailed such substantial government interference in the money market, and was suspicious of the amount of political influence which the scheme would place in the government's hands, unless money were to be given to every company which applied for it, in which case the money might be lost in 'bubble schemes'.[2] But by February 1847, there were 500,000 labourers being paid £800,000 a month under the Labour Rate Act, and Stanley withdrew his opposition to Bentinck's proposals, encouraged by the knowledge that they were backed by Herries and 'King' Hudson, the railway magnate.[3] On 4 February, Bentinck introduced his bill in the Commons and was 'loudly cheered by both sides'.[4] Russell hinted that he would accept the bill, but the Peelites protested that to do so was to hand the government of the country over to the Protectionists, and on the eve of the second reading, Russell told his party that he would resign if the bill were carried.[5] The bill was thus defeated by a vote to decide, so Bentinck complained, 'not whether the measure was in itself good and efficient for its own purposes, but whether Lord John Russell or I were to govern Ireland'.[6] There were, of course, other objections to the bill, one of them that the Irish members were adamant against it. Stafford O'Brien, the Irish Protectionist, canvassed against the bill, and a deputation of 40 Irish members, unwilling to sacrifice immediate food relief for the more distant benefits of railway construction, asked Bentinck to postpone it.[7] More than 100 members of the Protectionist party did not bother to vote for the bill. The division clearly revealed the Protectionists' waning

---

[1] Bentinck to Stanley, 28 September 1846. Derby Mss, 132/13.

[2] Stanley to Bentinck, 2 October 1846 (copy). *ibid.* 177/1.

[3] Bentinck to Stanley, 19 December 1846. *ibid.* 132/13; Stanley to Bentinck, 30 December 1846 (copy). *ibid.* 177/1.

[4] Disraeli, *Bentinck*, 380. For the speech, see *Hansard*, 3rd Series, lxxxix, 773–802.

[5] Russell to Wood, 7 January 1847. Gooch, *Later Correspondence*, i, 169–70.

[6] Bentinck to his father, 19 February 1847. Portland Mss, PWH/226.

[7] Stanley to O'Brien, 14 February 1847 (copy). Derby Mss, 177/1; Disraeli, *Bentinck*, 387. Of the 70 Irish members who voted on the bill, only 37 supported it, including 17 of 23 Repealers (Nowlan, *Politics of Repeal*, 135).

confidence in Bentinck. Despite his enthusiasm for the bill, Herries would not give Bentinck a letter of support to be read in the Commons.[1] Bentinck's inability to argue his case in detail dismayed his followers.[2] Ashburton told Stanley that Bentinck hazarded too many bold projects to win the trust of the party: 'he does not seem aware that the business of a party leader is not to find plans and measures, but to find fault'.[3] Lord Brougham rejoiced that 'this volunteer chancellor of the Exchequer' was beaten, since his removal from the leadership would improve the chances of Conservative reunion.[4] But no one challenged his position, and Bentinck stumbled on.

The other Protectionist quarrel with the government was over the Poor Law Bill. When it came to the House of Commons in March, Stanley rallied the Protectionist party to the defence of the Irish landowners. The bill gave the tenant power to deduct from his rent a certain proportion of the rate paid by the tenant in the first instance. Stanley drew up an amendment which would have debarred any occupier of rateable property from making this deduction, an amendment which he regarded as a *quid pro quo* for the sacrifice which landed property made in paying for outdoor relief. The amendment was lost in the Commons by only three votes, but Stanley could not find support for it in the Lords and abandoned it. When it came to the test, his majority in the House of Lords collapsed.

Stanley had adopted his first nakedly Tory posture since his resignation from Peel's cabinet. However just his claim that without his amendment the Poor Law would mean so lavish an outlay of money that it would 'prove fatal to all property and equivalent to an Agrarian Law',[5] he had identified himself with

[1] Herries to Bentinck, 3 and 4 February 1847 (copies); Bentinck to Herries, 4 February 1847. Herries Mss, NRA/21a.

[2] 'The railway debate and the speech of George Bentinck have thrown the Protectionists into consternation and dismay. Any remaining illusion about him has been entirely dissipated by the display of his intemperance and incapacity... they don't know how to shake him off. It is pretty clear that there is no cordiality between him and Stanley' (Greville, iii, 60).

[3] Ashburton to Stanley, 24 January 1847. Derby Mss, 147/15.

[4] Brougham to Lord Granton, 11 February 1847. E. G. Collieu, 'Lord Brougham and the Conservatives', in H. R. Trevor-Roper (ed.), *Essays in British History Presented to Sir Keith Feiling* (London, 1964), 208–9.

[5] Stanley to G. Hope, 28 March 1847 (copy). Derby Mss, 177/2.

the Irish landlords and, by implication, with Protestantism, absenteeism, and rack-renting. The railway bill had failed to win the support of the Irish radicals and, to the relief of many members of his party, Stanley had turned his back on them. The narrowness of the amendment's rejection in the Commons revealed the appeal of a hard anti-Irish line. Indeed, only Bentinck's blundering prevented the amendment from being accepted, and his reputation plummeted still lower, as one Protectionist pointed out to Stanley:

There was, it is true, no doubt for a large part of the Evening a majority in favour of it, and continued there until destroyed by himself [Bentinck], by two speeches, the first unnecessary altogether and driving some people away by its unjustifiable violence, the other, necessary no doubt, but most unnecessarily long...driving others away by boring them.

But the question being one on which both sections of the Party are agreed, why had we so wretched a muster? The answer is simple. No one knows better than you the absurdity of the twaddle about 'no party', and that bodies of men...can effect nothing unless organised and directed...But organised and directed by George Bentinck the bulk of the Conservative party will not suffer themselves to be. They won't come down when he asks them and no one else, as things stand, will take upon himself to organise and direct them, or even to ask them to attend, except by speaking to them as opportunities occur.[1]

During the debate on the amendment, Graham noticed in Bentinck 'symptoms more marked and decided than heretofore of a Mind off the Balance'.[2] A couple of nights later, when Bentinck launched an unexpected attack on Labouchere, chief secretary for Ireland, he was hooted by his own party, whom Greville reported to be 'overwhelmed with shame and chagrin'.[3]

Bentinck's religious opinions were as offensive to the Tory squirearchy as his erratic behaviour. In April, he enthusiastically supported a private member's bill repealing the penal clauses attaching to Catholics. Only eight Protectionists voted for the

[1] G. Hope to Stanley, 5 April 1847. *ibid.* 134/1. Stanley and Beresford agreed that Bentinck had incurred the defeat of the amendment (Stanley to Beresford, 10 April 1847 (copy). *ibid.* 177/2; Beresford to Stanley, 6 April 1847. *ibid.* 149/1).
[2] Graham to Peel, 30 March 1847. Peel Mss, Add. Mss 40453, ff. 209–10.
[3] Greville, iii, 71–2.

bill, which was defeated by a Peelite–Protectionist combination. Newcastle was disappointed that Bentinck had announced himself so much at variance with his party,[1] but it was fortunate for Stanley, who was in favour of the bill, that it never reached the Lords. Irish issues were providing a common ground for Peelites and Protectionists. In a tiny House, 27 Peelites had supported the rating amendment to the Poor Law, and 26 of them voted against the Roman Catholic relief bill. Of these, 15 had voted against the Maynooth grant in 1845, but the other 11 had either voted against their convictions then or had changed their minds since. Either way, the sign was distinctly encouraging to the Protectionists. Yet Goulburn was the only leading Peelite to side with the Protectionists on either occasion: anti-Catholicism was always more powerful on the back benches than with men of official experience.

On other issues, the two wings of the Conservative party continued to go their separate ways. The Ten Hours bill, passed at long last, earned the stubborn resistance of the non-interventionist Peelites and the almost solid support of the Protectionists. And when the expected Peelite support for Stanley's amendment to the Colonial Spirits Duties Bill in the Lords was wanting, even Lord Brougham gave up hope of a Conservative reconciliation before the elections.[2]

The 1847 election was one of the most lack-lustre of the century. The dissensions within the Protectionist party strengthened the hand of the government; Radicalism was impotent (only one Chartist was elected); and Russell had taken no great liberal steps to frighten the country into a conservative reaction. In the months before the election corn prices remained high, thanks largely to the failure of the root crops and the high wages which accompanied the railway boom. Wheat prices soared to 114s. in the London Corn Exchange on 17 May, in startling contrast to the 50s. which protected corn had fetched a year earlier. Even in the counties, the Protectionists felt that they were

---

[1] Newcastle to Stanley, 20 April 1847. Derby Mss, 147/14.

[2] Brougham to Ellenborough, undated. Ellenborough Mss, PRO 30, 12/21/8. See also Bentinck to Disraeli, 24 April 1847: '*Nine Peelites* every man voted against Stanley in the H. of Lds. yesterday; *not one* with him!!! So much for conciliation' (Hughenden Mss, B/XX/Be/27).

fighting uphill. Stanley concluded, therefore, that nothing could prevent Conservative losses.

I do not... see on public grounds any justification of an *active* opposition to the Government as at present composed; and an active opposition would be the only legitimate ground, under present circumstances, for the reunion of the Conservative forces. I must see my way to the probability of cordial co-operation in Office, before I make any serious attempt to eject its present holders. Personally, you are well aware, I have no wish to play the part of Leader of any party, or of any combination of parties... The Whig party must therefore, I presume, gain strength; and the Conservative party be again re-united, if ever, by a sense of common danger.[1]

As Greville remarked, the Conservative split made a Whig government a necessity.[2] No issue predominated at the elections, and the general confusion of parties, persons, and principles left the electorate indifferent. 'There is no supreme party, no all-powerful statesman', *The Times* commented, 'warranted to save the nation, or at all events to assure one class from the general reverse. There is no longer the banner of reform, and the phalanx of Conservatism.'[3] Stanley found himself 'watching, rather than opposing, Government which I cannot trust' and distrusting his own followers' outbursts against 'Popery'.[4] Beresford believed there never to have been 'so blind an election... Supiness is the order of the day among most Conservatives'.[5] Finding Protectionist candidates cost him great effort for little reward. 'The lukewarmness and shiftiness of those I have to deal with is most disheartening.'[6]

There were fewer seats contested in 1847 than in any other nineteenth-century election: only 235, or 36 per cent, of the total 656. This was partly a reflexion of the blurred distinction between the parties and the consequent disruption of conventional alliances in many constituencies. *The Times* complained of 'the

---

1 Stanley to Hope, 7 April 1847 (copy). Derby Mss, 177/2.
2 Greville, iii, 95–6.
3 *The Times*, 23 July 1847.
4 Stanley to Croker, 7 June 1847 (copy). Derby Mss, 177/2.
5 Beresford to Croker, undated. Jennings, *Croker*, iii, 118.
6 Beresford to Stanley, undated. Derby Mss, 149/1.

want of a decided and specific policy as to measures in the addresses of most of the candidates'.[1] Some Protectionists affirmed an undying faith in the Corn Laws,[2] but the majority were circumspect in their statements. E. B. Denison defended his vote against repeal, but said that years must elapse before the validity of free trade could be tested;[3] his caution did not prevent the West Riding from returning to its Liberal tradition by sending Lord Morpeth and Cobden to Westminster. Denison's position was the standard one adopted by Protectionists throughout the country. Free trade played so minor a part that George Lewis was able to tell his constituents in Herefordshire, if with some exaggeration, that 'the adherents of all political parties seem now to be agreed in the maintenance of the principles of Free Trade'.[4] That seemed, indeed, to be the lesson of the elections: Disraeli said that the landed interest must turn its attention to measures of compensation,[5] and few Protectionists went beyond a pledge not to tamper with the Navigation Laws.

If any issue aroused the electorate, it was, in Beresford's words, 'the proper and just old No Popery cry',[6] which was taken up by Protectionists and Dissenters throughout the country, despite the fact that the government had done nothing to encourage the Irish radicals. Both Stanley and Bentinck deplored the exploitation of Protestant bigotry, without being able to stop it. In an article based on a letter from Stanley, Croker dissociated the *Quarterly Review* and the party leadership from those who made a vote against the Maynooth grant and a promise not to vote for the payment of the Irish clergy tests of Conservatism. The label was not only unjust, but would 'distract and weaken a party which it is our first duty to reunite and consolidate'.[7] The *Illustrated London News* believed that the prominence of the anti-Catholic issue proved the want of subjects of

[1] *The Times*, 24 July 1847.

[2] *The Times*, 12 August 1847.

[3] *Illustrated London News*, 14 August 1847. Disraeli took the same ground (*The Times*, 25 May and 21 June 1847).

[4] G. C. Lewis, *Addresses and Speeches of Sir George Cornewall Lewis Relative to the Election for the County of Hereford in 1852* (London, 1857), 6.

[5] *The Times*, 21 June 1847.

[6] Beresford to Croker, undated. Jennings, *Croker*, iii, 118.

[7] *Quarterly Review* (June 1847), 309.

real controversy,[1] but for zealots the issue was real enough.
When the Maynooth Bill had been passed, protestant associations in every part of England and Scotland had resolved to make
its repeal the dominant issue at the next elections. From May
1846, until the elections, the National Club, in conjunction with
the Protestant Association, flooded the country with pamphlets
urging the return of anti-Maynooth candidates. At a great meeting in London on 12 May 1847, it called for the return of 'Protestant candidates'. Since the National Club was little more than
a dining club, and the Protestant Association was in debt, neither
was an efficient instrument of electoral management.[2] Still, their
agitation had its effect. Gathorne Hardy, a Peelite who was invited by the Bradford Conservative Association to stand as a
united Conservative candidate, refused to pledge himself against
concessions to the Catholics, lost the support of the Bradford
operatives, and was defeated by a Liberal.[3] Beresford tried to
persuade three constituencies to run the Peelite, Montagu Gore,
as a Protectionist, but despite Gore's promise to provide £3,000
for expenses, all three refused him because of his vote for
Maynooth.[4]

Many Protectionists were tempted to enter into an alliance
with Dissent on the anti-Catholic issue. In April, a national
education conference of Dissenters condemned the government's
legislation making increased grants available to schools which
taught the Authorised Version of the scriptures and called on the
electorate to return candidates who were aware that state aid for
religious purposes was a threat to religious liberty. A Dissenters Electoral Committee was established, and in some northern
industrial towns the Liberal party was on the verge of collapse.
Dissenters in Leeds, Huddersfield, and Newcastle put forward
candidates of their own against the Liberal nominee.[5] Stanley
advised the party not to participate in a temporary alliance with
men who were no more friendly to the Tories than they were to

[1] *Illustrated London News*, 24 July 1847.
[2] *The Times*, 13 May 1847.
[3] A. E. Gathorne-Hardy (ed.), *Gathorne Hardy, First Earl of Cranbrook, A Memoir* (London, 1910), i, 58–73.
[4] Beresford to Stanley, undated. Derby Mss, 149/1.
[5] *The Times*, 20 and 28 May, 12 July, 1847.

the Whigs, but the advice was not everywhere heeded. In Herefordshire the Low Church and Dissent combined against George Lewis without, however, defeating him.[1] The Peelite, Monckton Milnes, was successful at Pontefract notwithstanding the fact that 'the Clergy and the Methodists entered into a holy league against me, and spared neither truth nor money to turn me out for what the fools call my Popery'.[2] In Leeds and Lambeth, the Protectionists ousted Liberals by combining with the Dissenters, but the tactics were fruitless in South Essex and Derby.[3]

The usefulness of the Protestant issue for the Protectionists was considerably diminished by Bentinck's speech at King's Lynn advocating the payment of the Catholic clergy out of Irish land. Placards warning Dissenters against the 'Popish' party of Stanley and Bentinck and an anti-Bentinck leaflet were distributed in Nonconformist constituencies.[4] It is unlikely that the outcome of many elections rested on the religious issue. Stanley and Bentinck agreed that Protestantism had not gained the party any seats.[5] Bonham believed that Maynooth defeated several Peelites,[6] but the evidence for this conclusion is hard to find. There were only 10 unsuccessful Peelites, none of them in a constituency where Protestant fervour seems to have been particularly strong. Charles Round, the Protectionist brought forward by the Low Church party at Oxford University, failed to defeat Gladstone.[7]

---

[1] Lewis to Sir Edmund Head, 2 July and 5 August 1847. Lewis, *Letters*, 154–6.

[2] Reid, Milnes, i, 380.

[3] E. Baines, *The Life of Edward Baines* (London, 1851), 332; J. Maynall, *The Annals of Yorkshire* (London, 1878), i, 546–7; Stanley to Beresford, 5 August 1847 (copy). Derby Mss, 177/2.

[4] Beresford to Stanley, undated. *ibid.* 149/1.

[5] Bentinck to Stanley, 7 August 1847: 'The No Popery cry has not saved or gained us a single member – lost us Liverpool, Westminster, Cambridge town, Canterbury, and God knows how many places besides; it is absolutely worthless for good, but hangs round the neck of the party for evil and must eventually drown it ...I faced the cry and the effect was that after a four days' canvass, I found that I should only have lost seven votes by so doing' (Derby Mss, 132/13); Stanley to Bentinck, 10 August 1847 (copy). *ibid.* 177/2.

[6] J. B. Conacher, 'Peel and the Peelites, 1846–50', *English Historical Review* (July 1958), 437.

[7] For a detailed account of this contest, see S. Northcote, *A Statement of Facts Connected with the Election of the Right Hon. W. E. Gladstone as a Member for the University of Oxford in 1847, and with his Re-elections in 1852 and 1853* (London, 1853) (Bodleian Gough Adds. Oxon.) and various manuscript items in *Papers Relating to the Proceedings of the University*, 1847 (*ibid*).

Sidney Herbert was returned without a contest for South Wiltshire because the clergy, though strong against Maynooth,
fought shy of alliance with Dissent.[1] Graham called Cardwell's
victory at Orange Liverpool 'at once the discomfiture of bigotry
and of Protection',[2] while Lincoln successfully repelled the 'No
Popery' blast at Falkirk District.[3]

The Peelites returned almost 100 members, a reduction of
only about 20 in their ranks, and one of the reasons for their
doing so well was the support which they received from the
Whigs: Goulburn, Gladstone, Cardwell, George Smythe, and
Sir George Clerk all received Whig assistance.[4] In addition,
Stanley kept his party from running candidates against the Peelites 'except in cases where a flagrant breach of trust has excited
strong feeling in the Elective body, and where a fair chance is
presented of replacing them by staunch Protectionists'.[5] On this
ground he hoped to defeat Granville Somerset at Monmouth-
shire, but even there Somerset shared the representation with a
Protectionist in an uncontested election.[6] Protectionists stood
against Peelites in only ten constituencies, and were defeated in
all of them but Shrewsbury and Shaftesbury. Elsewhere, the
Peelites had the advantage of being the established local representative.

The election produced little change at Westminster. Contemporaries were struck by the emergence of a business, particularly
railway interest in the Commons – in itself an ill-omen for the
landed interest – and by the large turnover in personnel, but the
balance of parties remained about the same. The Whigs gained a
clear majority in the Commons, but they were still at the mercy
of their Radical and Irish supporters, both of whom increased
their representation slightly. Exact calculation of the returns is

[1] Herbert to Peel, 5 August 1847. Parker, *Peel*, iii, 488.

[2] Graham to Peel, 1 August 1847. *ibid*. iii, 487–8.

[3] Lincoln to Peel, 16 July 1847. *ibid*.

[4] Bentinck estimated that Goulburn and Gladstone each received about 300
Whig votes, and that Cardwell, Clerk, and Lincoln succeeded through the Whigs
and Roman Catholics splitting in their constituencies. Smythe was 'brought in upon
[the Whig] Albert Conyngham's back; I do not suppose he got 250 votes of his
old party' (Bentinck to Croker, 8 September 1847. Jennings, *Croker*, iii, 131–2).

[5] Stanley to Beresford, 12 July 1846 (copy). Derby Mss, 177/1.

[6] Stanley to Beresford, 12 August 1847 (copy). *ibid*. 177/2.

impossible. Even contemporaries were unable to assess the relative strength of parties precisely. Gladstone estimated the number of Peelites at under 60, Bentinck at 85, and Beresford at 120; figures for the Protectionists ranged from the *Illustrated London News'* 201 to the *Morning Post's* 247.[1] It all depended on what you meant by 'Peelite' and 'Protectionist'. The terms were far from distinct in an election in which free trade had played so small a part. But even the Liberal figures ranged from 317 to 341.[2] The figures based on Dod's lists agree with those of the Whig whip, Tufnell, and as they strike a midway point between the extremes of various observers may be taken as near to the true state as we are likely to get. Tufnell gave the Liberals (of all shades) 336, the Protectionists 225–30, and the Peelites 85–90.[3] By Dod's classifications (he designated Peelites as Liberal Conservatives) there were 330 Liberals, 229 Protectionists, and 98 Peelites.[4]

The combined Conservative loss was thus about 50 seats. Although the Conservative organisation undoubtedly suffered from the split in the party, it is impossible to gauge the efficiency of party electoral machinery in normal conditions this early in the century. An exhaustive study of local conditions can alone yield a satisfactory picture of what happened in a general election in the nineteenth century. Even then, the evidence for making strong claims is lacking. Until, if it is ever possible, mid-nineteenth-century elections are better explored, one has to keep to the main paths and miss most of the trees. A few general trends are the most one can hope to discover.

Bentinck's claim that the absence of an anti-malt tax cry hurt the Protectionists is, at least, suspect.[5] The Protectionists swept the counties where the issue would have helped them, winning

[1] Gladstone memorandum of 29 November 1876. Gladstone Mss, Add. Mss 44778, ff. 76–83; Bentinck to H. Bentinck, 18 August 1847. Bentinck Mss, PWL/417; Bentinck to Stanley, 19 August 1847. Derby Mss, 132/13; *Illustrated London News*, 11 September 1847.

[2] The *Sun* gave the Liberals 341, the *Morning Post*, 317 (Bentinck to Stanley, 19 August 1847. Derby Mss, 132/13).

[3] Gash, *Reaction and Reconstruction*, 192.

[4] Dod may slightly exaggerate the Peelite strength. Some Peelites were too independent to be susceptible to party classification.

[5] Bentinck to Stanley, 7 August 1847. Derby Mss, 132/13.

42 of the 48 'agricultural' and 47 of the 59 'mixed' county seats. In the 'industrial' counties they did poorly, as in Lancashire, where they lost all four seats.[1] They lost both seats in Cheshire North, which surrounded the manufacturing towns of Macclesfield and Stockport, but held both seats in the purely agricultural southern division of the county. Derbyshire returned two Liberals for the iron and coal area of the Northern division and two Protectionists for the south. In some northern counties, notably Cheshire North, Lancashire South, and the West Riding, the Anti-Corn Law League's registration drive of 1844–5 seems to have borne fruit.[2] In a few southern counties, the high corn prices may have kept the farmers from taking revenge on the Peelites.[3] The election made distinct the division between the Liberals and the Protectionists as the urban and landed parties. The Liberals had a net gain of 21 borough seats; only 5 of the 17 boroughs which they lost went to Protectionists. Free trade was vindicated in the towns and the Protectionists reduced to the landed rump of Peel's great Conservative party.

One possible trend at the elections was a return to electoral allegiances of the mid-1830s. The rise of the Conservative party in the 1830s was the result of a variety of factors. Three of the most important of them no longer applied: the leadership of Peel, the fear of radical changes in the constitution, and the threat of the Anti-Corn Law League. Liberals who had gone over to Peel returned to their party. The example of Frome, a small borough in Somersetshire, is instructive. In the terminology of

[1] The counties are divided into these three categories according to a table compiled from the 1831 census in P. Deane and W. A. Cole, *British Economic Growth, 1868–1959* (Cambridge, 1962), 103.

[2] H. Ashworth, *Recollections of Richard Cobden and the Anti-Corn Law League* (London, 1876), 283. The League was said to have invested £250,000 in freeholds in Lancashire, Yorkshire, and Cheshire, thereby gaining 5,000 votes (R. A. J. Walling (ed.), *The Diaries of John Bright* (London, 1930), 75).

[3] Herbert believed this to be true in South Wiltshire, where he was re-elected 'without so much as a threat of opposition...in a purely agricultural constituency which was expected by the Protectionists to take signal revenge upon a member of your Government' (Herbert to Peel, undated. Lord Stanmore, *Sidney Herbert, Lord Herbert of Lea* (London, 1906), i, 81). Stanley, however, had been advised not to put an outsider against the sitting, resident member (Nelson to Stanley, 8 March 1847. Derby Mss, 150/16) and the seat is one of those in which Stanley's policy not to oppose Peelites was followed.

Dod, Frome returned a Liberal in 1832, a Liberal Conservative in 1835, a Conservative in 1837, and a Protectionist in 1841, the representative in each parliament being the same Thomas Sheppard. In 1847, a Liberal, Robert Boyle, was once again elected. Middlesex presents a similar picture. In 1832 and 1835, Colonel Thomas Wood, a Conservative, failed to dislodge either of the Liberal members. In 1837 and 1841, he shared the representation with a Liberal. In 1847, he lost again and two Liberals were returned. This electoral pattern of Conservative fortunes is reflected in a number of constituencies.[1]

To contemporaries, the great feature of the elections was that no party was placed firmly in control of the House of Commons. Nor had the election shed much light on what were to be the important questions discussed there. The radical *Illustrated London News* observed with satisfaction that 'the country has returned a House of Commons less distinctly marked by old party divisions than any that has sat for the present century' and added, with more accuracy, that 'practicality predominates, physical and material interests are getting the advantage of theory…and of party'.[2]

[1] Notably in Barnstaple, Bedford, Harwich, Kingston-upon-Hull, Lincoln, Pontefract, Reading, Rochester, Southampton, Surrey East, and Surrey West.

[2] *Illustrated London News*, 20 November 1847.

5

FROM BENTINCK TO DISRAELI

DOWN TO the elections of 1847, Stanley had done nothing in particular and done it very well. His position ever since Peel's resignation had been that the electorate must decide the tariff question, and that until its decision was registered at the polls the organisation of a permanent Protectionist party was not only impractical but wrong-headed. In silencing the anti-malt tax cry and in preventing a head-on collision between Protectionists and Peelites at the elections he had won two decisive victories over Bentinck. The way was thus left open for a gradual reunion of the Conservative party, Stanley's fundamental political object, should free trade be confirmed by the electorate. So it appeared to have been. More than two-thirds of the members of the new House of Commons were free traders. After a year in which he had studiously abstained from dogmatic statements of attachment to the Corn Laws, Stanley was free to wean his party away from protection in the autumn of 1847, without seriously damaging his political reputation. He would merely have been accepting the facts of the matter. Had he done so, and come into power in 1852 rid of the albatross of protection, the subsequent history of political parties in England might have been quite different. But various circumstances made it possible to reject the results of the elections as a verdict in favour of free trade. Two coincident events, a sharp drop in agricultural prices and the financial crash of the autumn of 1847, convinced Stanley and Bentinck that if the elections were held again a very different result would be obtained.

In the autumn of 1847 the economy passed through a bad season. As prices fell, the unemployment figures rose. The export trade languished and the Bank was exposed to a heavy drain on its gold reserves. Recourse to greater direct taxation, the Manchester School's next object now that the Corn Laws had been repealed, seemed to be the inevitable method of supplying the loss of customs revenue from the Exchequer. In these straitened circumstances free trade might quickly be discredited. In May the Protectionist agent in Liverpool had expected a reaction against free trade to appear there in three years' time, but by the following November he believed it already to have set in.[1] Adherence to the Corn Laws was, then, perhaps the only, certainly the easiest, way to keep together a strong Conservative party for the approaching 'struggle between the Democratic and Aristocratic (and Monarchical) principles'.[2] Even Lord John Manners, who throughout 1847 had pleaded with Stanley and Disraeli to renounce protection, saw that the wind was blowing in a new direction.

It seems to me that on the three great fields of inevitable debate we have a clear and ascertained superiority. Ireland, Free Imports, Currency; heretofore we have been assailed, henceforward, that is if I had my way, we are the assailants; Bright and Villiers and Thompson Smith are not half the men to defend as they are to attack... It is clear that they must admit the present failure of their grand scheme of Free Imports.[3]

By such reasoning Stanley came to the decision to continue his policy of wait-and-see for another year. Though in the long term it might be wiser to let the tariff issue fade away, in the short term, especially considering the mood of the party, the reward for not doing so was potentially too rich to be thrown away.

The financial crisis of 1847 was the worst that England had experienced since the panic of 1825. The speculative orgy of 1845, encouraged by a competitive Bank rate of $2\frac{1}{2}$ per cent, lower than the market rate, surpassed the excesses of 1825.[4]

---

[1] Henry Chapman to Bentinck, 3 May and 4 November 1847. Bentinck Mss, PWL/69. See also Bentinck to Disraeli, 5 October 1847: 'Free Trade seems working mischief faster than the most fearful of us predicted and Manchester Houses, as I am told, "failing in rows" ashamed to do penance in public are secretly weeping in sackcloth and ashes and heartily praying that Peel and Cobden had been hanged before they were allowed to ruin the country' (Hughenden Mss, B/XX/Be/36).

[2] Stanley to Croker, 12 September 1847. Jennings, *Croker*, iii, 134–6.

[3] Manners to Disraeli, 8 November 1847. Hughenden Mss, B/XX/M/14.

[4] C.N.Ward-Perkins, 'The Commercial Crisis of 1847', *Oxford Economic Papers* (1950), 76.

By 1846, the boom had slackened and when the good harvest of 1847 tumbled wheat prices to 45s. by the end of August, the failure of corn dealers in Liverpool and London began. The effects spread to financial houses who had extended them credit and 'like a house of cards the over-strained credit structure collapsed'.[1] Too late to influence the elections, the crisis nevertheless was welcome fodder to the Protectionists. Free trade had brought increased food imports,[2] which, not being paid for by an expanded export trade, had resulted in a crippling drain on the Bank's gold reserves. From 1815 to 1842, England had maintained a favourable balance of trade, but in the five years under Peel the trade deficit mounted to £35,677,941.[3] Between 23 January and 17 April 1847, the Bank's bullion reserve in the issue department dwindled from £13,400,000 to £9,200,000. Peel's restrictive Bank Act of 1844 came into effect for the first time and 'assets other than bank notes became almost unmarketable',[4] while the interest rate rose to 8 per cent.

The 1844 act embodied the principle that paper circulation should vary in amount exactly as the circulation would vary if it were in metallic currency.[5] By restricting circulation and confining the issue of notes almost exclusively to the Bank of England, Peel intended to control the flow of gold out of the country and avoid financial panics. When high prices in England caused a drain of gold to foreign countries, the circulation would contract, lowering prices in England, cutting down imports and increasing exports, and in the end restoring the balance of trade and arresting the drain of gold. The bill was supported by the free traders who believed that the contraction of the currency would lower agricultural rents and make it difficult for landowners to pay the interest on their mortgages. By lowering the prices of manufactured goods, the bill might also swell the demand for the repeal of the Corn Laws. Charles Newdegate warned

[1] *Ibid.* 78.

[2] In the first nine months of 1847, there were increases of 35 per cent in butter imports, 100 per cent in live animals, and 300 per cent in grain and flour (*The Times*, 26 November 1847).

[3] *Quarterly Review* (September 1847), 559.

[4] Ward-Perkins, 78.

[5] For a discussion of the act see B. Holland, *The Fall of Protection, 1840–50* (London, 1913), 140–58.

Conservatives that the bill endangered the mixed aristocracy of birth, intellect, and wealth by which England was governed: the bill was part of a system which would end in 'the construction of an aristocracy of mere wealth, by raising the value of money above other capital to the extinction of the present mixed aristocracy'.[1] Insofar as it was in the interest of the financiers, as holders and lenders of money, that money should be dear while other things were cheap, since the contraction of currency increases the power of gold over produce, the Bank Act posed some danger to the agriculturalists. But the subject was too dry, the details too complex, and the consequences too indirect for the bill to arouse the agriculturalists' opposition in 1844.

In the autumn of 1847 the Protectionists were made aware of the action of the Bank Act. To them it appeared obvious that the combination of the Bank Act and the repeal of the Corn Laws had produced the crisis. Bentinck commiserated with the Duke of Rutland, on whose mortgage the interest had risen by 33 per cent, but he thought 'nothing as likely to rouse the landed Aristocracy from their apathy and to weaken their idolatry of Peel so much as this warning note of the joint operation of his Free Trade and Restrictive Currency Laws'.[2] But the Protectionists' belief that they would benefit from the crisis in a new election was perhaps ill-founded. In 1826, when currency questions attracted much more notice than in the 1840s, Sir James Graham remarked that the subject was 'foreign to the tastes of the country gentlemen'.[3] The Protectionist party was deficient in members able to debate financial matters in detail. Monckton Milnes' father saw little advantage accruing to the party from the crisis since 'neither Lord George nor Dizzy can argue it aright, the former so extravagant and unfair in his way of stating it, and Dizzy so unpractical'.[4] The crisis was, at any rate, not entirely the result of the interaction of free imports and a diminishing gold stock. Unemployment in manufacturing areas was greatly increased by a short American cotton crop in 1845–6, which sent the price of cotton soaring and depressed England's leading

[1] 13 June 1844. *Hansard*, 3rd Series, lxxv, 832.
[2] Bentinck to Disraeli, 30 April 1847. Hughenden Mss, B/XX/Be/33.
[3] A. B. Erickson, *The Public Career of Sir James Graham* (Oxford, 1952), 52.
[4] Reid, *Milnes*, i, 401.

manufacture, the textile industry.[1] A committee of the House of Commons, in an admittedly shallow inquiry and report, acquitted the Bank Act of responsibility for the crisis and blamed it on deficient harvests and the diversion of capital into railway-building. The Protectionists would have been at pains to refute the *Illustrated London News'* explanation of the crisis: that capital had been devoted to railways which would in time return large profits, but which for the moment had been taken out of commercial transactions, and that the crisis was therefore the natural result of the transition which the country was making from agriculture to industry. For a few years, before industry developed fully to its new trading prominence, there was bound to be an adverse trade balance. The remedy was not to return to the Corn Laws, but 'to retrench, to work hard, to produce and sell, in order to bring back by the course of trade the gold we have parted with'.[2] There was sounded the mid-Victorian gospel, soon to drown out the old Protectionist creed.

The 1847 panic not only replenished the Protectionists' faith, but by drawing renewed Protectionist attacks on Peel's record, poured salt in the Conservative party's wounds. Lord Ellenborough declined Stanley's invitation to dinner in November because of the *Morning Herald's* campaign for the repeal of the Bank Act.[3] The 'No Popery' campaign of some Protectionists during the elections had already widened the Conservative split. Peelite sensibilities were offended by the Protectionists' anti-Catholic outbursts, and also by Bentinck's support for the Radical, Bernal Osborne, at Middlesex against their candidate, Colonel Wood, a renegade from the Protectionists.[4] 'The party to which we belonged has gone to the dogs,' Arbuthnot wrote, '...there is no likelihood of its reuniting in our lifetime.'[5] Peel had renounced ties with any party, so that the Peelites were a loose group of men to be bartered for, and the competition for

---

[1] Ward-Perkins, 78.

[2] *Illustrated London News*, 9 October 1847.

[3] Ellenborough to Stanley, 9 November 1847. Derby Mss, 137/7.

[4] See Lincoln to Peel, 7 August 1847. Peel Mss, Add. Mss 40481, ff. 416–17. Bentinck sent Osborne £100 which was returned to him (P. H. Bagenal, *The Life of Ralph Bernal Osborne, M.P.* (London, 1884), 80–1).

[5] Arbuthnot to Graham, 23 July 1847. Peel Mss, Add. Mss 40452, f. 223.

their allegiance hotted up. In April, Russell had dismissed the suggestion that he make room for two or three Peelites in his cabinet as an attempt 'to make matters better than well',[1] but in July the Peelite, Dalhousie, accepted the non-party appointment to the Governor-Generalship of India, and Stanley, while not accepting the *Morning Chronicle*'s statement of a coalition between Whigs and Peelites, believed that there was 'a very good understanding between the Government and many of Peel's followers'.[2] On the main questions which would arise in the 1848 session, the admission of Jews to parliament, an increase in direct taxation, and the repeal of the Navigation Laws, the Peelites and the Protectionists were divided from each other. The *Quarterly Review*, hitherto an advocate of reconciliation, concluded that the Conservative schism was irreversible. The only hope of curbing the government's 'destruction' lay in a firmly united Protectionist party.[3]

The party was itching for a fight. Lord John Manners, anticipating an onslaught upon the remaining customs duties, the Navigation Laws, and 'half a hundred other systems and institutions', wanted to upstage the government and 'call away the destined besiegers to defend their own crumbling places of strength'.[4] Stanley wished to avoid defeating the government, not only for personal reasons,[5] but, more important, because he feared that a Protectionist government would provoke a Radical revival. His fears were shared by Graham, who was determined to prevent a Tory government because of 'the great impetus it would give to reform, and the vast power the Radical and subversive interest would acquire'.[6] In the late 1830s Wellington had conceived it to be true Conservative policy to keep the Whigs in power, where they could be held in check by the opposi-

---

[1] Broughton, *Recollections*, vi, 187.

[2] Stanley to Brougham, 20 August 1847 (copy). Derby Mss, 177/2.

[3] 'Jewish Disabilities' and 'Parliamentary Prospects', *Quarterly Review* (September 1847), 526–40 and 541–78.

[4] Manners to Disraeli, 8 November 1847. Hughenden Mss, B/XX/M/14.

[5] Stanley to Lambert, 5 January 1848: 'I cannot share in the desire you express to see me at the head of the affairs of this Country – little as I should court such a post at any time, I do not think I ever recollect a period at which it would be so little inviting an object of ambition as the present' (Derby Mss, 177/2).

[6] Greville, iii, 196.

tion. The argument rested on the assumption, supported by some experience, that a liberal or left-wing party will behave more radically out of office than in. From 1847 to 1851 Stanley acted, if less explicitly than Wellington, on the Duke's principles. Only in the Lords, if at all, were the Protectionists strong enough to defeat the government. But to do so, as Peel had seen in the late 1830s, was to run the risk of raising a radical cry of 'the peers against the people' and provoking an attack on the upper chamber. Thus, in 1849, the Navigation Laws were repealed, when 'the prudence of the Lords got the better of their desire to restore the Corn Laws'.[1]

In the late 1840s a defensive position had its merits. Ireland was smouldering with resentment at English rule, and the Radicals were sharpening their attack on aristocratic strongholds by advocating direct taxation on landed income and retrenchment in the services and the colonies – traditional preserves for younger sons of the gentry. The Protectionists could not take office without the promise of a dissolution, and in 1849 Cobden warned them that if they defeated the government he would lead the fight at the elections against the whole system of aristocracy.[2] The familiar accusation against Stanley, that he behaved with boyish indifference to politics, negligent of the interests of his party, misses the mark. As long as there were, in reality, two conservative parties in the country, it was arguable that the business of the Tories was to temper the forward tendencies of Whiggery in opposition. The hitch in the argument is that if the policy is followed indefinitely it will eventually destroy the parliamentary system, since in order to discharge the function assigned to it an opposition must be powerful. It must be a threat to the government in power. Otherwise it neither inhibits the government nor attracts public support. Clever young men will not throw in their lot with a party which makes a virtue of renouncing the prizes of public life. Stanley was quite aware of the danger. Though his caution inspired mistrust and some grumbling among the more ambitious of his followers,

---

[1] Cornewall Lewis to Sir Edmund Head, 10 June 1849. Lewis, *Letters*, 204–9.

[2] Speech at Leeds, 18 December 1849. Bright and Rogers, *Speeches by Cobden*. i, 411–33.

all Stanley wished to ensure was that the Protectionists should not take office until they had acquired the strength to govern on Conservative principles. If a right-wing government acts as an impetus to the revival of radicalism, how much more so does a weak right-wing government.

In the autumn of 1847, the chief source of weakness in the Protectionist party, apart from its want of front-bench experience and ability, was the uncertainty of its leadership in the House of Commons. At the end of October, Stanley asked Bentinck to take a more decided lead by issuing notices and calling meetings of the Commons' party in his own name, instead of leaving it to Stanley to hold meetings of Protectionists in both Houses.[1] It was a foolish request, since the City had just returned Baron Meyer de Rothschild to parliament. Since 1830 Bentinck and Stanley had consistently voted for the admission of Jews to parliament. Opposition to that reform, which had three times been blocked by the House of Lords, had been led by the Tories, Inglis, Spooner, Plumptre, and Colonel Sibthorp, all of whom were now sitting on the Protectionist benches. Having lost the battle to keep parliament Anglican, and then Protestant, they were still fighting to keep it Christian. In December 1847, the government brought in its bill to admit Jews, and Bentinck and Disraeli accounted for half of the Protectionist votes in its support.[2] Bentinck's day was over, although, thanks once more to the Lords, Rothschild's was not yet to begin. Stanley and others had tried to persuade Bentinck merely to record a silent vote for the measure,[3] but Bentinck delivered a slashing speech against religious intolerance. 'The strongest proof of the virtual deposition of Lord George', Peel wrote some time later, 'was the disinclination of the House to listen to him. I hope to see Inglis in his proper place as the leader of a real old Tory, Church of England, Protectionist, Protestant party.'[4]

Bentinck, too, thought that the party would be better served

---

[1] Stanley to Bentinck, 27 October 1847 (copy). Derby Mss, 177/2.

[2] The others were Thomas Baring and Milnes Gaskell. 11 Peelites supported the bill. 41 Peelites and 138 Protectionists opposed it (Beresford to Stanley, undated. Derby Mss, 149/1).

[3] Bentinck to Disraeli, 3 November 1847. Hughenden Mss, B/XX/Be/40.

[4] Peel to Graham. 2 January 1848. Parker, *Graham*, ii, 62.

by Lord Ashley or Inglis at the helm. He was as fed up with the party as the party was with him.

I am lowspirited at seeing the Party occupying itself about the admission or exclusion of an individual from Parliament at a moment when the great Commercial Empire of the World is engaged in a life and death struggle for existence. It is tea table twaddling more becoming to a pack of Old Maids than a great Party aspiring to govern an Empire on which the Sun never sets.[1]

Just at the time of the Jewish question, Beresford's Protestantism was inflamed by the first rumours that the Whigs and the Pope were negotiating to create Catholic sees in England, an issue which could conceivably be used to build a Protectionist majority in the country.[2] But there was no 'Protestant' of sufficient stature to lead the party. The party's two most skilful debaters, Disraeli and Thomas Baring, had supported the Jews. They were also the foremost opponents of the government's finance bill in the following February, a fact which, as Lord John Manners wrote to Disraeli, ought not to be lost upon the 'Protestants'.

I hope, too, the fact you note, of all the speaking on our side coming from supporters of religious liberty, will not be lost upon the squires. A month ago I asked a furious friend of mine if he thought the party was likely to be strengthened by the exclusion of you, G.B., T. Baring and Milnes Gaskell? It would be almost worthwhile to absent yourselves from the Navigation Laws debate in order to let the highfliers see what their real capacity is.[3]

Immediately after the vote on the Jewish bill, Beresford informed Bentinck that he no longer commanded the allegiance of the party.[4] Augustus (formerly Stafford O'Brien) had seceded from the party in September in protest against Bentinck's leadership,[5] and Stanley was aware that Bentinck had alienated many

[1] Bentinck to Disraeli, 14 November 1847. Hughenden Mss, B/XX/Be/42.
[2] See the debate, particularly Gladstone's speech, on the Diplomatic Relations Bill in January 1848.
[3] Manners to Disraeli, 7 February 1848. Hughenden Mss, B/XX/M/24.
[4] Beresford to Bentinck, 19 December 1847 (copy). Derby Mss, 149/1; Bentinck to Stanley, 24 December 1847. *ibid.* 132/13.
[5] C. Whibley, *Lord John Manners and his Friends* (London, 1925), i, 287. Stafford to Manners, 27 November 1847: 'You wonder why Clive, etc., will not

members of the party by the distance he kept from them.[1]
Bentinck had come to the leadership by default and had protested
at the time that his religious views disqualified him for it. He
owed his position, as he said, to the fact 'that England has proved
to be so degenerate that, in the face of an emergency, she has
produced, so far as I can see, no new leaders to take my place'.[2]
To hold a position on sufferance is always uncomfortable. Rather
than wait to be formally cashiered, Bentinck sent a letter of
resignation to George Bankes, explaining that he felt 'like a
caged bird escaped from his wired prison'.[3] For all his defects
as a leader there is no doubt that Bentinck was badly treated by
the party, especially by Beresford and the *Morning Herald*.

Appointed on account of my uncompromising spirit, I am dismissed
for the same reason...In April, 1846, they would have me, *nolens
volens*, for their leader. I in vain warned them that my religious
differences from them, as well as my want of capacity to lead a party,
alike disqualified me for the office. I foretold all that has since come to
pass – all in vain – ...and now...I read in their *Morning Herald* that
'Lord George Bentinck has thrown over his party'!

However, the great Protectionist party having degenerated into a
'No Popery', 'No Jew' party, I am still more unfit than I was in 1846
to lead it. A party that can muster 140 on a Jew Bill and cannot muster
much above half those numbers on any question essentially connected
with the great interests of the empire, can only be led by their antipa-
thies, their hatreds and their prejudices; and I am the unfittest man in
the world to lead them. Beresford, Newdegate, and Mr. Phillips of the
Morning Herald have raised all this artificial zeal in the cause of religion
...I am necessarily the first victim.[4]

A small group of the most able men in the party, who resented
Beresford's underhand tactics in asking Benthinck to resign without the approval of Stanley or the party, attempted to persuade

join us, and the wonderful thing is that you will never see how we are despised, and
how G. B.'s name is a byword or scoff among the Clubs. I do not believe that there is
any believer in him throughout the whole world except you' (*ibid*. i, 289).

[1] Stanley to Arbuthnot, 17 October 1847 and to Wellington, 17 October 1847
(copies). Derby Mss, 177/2.

[2] Bentinck to Croker, 5 October 1847. Jennings, *Croker*, iii, 146.

[3] Bentinck to Stanley, 24 December 1847. Derby Mss, 132/13.

[4] Bentinck to Croker, 26 December 1847. Jennings, *Croker*, iii, 158–60.

Bentinck to continue.[1] Stanley asked Beresford for a list of those who had complained of Bentinck to him, but received no reply.[2] Stanley made no attempt, however, to assist those who were trying to force Bentinck back on the party. He told Bentinck that while he wished him to continue to play a prominent part in the Commons, he expected 'that the "wild Bird" once more at liberty will wing his way rather more than of late to Newmarket'.[3]

Bentinck's fall was not a loss to the party. Arbuthnot found him to be 'with all persons the stumbling block' to reunion.[4] Forthright, honest, and indefatigable in the daily routine of parliamentary business, Bentinck was too poorly educated and too inexperienced in the ways of the House of Commons ever to have established his authority over that body or his party. Like Stanley, and unlike Disraeli, he took little interest in the organisation of the party in the country.[5] Energy, sincerity, and assiduous labour could not supply the place of political *savoir faire* and tactical sense. Cornewall Lewis, criticising Disraeli's eulogistic biography of 1851, found it 'impossible to make a hero out of Bentinck'.[6] Impetuosity led Bentinck on several occasions to embarrass his party by crude outbursts in the Commons. His hatred of compromise and 'dealing' was more suited to his famous reform of the Turf than to the delicate job of controlling a party and influencing the House of Commons. Even a warm admirer, Lord John Manners, was ill at ease in his company.

There was something in his stern vehemence which frightened my commonplace and yielding nature, so that I never ventured to argue out a question with him... A few civil words, a specious letter, would in '47

[1] The principals in this group were Disraeli, Herries, Granby, Henley, Bankes, Miles, Christopher, Stuart, and 'King' Hudson.

[2] Stanley to Beresford, 18 January 1848 (copy). Derby Mss, 177/2.

[3] Stanley to Bentinck, 26 December 1847 (copy). *ibid.*

[4] Arbuthnot to Stanley, 19 October 1847. *ibid.* 116/5.

[5] Just before the vote on the Jewish bill, Beresford, who was establishing a central registration office in London with county branches, wrote to Stanley that Bentinck 'seems to look upon anything of the sort as quite insignificant. He talks as before, of our having some *great and comprehensive Plan* that will attract the country... and that the very attention to Registration is old woman's work' (Beresford to Stanley, undated. Derby Mss, 149/1).

[6] Lewis to Sir Edmund Head, 21 December 1851. Lewis, *Letters*, 247–50.

have given him the enthusiastic support of Young Ireland. You remember his terrific rebuff to some overtures from that party; and so throughout his career. I don't think he ever gained a speech, a vote, an election, or an adherent by holding out a dubious light or concealing a single opinion...money he always seemed to contemn...He was the Strafford of the 19th century.[1]

The search for a successor to Bentinck occupied and distracted the party for the whole of 1848. A half-hearted attempt was made in January to have Goulburn fill the vacancy, for which Beresford and Graham thought his Church-of-England conservatism and his protectionist leanings suited him, but Goulburn stuck to his position that reunion must be the natural outcome of combination in divisions of the House of Commons.[2] Stanley acknowledged that the currency issue and the repeal of the Navigation Laws were bound to keep them apart.[3] Disraeli's name was not, at the beginning of 1848, even canvassed. His standing with the party may be gauged by Croker's opinion that all Bentinck's shortcomings were the result of his having been guided by Disraeli.[4] Stanley, partly influenced by an episode years before involving his son with Disraeli,[5] had a low opinion of Disraeli. 'I know Disraeli has the feeling that I dislike him,' Stanley wrote to the Earl of Wilton. 'I certainly have no personal prepossession in his favour.'[6] Bentinck wished to see Bankes restored to the place he had held at the beginning of 1846, and Bankes was eager to comply, but he had the backing neither of Disraeli's circle nor of the old guard, and Stanley quickly assured him that he was not a candidate.[7] The choice was thus narrowed to Herries, the almost antedeluvian Canningite, who had regained a seat at the 1847 elections, and the Marquis of Granby,

[1] Manners to Disraeli, 12 October 1850. Hughenden Mss, B/XX/M/67. For a lengthy, balanced appraisal of Bentinck, see Greville, iii, 222–34.

[2] Beresford to Stanley, 27 December 1847. Derby Mss, 149/1; J.B.Conacher, 'Peel and the Peelites, 1846–50', *English Historical Review* (July 1958) 439.

[3] Stanley to Phillips, 9 January 1848 (copy). Derby Mss, 177/2; Peel to Graham, 12 January 1848. Parker, *Graham*. ii, 63.

[4] Croker to Brougham, 10 October 1847. Jennings, Croker, iii, 148–9.

[5] See R.Blake, 'The Rise of Disraeli' in Trevor-Roper, *Essays in British History*, 226.

[6] Stanley to Wilton, 26 February 1848 (copy). Derby Mss, 177/2.

[7] Stanley to Bankes, 23 January 1848 (copy). *ibid.*

eldest son of the Duke of Rutland and brother of Lord John Manners. 'We are at a low ebb,' Graham scoffed, 'when Herries reappears in a first-rate part on the stage: but the Country Party led by Bankes and Stafford O'Brien would indeed be the conversion of Tragedy into Farce.'[1] Herries, though greatly respected by the party, was disqualified by his support of the Jews,[2] and so Stanley was left to press the diffident Granby into service. Granby was the staunchest of Protectionists, one of the few Conservatives to have resigned from the Royal Household when Peel introduced the repeal of the Corn Laws. Heir to a famous dukedom, and admired for his reliability and common sense, Granby's genial and unassuming nature stood him in good stead with his colleagues. So quiescent had he been during his ten years in the Commons that he had made no political enemies and could count on Bentinck's sympathy, no small recommendation in Stanley's eyes. On 9 February the party elected him leader, but Granby was too conscious of his mediocrity to accept the position.[3]

Having refused to consider, not altogether unwisely – it is one of the strengths of the party system that leadership must be earned by the demonstration of loyalty and trustworthiness – their 'only man of talent',[4] the party laboured through the 1848 session without a leader in the Commons. Disraeli's position was raised by the indeterminate contest for the leadership. A number of Protectionists who had followed Bentinck to the end now formed a small coterie around him – Disraeli called them his 'Imperial Guard'[5] – and were to be his lieutenants during the next year in his successful bid for the leadership. Those Protectionists who had been offended by Beresford's use of the press against Bentinck looked to their new favourite to counteract

[1] Graham to Peel, 15 January 1848. Peel Mss, Add. Mss 40452. ff. 252–5.

[2] Herries' Jewish sympathies infuriated Beresford. 'He says they are better than Roman Catholics!! Now bigoted Protestant as I am, I prefer a Christian to a Jew or infidel' (Beresford to Stanley, undated. Derby Mss, 149/1).

[3] Malmesbury, *Memoirs*, i, 205–7. Greville's opinion was that 'except his high birth' Granby had 'not a single qualification for the post' and reported that when the Protectionists elected him 'all the world [was] laughing at their choice' (Greville, iii, 123).

[4] *Ibid*. iii, 114.

[5] He numbered them at 50 (Whibley, *Manners and his Friends*, i, 298).

Beresford's influence over Stanley. Charles Newdegate, the assistant whip, was torn between his sympathies for Beresford's opinions and his feeling that Disraeli was necessary to the party.

I see that many impartial men think that Disraeli's talent fairly entitles him to the position he desires; but many distrust him...Beresford declares that Disraeli's appointment would be fatal to the party. I think it would be injurious, but I see that without him we shall be very weak and cannot calculate upon the line he and his supporters might take if he were rejected...Beresford is inclined to be *too hasty* in this matter.[1]

The memory of how, with his small band of Young Englanders, Disraeli had turned on Peel when Peel had ignored him, was a large consideration in the Protectionist party's begrudging decision to accept him as leader.

The 1848 session of parliament furnished for Disraeli a favourable setting in which to stake his claim upon the leadership. The bill to repeal the Navigation Laws was the first opportunity for a full Protectionist offensive since 1846, while in other fields, notably the proposed increase in the income tax and the management of the Colonial Office, the government ran amuck of the Radicals and the Peelites. In the 1848 session the Whig–Radical–Peelite alliance showed signs of disintegration. If the Protectionists were to profit from this development, it was obvious that they could not remain unorganised. By a sustained devotion to parliamentary debate, Disraeli forced the party to recognise his necessity.

Irish questions provided few opportunities for either Disraeli or the Protectionist party to make their mark. When Macaulay was defeated at the 1847 elections, Lord Granville took his place in the cabinet, which thus became the most purely aristocratic since the days of Henry Pelham. Nowhere was the landed bias of the government more conspicuous than in its treatment of Irish questions. At the beginning of 1847, the new friendship between Catholic and Protestant, gentry and tenant farmer, which was expressed in the meeting of the landlords' Reproductive Works Committee and Young Ireland's new Irish Confederation in January, seemed to foretell the emergence of a united Irish

1 Newdegate to Stanley, 22 January 1848. Derby Mss, 148/1.

parliamentary party. But cooperation foundered on the Poor Relief Bill of that year, which the landlords opposed and the Radicals supported.[1] Thereafter, the force of Irish nationalism in the English House of Commons was eclipsed, until the arrival of the Tenant Right party in the elections of 1852. O'Connell's death in May 1847, left the Repeal Association in his son's inexperienced hands. Young Ireland, now the Irish Confederation, superseded it in importance. The two organisations remained separate, despite recurrent attempts at amalgamation, and the Confederation itself split into a nationalist faction which still sought repeal and a left-wing group which turned its attention to the land problem and the securing of tenant right. In these circumstances, Russell was able to follow a conservative policy towards Ireland. Although at various times he displayed a desire to introduce radical reforms for Ireland, the conservatism of landlords like Palmerston and Lansdowne was too strong for him to overcome.[2]

In November 1847, parliament was recalled early to deal with a fresh outbreak of agrarian crime in Ireland. Lord Clarendon, the lord-lieutenant, persuaded Russell to introduce a Crime and Outrage Bill, by which lords-lieutenant of the counties were empowered to proclaim a disturbed area and bring additional police into the district, and which imposed two years' imprisonment for the possession of unlicensed arms in a district so proclaimed. Stanley received the measure enthusiastically, although he chided the government for acting so tardily. 'If we were not the most forbearing set of men in the world', he wrote to Lord Ellenborough, 'we could not so long have refrained...from attacking the Government upon their insane abandonment of an Arms Bill for the first time since the Union.'[3]

In 1848, the Irish Confederation became more outspokenly revolutionary than any previous Irish nationalist movement, especially in the leaders of the *United Irishman*, a Young Ireland newspaper founded by the tenant-right agitator, John Mitchel,

---

[1] Nowlan, *Politics of Repeal*, 125–37.
[2] See Russell to Clarendon, 10 November 1847 and to Lansdowne, 18 November 1847. Walpole, *Russell*, i, 464 and 467.
[3] Stanley to Ellenborough, 12 April 1848 (copy). Derby Mss, 178/1.

in February. The national–liberal revolutions in Europe affected the Irish imagination, and on 20 March a great public demonstration was held in Dublin in favour of Franco–Irish friendship. Already worried by signs of a Chartist revival in England, the government acted quickly. In April, Russell gained the plaudits of the Protectionists for his Crime and Government Security Bill, which made the advocacy of republicanism a transportable felony, a course which Stanley had urged on the government from the appearance of the first number of the *United Irishman*.[1] That paper was suppressed and Mitchel sentenced to fourteen years' transportation. The leaders of Young Ireland fled Dublin for the south. Clarendon fed the cabinet reports of a 'rebel army' and 'planned insurrection' and succeeded in getting parliament to suspend Habeas Corpus for Ireland in July. Panic-stricken, Smith O'Brien staged a confused attempt at rebellion at Ballingarry on 29 July, which the government easily crushed. It was the end of Young Ireland and, as it proved, of the movement begun by O'Connell to repeal the Union.

Firm government in Ireland ensured that the moratorium on Irish questions continued. Stanley seemed to be calling the tune in Ireland. But the Protectionists succeeded, with Radical support, in forcing Charles Wood to withdraw his proposal to double the income tax and, at the expense of parliamentary usage so protracted the debates upon the preliminary resolutions for the repeal of the Navigation laws, that the question was postponed for a session. When the income tax debates revealed that the government could no longer rely on the goodwill of the Radicals, the weakness of the Whigs' position was manifest. 'I do not know which cuts the worst figure', Stanley mused, 'Louis Phillipe and Co. in their abandonment of the cause without a struggle, or our ministers in their...sudden abandonment of their additional Income Tax. They would have been infallibly beaten.'[2] In February, Bentinck's casting vote as chairman enabled the sugar committee, which Bentinck had harried the government into appointing, to recommend the return to a

---

[1] Stanley to Desart, 20 April 1848 and to Lord Grey, 12 April 1848 (copies). Derby Mss, 178/1.
[2] Stanley to Newcastle, 2 March 1848 (copy). *ibid.* 177/2.

differential duty on the import of sugar. Cobden lamented at the end of the session that Russell had abused a majority which he could have commanded for liberal measures by passing coercion bills for Ireland.

He has allowed himself to be baffled, bullied and obstructed by Lord George Bentinck and the Protectionists, who have been so far encouraged by their success in Sugar and the Navigation Laws, that I expect they will be quite ready to begin their reaction on Corn next session, and we may have to fight, the Free Trade battle all over again.[1]

In June, Russell brought in a bill to reduce the sugar duty from 13s. to 10s. Sir John Pakington introduced a Protectionist amendment against the bill on which the government was widely expected to be beaten.[2] When the amendment was lost by fifteen votes, the Protectionist balloon was discovered to have leaks.

Bentinck, who believed that 'Free Trade will break down and Protection eventually triumph through the Sugar Duties',[3] blamed Stanley for the party's poor showing: 'What a moment for the Party to be divided by a pusillanimous House of Lords Leader drivelled and dribbled through Miles in the Commons advocating *three years more of Fair Trial to Free Trade*!!! This is downright Peelism.'[4] It was indeed. Stanley was not yet prepared to take office. After the division on Pakington's amendment, Greville wrote meanly of Stanley's conduct:

It is pretty generally understood now that Stanley has never had the least notion of forming a Government, nor even of making the attempt. Had the event occurred [the resignation of the government] he would have made a pirouette and whisked off; having done his mischief and had his fun, he would have considered his work over. It was very significant that while all the world was fancying he meditated becoming Prime Minister, he accepted the office of Steward of the Jockey Club, to which high dignity he is this day to be promoted.[5]

The Derby Papers contain no reference to this episode. But by Bentinck's evidence, Greville has got it wrong. Stanley was not

---

[1] Cobden to G. Combe, 23 July 1848. Morley, *Cobden*, i, 520–1.
[2] See Greville, iii, 195–9.
[3] Bentinck to Disraeli, 26 January 1848. Hughenden Mss, B/XX/Be/49.
[4] Bentinck to Disraeli, 12 March 1848. *ibid.* B/XX/Be/52.
[5] Greville, iii, 204–5.

making mischief; he was preventing mischief by using Miles as his representative in the Commons. For Stanley, the mischief would have been to defeat the government when there was no plausible alternative to it: a broadly-based Conservative party was the essential, at any rate highly desirable, precondition of power.

That primary concern of Stanley led him into a minor quarrel with Bentinck and others, which is indicative of the tensions in the Protectionist party. At the beginning of the 1848 session Stanley gave Beresford permission to put back the word 'Conservative' instead of 'Protectionist' in the party's circulars. Bentinck protested violently to Stanley:

I know nothing of *this* 'Conservative Party'. I gave my adherence to the '*Protectionist Party*' and to no other. At the suggestion if I recall right of Miles the term '*Conservative*' was repudiated '*as a byword of reproach*' and '*Protectionist*' substituted; justly branded as such by Disraeli, I acknowledge nothing in the '*Conservative Party*' but 'an Organised Hypocrisy'.[1]

Lord John Manners was hardly less upset by the change:

To the Protestant it smells of Maynooth – to the Protectionist of Free Trade – to the Churchman of demolished bishoprics and cut-down Cathedrals – to all of cowardice, treachery and imbecility.[2]

Such strong feelings were not to be overcome, and for the next four years the party went by both names.

During the same period the Peelites struggled to maintain their separate identity. Peel himself acted in close conjunction with the Whig cabinet, especially on Irish affairs, but persistent rumours of a Whig–Peelite government were not fulfilled. In January 1849, Russell's offer of cabinet places to Graham and Lord St Germains were refused. Graham impressed upon Russell that he had no personal objection to him, but having once injured the Whig party by defecting from it he was anxious to avoid being placed under the same necessity again. It is a mark of the growing liberalism of the Peelites that Graham's objec-

[1] Bentinck to Stanley, 4 February 1848. Derby Mss, 132/13.
[2] Manners to his brother, February 1848. Whibley, *Manners and his Friends*, ii, 86.

tions were to the conservative members of the cabinet, particularly Palmerston at the foreign office.[1] Greville noted that the Peelites were 'disengaging themselves from their chief without joining the Tories and...so conducting themselves as to make any junction with the Whigs very difficult'.[2] Graham was not surprised when, except for himself, Peel, and John Young, all the 'front-bench' Peelites voted for Pakington's sugar amendment, since 'they were impatient, could no longer be restrained and were resolved to join the Protectionists'.[3] That was a misinterpretation. Gladstone voted against the reduction in the sugar duty, not on protectionist grounds, but because the government was decreasing the revenue without pledging itself to any retrenchment to make it up. He was furious with Peel for voting with the government merely to keep out the Protectionists, since he did not believe them to be capable of restoring the Corn Laws.[4] Gladstone was by this time also a prominent critic of the Colonial Office, but Graham was wrong to detect a predeliction among the Peelites to rejoin the Protectionists. Most of them took little part in the debates of 1848 and left long before the session was over, behaviour which puzzled Lord Clarendon.

I don't understand the Peelites, for they seem ill disposed to the Protectionists, and Lincoln and Co. are writing articles in the *Chronicle* that will never be forgiven; yet they are throwing off the man who alone gives them importance in the country. I know they are angry with Peel, and complain of his selfish determination neither to act as they wish nor to advise them what they should do; but they are acting as if they meant to isolate themselves. Their course is not one which can lead to fusion with the Whigs.[5]

Protectionist efforts to secure Peelite cooperation were futile. Shortly after Goulburn had resisted their overtures in January 1848, he and Gladstone arranged to discuss the business with Bankes, Granby, Lyndhurst, and Ellenborough. The meeting did

---

[1] Graham to Peel, 16 January 1849. Peel Mss, Add. Mss 40452. ff. 315–20.
[2] Greville, iii, 205.
[3] *Ibid*. iii, 196.
[4] Gladstone memorandum of 12 December 1848. Gladstone Mss, Add. Mss 44777, ff. 278–80.
[5] Clarendon to Lewis, 2 July 1848. Maxwell, *Clarendon*, i, 291.

not, however, take place, because it was apparent that the forthcoming repeal of the Navigation Laws would render agreement
useless.[1] Londonderry's habitual attempts to lure Goulburn or
Graham with hints of the leadership remained fruitless: Bentinck and Disraeli stood in the way.[2] At the end of 1848, Abraham
Hayward, whose position as writer for the *Morning Chronicle*
brought him into close association with the Peelites, discounted
talk of reunion. 'The leaders of the two sections are as wide as
poles assunder, and, of course, Peel's friends will not allow him
to be assailed with impunity.'[3]

In 1849 the disintegration of the Peelites proceeded apace.
On the repeal of the Navigation Laws, the Jewish bill, the Canada
Rebellion Losses Bill, and a motion of censure on the administration of Vancouver Island, the party fell to pieces. Peel, Graham,
Young, and St Germains consistently upheld the government,
but on three of the bills Goulburn deserted them, Gladstone
on the latter two. But formal negotiations for reunion did not
occur again until Stanley was asked to form a government in
1851. The *Morning Herald* became even more vindictive with
the suggestion that the Peelites should be excluded from the
Carlton Club. Stanley became more avowedly protectionist in his
language. And even Lord Londonderry, after making a final
personal appeal to Graham in January 1849, became at last
weary and disheartened and quit active politics.[4]

Early in the 1848 session, Bentinck remarked to Croker that
'nothing but the pitiful disunion of the Protectionist party could
prevent the Whig Government and the entire Free-Trade policy
from being overthrown'.[5] That was delusion, but the party
suffered from the want of direction which could be supplied only

[1] Gladstone memorandum of 12 December 1848. Gladstone Mss, Add. Mss
44777, ff. 278–80.

[2] Londonderry to Disraeli, 1 July 1848. Hughenden Mss, B/XX/V/5; Graham
to Peel, 25 September 1848. Peel Mss, Add. Mss 40452, ff. 278–83.

[3] Hayward to Lady Charleville, 11 November 1848. H.E.Carlisle (ed.), *A
Selection From the Correspondence of Abraham Hayward, Q.C.* (London, 1886), i,
133.

[4] Londonderry to Disraeli, 11 March and 16 May 1849. Hughenden Mss,
B/XX/V/10, 13.

[5] Bentinck to Croker, 2 March 1848. Jennings, *Croker*, iii, 167–8.

by an official leader in the House of Commons. Bentinck continued to act a leading part in the debates, but he had stopped attending party meetings. When Stanley asked him to attend one in May, he refused: 'having been unharnessed by others I will never submit to being harnessed again'.[1] Disraeli was even more prominent in debate than Bentinck, but Stanley was not in communication with him. The organisation of the Commons party had collapsed. From 1846 until the elections of 1847 Stanley had presided over weekly meetings of the party in both Houses; in 1848 those meetings ceased. What direction the party received came from the whips, Beresford and Newdegate, with the result that there was 'no longer any cohesion among the Old Party except on the Jew Bill'.[2] The strength of that bond was illustrated by the failure to find a seat for Lord John Manners, one of the party's best speakers, but a pro-Jew, until 1850, despite his obvious qualifications to fill the vacancy created at King's Lynn by Bentinck's death in September 1848. When Disraeli received no support after a brilliant speech on commercial policy in February, Manners concluded that 'the Beresford rot has infected many'.[3]

The disarray of the party alarmed Croker.

> The Conservative party, that might have been abundantly capable of counteracting and correcting the disorganising tendencies of the Whigs, is itself so disorganised by apostasies, jealousies, disgusts and the almost despair of good faith, principle or honour in public men, that it – the only solid basis of government in this country – seems rather an addition than an antidote to the danger.[4]

Disraeli was the beneficiary of this alarm. By speaking forcefully on every major issue, he compelled the party to take notice of him. In 1859, Graham called Disraeli 'the red Indian of debate' who 'by the use of the tomahawk' had cut his way to power.[5]

[1] Stanley to Bentinck, 17 May 1848 (copy). Derby Mss, 178/1; Bentinck to Stanley, 18 May 1848. *ibid*. 132/13.
[2] Bentinck to Michele, 16 April 1848. R. Lucas, *Lord Glenesk and the 'Morning Post'* (London, 1910), 31.
[3] Manners to Disraeli, 21 February 1848. Hughenden Mss, B/XX/M/25.
[4] *Quarterly Review* (June 1848), 250.
[5] *Hansard*, 3rd Series, cliv, 267.

The sting of his speeches was such that Bentinck reported that 'Cobden writhes and quails under him just as Peel did in 1846' and predicted that 'spite of Lord Stanley, Major Beresford and Mr. Phillips and the *Herald*, it will end before two sessions are out in Disraeli being the chosen leader of the party'.[1] In July Stanley wrote his first letter to Disraeli, accepting an invitation to dinner, and a month later he asked him to sum up the session in the House of Commons. Disraeli did so with such flair that even Beresford praised his speech to Stanley as 'very able and forceful', and then, in a telling phrase, added that Disraeli was wrong to think that he could climb to the leadership by ability alone.[2] Stanley accepted the force of Beresford's innuendo.

As the leadership of the House of Commons, I consider it so entirely in abeyance that any man is entitled to *bid* for it, in the only mode in which it can be obtained, by the display of superior ability and power in debate; but these will not do alone, and personal influence must be added to them to enable anyone to hold the post; and in this respect Disraeli labours under disadvantages which I do not think he can overcome.[3]

Like Canning thirty years earlier, Disraeli had made many political enemies. Like Canning, Disraeli suffered from the reputation which a man of sharp, destructive wit and openly-displayed ambition so easily gains, a reputation for want of political principle and for placing self-interest ahead of the interests of the party and the nation. And like Canning, Disraeli was handicapped by low birth and modest means in a party which paid great attention to such matters.

By February 1849, when the party gathered to consider the leadership question again, Disraeli had attracted a substantial body of support. The death of Bentinck in the previous September was believed by many, who saw Bentinck as Disraeli's link with the Tory aristocracy, to have dealt a fatal blow to Disraeli's ambition,[4] but Bentinck had used up his influence in that quarter.

1 Bentinck to Croker, 2 March 1848. Jennings, *Croker*, iii, 167.
2 Beresford to Stanley, undated. Derby Mss, 149/2.
3 Stanley to Beresford, 2 September 1848 (copy). *ibid*. 178/1.
4 See, for example, Graham to Peel, 25 September 1848. Peel Mss, Add. Mss 40452, ff. 278–83; also Herbert to his wife, 29 September 1849. Stanmore, *Herbert*, i, 89.

His death solidified the support for Disraeli from among his old following. 'King' Hudson, Christopher, the Miles brothers, Stuart, and Bankes all pressed Disraeli's claim on Stanley and Beresford.[1] During the latter months of 1848, Disraeli had also gained powerful aristocratic allies. The Duke of Newcastle, Lord Malmesbury, and the Earl of Mandeville urged Stanley to bow to the inevitability of Disraeli. 'To me it appears to be perfectly clear', Newcastle wrote, 'that we must of necessity choose the cleverest man that we possess.'[2] Even the leader of the High Church party, Robert Inglis, had come round.[3] Most unexpected of all, Phillips of the *Morning Herald* began to work on Disraeli's behalf in Scotland, especially among the Low Church party. Phillips had decided that Conservative reunion was past recall – he had done his bit to make it so – and that Protectionist and Protestant should pull together behind Disraeli. It was strange reasoning, but not to be scoffed at, since Phillips was able to persuade the National Club to vote its confidence in Disraeli.[4]

Disraeli's new support still left him with the trust of only about one-third of the party. Beresford and Newdegate remained as antagonistic as ever and Stanley clearly hoped to avoid having to accept him. Beresford shrewdly suspected Disraeli's protectionist principles and saw in the intrigue to force him on the party a plan to rid the party of its commitment to the Corn Laws.[5] For Stanley, the main objection to Disraeli was that he was 'the most powerful *repellent* we could offer to any repentant or hesitating Peelites'.[6] In some quarters the fixation on the Peelites was so

[1] The activities on Disraeli's behalf may be followed in Monypenny and Buckle, iii, 115–41 and in Disraeli's letters to his sister throughout January. R. Disraeli (ed.), *Lord Beaconsfield's Correspondence with his Sister, 1832–1852* (London, 1886), 218–19.

[2] Newcastle to Stanley, 7 January 1849. Derby Mss, 147/14.

[3] Richmond to Stanley, 21 January 1849. *ibid.* 131/13.

[4] Phillips to Disraeli 18 November 1848 and 4 February 1849. Hughenden Mss, B/XX/P/223, 232.

[5] Hardinge told Beresford that Disraeli had been coquetting with Palmerston in the autumn, and when the latter protested their divergent opinions, 'D. challenged Lord P. to produce one sentence in any of his speeches in which he had ever advocated Protections *per se.*' Beresford's friends had taken up the challenge and were unable to refute Disraeli's claim (Beresford to Stanley, undated. Derby Mss, 149/2). Stanley agreed that the story, if true, disqualified Disraeli (Stanley to Beresford, 23 January 1849 (copy). *ibid.* 178/1).

[6] Stanley to Christopher, 8 January 1849 (copy). *ibid.*

obsessive that Henry Baillie, a friend of Disraeli, could suggest making Sir John Pakington leader, a man whose single qualification for the post was that 'all his liaisons are with Peel's party, whilst all his votes have been with yours'.[1]

Stanley ignored Stuart's advice to name Disraeli as his choice and thereby rally the party around one man.[2] Instead, he modified the Duke of Richmond's suggestion that the party be content with a 'shadow cabinet' of five or six members,[3] and proposed that the party be jointly led by Granby, Herries, and Disraeli. He had tried in vain to persuade Granby to take the leadership alone, and since Herries considered himself too old for the job, the tripartite solution was adopted. It was, of course, a nonsensical arrangement. Disraeli soared above the other two men in the Commons. He had, in effect, been made leader. A month later, at a Protectionist banquet at Merchant Tailors' Hall, he met the redoubtable Croker for the first time.[4]

[1] Baillie to Disraeli, 30 November 1848. Hughenden Mss, B/XX/Be/145.
[2] Stuart to Stanley, 23 January 1849. Derby Mss, 149/4.
[3] Richmond to Stanley, 21 January 1849. *ibid*. 131/13.
[4] Disraeli memorandum of the 1860s. Hughenden Mss, A/X/A/23.

6

THE PROTECTIONIST REVIVAL

FROM 1849 to 1852, two undercurrents ran in English politics: from the left, a revivified Radicalism, expressed in England by the Financial Reform Association, under the leadership of Cobden and Bright, and in Ireland by the Tenant Right movement; from the right, a sustained agitation for a return to agricultural protection, stimulated by three years of low agricultural prices.

The new Radical activity was a continuation of the Anti-Corn Law League's attack on the political power of the landed class, but it was, in Cornewall Lewis' phrase, 'a very Philistine Radicalism',[1] which sought the extension of the franchise only in order to carry out its programme of increased direct taxation on real property, the removal of all remaining customs duties, and retrenchment in government expenditure. The movement lacked focus. Cobden was primarily interested in financial reform, while Bright was almost single-mindedly interested in parliamentary reform for its own sake. In June 1849, exasperated by the emphasis which the parliamentary Radicals placed on old-fashioned political and constitutional reforms, Cobden struck out on his own and formed the Freehold Land movement. But there were too few artisans able to sink £40 into a freehold merely in order to enjoy the luxury of a vote for the movement to succeed. Divided in its aims and organisation, and thinly represented in the House of Commons, Radicalism was little more than a nuisance to the Whig government. In 1849, Hume's annual motion for the ballot, triennial parliaments, and equal electoral districts was defeated by 286 votes to 82, and again in 1850 by 242 to 96.

Russell had more to fear from the right, powerful in the Commons under Disraeli's attacking lead, and capable at any time of using its majority in the Lords against the government. At the beginning of 1849 Stanley was prepared to resist the repeal of

[1] S. Maccoby, *English Radicalism, 1832–52* (London, 1935), 287.

the Navigation Laws and any proposal for Roman Catholic endowment 'totis viribus',[1] and in 1849 for the first time he gave serious, if somewhat melancholy, thought to the composition of a Protectionist government. The Whigs did not take the risk of offending English sentiment by introducing a measure for Roman Catholic endowment. and the Protectionists were unable to save the Navigation Laws. But so energetic was the Protectionist agitation in the country that the government was suspected of toying with the idea of imposing a small fixed duty on imported corn. The rumour persisted into 1850 because some Whigs, including the chancellor of the exchequer, Charles Wood, were known to be having second thoughts about complete free trade and because the government did not squash it by forthright denials. At six cabinet meetings in the autumn of 1849, however, when speculation about the government's intentions was at its peak, the Corn Laws were not even mentioned.[2] As Peel pointed out, strict adherence to free trade was not only the condition of Peelite support for the government, but also the only solid basis of Whig support in the country.

The government seems to have little prospect of acquiring strength. Their main source of strength will be the declared resolution of the Protectionists to restore Protection *as a principle*.

If the Government will tie the Protectionists to that stake, and will declare in express, unequivocal terms, without a lingering, retrospective look of affection at their budget of 1841, that they are against Protection, and that the test of party difference is now Protection or no Protection, they may hold their ground.[3]

Disraeli made the same assessment of the political situation as Peel. In March 1849, he came to the conclusion that if the agricultural distress continued after the next harvest 'Graham and Co. must give up progress and swallow a little moderate reaction'.[4] But Disraeli knew that protectionist dogma would ruin the party electorally and that the party must therefore find other ways of providing relief to the landed interest.

[1] Stanley to Granby, 14 December 1848 (copy). Derby Mss, 178/1.
[2] Peel to Goulburn, 4 December 1849. Goulburn Mss, II/20.
[3] Peel to Graham, 24 July 1849. Parker, *Peel*, iii, 523.
[4] Disraeli to his sister, 28 May 1849. R. Disraeli, *Beaconsfield's Correspondence*, 225–6.

The great test of the government's strength in 1849 was the bill to repeal the Navigation Laws. The end of preferential tariffs meant that the old Protectionist argument of the imperial government's duty to the colonies had become a free-trade argument for the repeal of those laws. Stanley, however, did not 'look upon the principle of free trade as so far recognised, and its adoption a *fait accompli*, as to be ready to follow it out to an inference that the Navigation Laws should be sacrificed'.[1] That represented a significant shift from his attitude in 1846, when he had argued that the government's sugar legislation had to be accepted in order that the free-trade policy should be played out. The bill to repeal the Laws passed the Commons by only 61 votes, a small majority for a free-trade measure in the 1847 parliament. Expectations that the government would be beaten in the Lords, however, were not fulfilled, despite a full-blooded defence of the old system from Stanley. Bright thought that the Lords were unwilling to put Stanley in office.[2] And the crisis provides an early illustration of Prince Albert's regard for the Peelites as the 'king's party'. He wrote to the Duke of Wellington begging him to consider the evil results of rejecting the bill, namely that the Protectionists would be given a chance to form a government.[3] For Disraeli, who was excited by the fact that a Protectionist cabinet was in embryo,[4] the result was a bitter disappointment, but Stanley was probably relieved when the government scraped home by ten votes.[5] There is one interesting aspect of the episode. When Stanley was planning a possible government, he made no provision for any Peelites. The idea of reunion was, for the moment, put aside, and Disraeli was told that he would be the leader of the government in the House of

---

[1] Stanley to Phillips, 9 January 1848 (copy). Derby Mss, 177/2.

[2] Disraeli to his sister, 24 April 1849. R. Disraeli, *Beaconsfield's Correspondence*, 223–4.

[3] Broughton, *Recollections*, vi, 239.

[4] Disraeli to his sister, 26 March 1849. R. Disraeli, *Beaconsfield's Correspondence*, 222–3.

[5] Henry Greville commented: 'Stanley surpassed himself – his peroration was very fine. I suspect he was greatly relieved at the certainty that the majority would be against him, for he must have been aware that he could not make a Government' (Viscountess Enfield (ed.), *Leaves from the Diary of Henry Greville* (London, 1883), i, 336).

Commons.[1] 1849 would have been an awkward moment for the Protectionists to take office. Disraeli was eager to wean the party away from the single idea of the Corn Laws, but the Protectionist revival was just beginning, and for the next three years Disraeli's career is the story of his failure to do so.

From 1849 to 1852, English agriculture suffered from its most severe depression since the end of the war. On 9 September 1848, wheat sold at an average of 56s. 10d., but thereafter prices underwent a steady decline. By 30 December they had fallen to 46s. 10d. and by September 1849, to 38s. 9d. On 4 May 1850, wheat fetched only 36s. 11d., the lowest price since 1836 and it remained around that low level until the spring of 1851. Not until the end of 1852 did prices begin to move sharply upwards again.[2] Agriculture was not alone in experiencing low prices, but it did so far more drastically than manufacturing. There was an unexpected coincidence of poor English harvests and abundant European ones. In 1845–6 and 1846–7 wheat imports were about 750,000 quarters. Then in the three years from 1848–9 to 1850–1 the figures rose to 5,295,000, 4,258,000, and 6,011,000 quarters.[3] The English farmer was caught. Despite poor harvests, prices were kept down by large foreign imports. The farmer sold only a little wheat and that at depressed prices. Livestock farmers were no better off than the growers of grain. Wool, for instance, which in the mid-1830s sold at 40s. a rod, in 1849 got only 23s. a rod.[4]

At the end of 1848 Lord Malmesbury, not the most sanguine of Protectionists, was 'quite sure that our principles are gaining favour with thousands who were carried away with the free trade cry in 1846',[5] and a year later Beresford reported that 'decidedly the feeling in favour of restoring Protection is getting very strong'.[6] Throughout 1849 and 1850 agricultural meetings were

[1] Disraeli to his sister, 26 March 1849. R. Disraeli, *Beaconsfield's Correspondence*, 222–3.
[2] T. Tooke and W. Newmarch, *A History of Prices and of the State of Circulation from 1792 to 1856*, v, 9–34.
[3] *Ibid.* v, 50.
[4] Christopher to Stanley, undated 1849. Derby Mss, 150/15.
[5] Malmesbury to Stanley, 3 December 1848. *ibid.* 148/1.
[6] Beresford to Stanley, 4 December 1849. *ibid.* 149/2.

held with the same frequency and favour as in the early months of 1846. The most important of these meetings was the one held on 1 May 1849, to establish the National Association for the Protection of British Industry and Capital.[1] 'The clamour of the Agricultural Meetings', Cobden told a gathering at Leeds, 'has at last aroused the sleeping dragon of free trade.'[2] He began a counter-agitation to repeal the malt tax and reform taxation in an attempt to drive a wedge between the landowners and the tenant farmers.

The Protectionist revival was marked by a string of by-election triumphs, beginning with a startling, one-sided victory over the Liberals at Cirencester in May 1848, a seat which the party had not bothered to contest at the elections a year earlier. In 1849, the Protectionists gained seats at Kidderminster, Reading, South Staffordshire, North Hampshire, and Cork. They had not contested Kidderminster in 1847, and had been badly beaten at Reading, where Maynooth was a major issue. But the most encouraging result was in November, at Cork, a seat held by the Liberals since 1832. 'The Cork election, I own', Beresford wrote, exulting, to Stanley, 'is beyond my hopes, it looks very much like reaction indeed. It was fought on Protectionist principles, and the triumph is a Protectionist one.'[3] Isaac Butt, the leading Protectionist in Ireland, was even more ecstatic.

Everything I saw in Cork has confirmed me in my belief of the possibility of reclaiming from priests and agitation the popular mind of this country to a moderate and national Conservative Protectionist party. One thing is plain, that if a general election occurred at this moment the great majority of the Irish members returned would be protectionists.[4]

The Protectionists benefited from the death of O'Connell and the divisions within the Irish nationalist movement. Butt saw that the party would have to overcome its repugnance to combination with Irish reformers if the victory at Cork was to be the beginning of permanent Protectionist strength in Ireland. Underneath the euphoria of 1849 lay the question whether English

---

[1] Irving, *Annals*, 161.   [2] The *Globe*, 22 December 1849.
[3] Beresford to Stanley, November 1849. Derby Mss, 149/2.
[4] Butt to Disraeli, 22 October 1849. Hughenden Mss, B/III/35.

Conservatism could reach some accommodation with the Tenant Right movement.

To many Protectionists it seemed unnecessary, in the midst of success, to deviate from a dogged adherence to the Corn Laws. Towards the end of 1848, the tenant farmers had once more taken up the repeal of the malt tax, but the party leadership remained adamant against it. At a meeting of the Protection Society in December, the Duke of Richmond dissuaded the farmers from discussing the question.[1] As prices continued to fall it became more difficult to muzzle them, as Newdegate reported to Stanley in February 1849.

> We have had a very determined spirit manifested by the farmers at the Protection Society today to agitate for the repeal of the malt tax. This has prevailed in several counties for some time and Cobden is fomenting it all.
>
> The fact is that the farmers see distress staring them in the face and will not submit to it quietly. They claim the promises which have been made by our Party, that we should attempt something for their relief; they will, as they told us plainly, with much regret join the Cobdenite party, as the only men who manifest any practical intention of assisting them in their difficulties. It was in vain that Miles, Stafford, Wodehouse, Christopher and I urged the fact that the public opinion of the country was ripening rapidly against free trade, and that the advantage to them from the repeal of the Malt Tax would be slight, that the revenue from it could not be spared, and that we would not join in the destruction of the means necessary for national defence and the maintenance of public credit.[2]

In 1850, when a motion for the repeal of the malt tax was about to be read, Stanley refused to see a deputation from the Association for the Total Repeal of the Malt Tax. He was right to believe that the farmers would derive scant benefit from the project. The principal effect of the malt tax was to raise the price of barley to the consumer who felt the weight of the tax in the cost of beer. If the malt tax were repealed, the price of beer would go down, but the farmer would benefit from the measure only if

---

[1] Beresford to Stanley, undated. Derby Mss, 149/2.
[2] Newdegate to Stanley, 6 February 1849. *ibid.* 148/1.

the price of barley remained high. By the evidence of increasing imports in the years 1846–50, it is probable that an increased demand for beer would stimulate the import of barley rather than keep up the home price.[1] When the tax was finally removed in 1880, the price of barley dropped.

The Earl of Malmesbury, Stanley's closest political friend in these years, accepted the official argument against repeal of the malt tax, which Newdegate had tried to impress upon the farmers, but, like Bentinck two years before, he criticised Stanley's pre-occupation with Whitehall and his unwillingness to seize political advantage from the farmers' discontent. He argued that since the Commons could not be persuaded to restore a corn duty the Protectionists ought to propose some other form of relief.

I am sure we think too much of parliamentary tactics when we often say it is not our business to suggest remedies. The country likes a man who does so. It takes it as a proof that he is ready and fit to succeed the Government he attacks. The rapid reputation that George Bentinck made rose far more from his apparent readiness to carry out plans of his own for the relief of certain interests, than in actual hard fighting.[2]

In 1850, Malmesbury was still trying to rouse Stanley.

I believe we must do everything with a view to the future General Election and look more to our party *out* of the House than *in* it. The former know we are now the weakest in Parliament... but they expect us to attest our principles as often as possible. If we do this I am sure they will come well to the hustings. I go farther than this and am convinced that although we must *generalise* on 'Protection', we ought to bring forward a positive proposition for the alleviation of our Burdens. It is expected of our Leaders in the country.[3]

By the time that Malmesbury wrote the second letter to Stanley, in February 1850, Disraeli's attempt to attach the party to a programme of relief independent of protection had failed.

[1] Quarters of barley imported:

1846	299,425	1849	899,760
1847	400,443	1850	1,554,860
1848	794,999		

(*Edinburgh Review* (October 1852), 552).

[2] Malmesbury to Stanley, February 1849. Derby Mss, 144/1.

[3] Malmesbury to Stanley, February 1850. *ibid.*

Disraeli's scheme originated in the mind of his independent radical friend, Henry Drummond. After Bentinck's death in September 1848, Drummond urged Disraeli to fill the intellectual vacuum at the head of the party.

> The men around you are at your mercy; they have not an idea touching any course of policy: all their ideas of parties are like those of rival attornies, rival public houses...in a country town. If you adopt a line of policy, they must follow you from mere helplessness; but if you adopt a line of policy to suit the party, it will sink you.[1]

During the 1849 session, Herries and Granby, despite Stanley's encouragement, had not interfered with Disraeli's leadership in the Commons. In August, Drummond, thinking Disraeli to be master in his house, sent to him a line of policy to take up. Finance had become the leading question of the day, and Cobden's statement that 'no statesman will ever again dare to propose a custom house duty, but will raise the whole of the necessary revenue upon articles of domestic growth' provided the Protectionist party with the point on which to close. The great danger facing the party was that the tenant farmers, despairing of redress any other way, would follow Cobden into direct taxation and reduced expenditure on the services and the colonies. Since neither policy would be accepted by the Protectionists, some other scheme of relief must be put forward, one which would 'get rid of the old names of Free Trade and Protection because they no more express the present ground of quarrel than those of Whig and Tory'. Drummond started with the assumption that the Protectionist party was assured of landlord support. To win the support of the tenant farmers and the urban workers he had drawn up a five-point programme: a graduated income tax and the repeal of those taxes (on malt, soap, bricks, and hops) which weighed on the working class; a sinking fund to be raised by the equalisation of the land tax; an *ad valorem* duty on imports; free trade within the empire; and an Extension of the franchise. Such a programme, Drummond believed, would throw over the Peelites and counter Cobden's appeal with a slogan of 'British versus Foreign Labour'.[2]

[1] Drummond to Disraeli, 8 November 1848. Hughenden Mss, B/XX/Be/143.
[2] Drummond to Disraeli, 22 August and 5 October 1849. *ibid.* B/III/2, 19.

Drummond's suggestions found a sympathetic mind. Disraeli wrote to the Duke of Newcastle that if the party continued to drift until the next election, the farmers would turn to the Financial Reform Association 'which really means nothing more than direct taxation and the confiscation of the Aristocracy'. Disraeli did not, apparently, share Drummond's interest in the urban workers' votes, since he discarded the proposals to extend the franchise and to remove the excise duties. But he took up the redistribution of local taxation and the establishment of a sinking fund. 'I would wish to build up the country party on two great popular principles – the redistribution of public burthens and the maintenance of public credit, and thus to associate the interests of the land with the general sympathies of the Country.'[1]

Disraeli raised a storm within the Protectionist party and in the agricultural community in the country by his proposals. They were first disclosed in mid-September 1849, at a private meeting in Aylesbury which, to Disraeli's surprise, was reported in the press. Disraeli suggested that the land tax be raised in every Welsh and English county to the Buckinghamshire level of 1s. 6d. in the pound. The increased annual revenue from this source, which he estimated at about £5,000,000, was to be used to establish a sinking fund. Disraeli hoped that the fund, by acting powerfully on the price of funds and facilitating the acquisition of money at a low rate of interest, would afford the farmers relief.[2]

There were several objections to the scheme. Counties like Warwickshire and Lancashire, where the existing land tax rate was only 3d., were bound to oppose the increase. In addition there was the danger that farmers might be induced to borrow heavily at a time when agricultural prospects made quick repayment improbable. The next turn of the Bank screw might then throw a large amount of landed property into the hands of the money lenders.[3] Finally, Disraeli appeared to be making a disguised assault on the traditional Tory view of taxation. 'I am

[1] Disraeli to Newcastle, 16 October 1849. Newcastle Mss, NeC/5477.
[2] Stanley to Disraeli, 22 September 1849; Disraeli to Stanley, 24 September 1849. Monypenny and Buckle, iii, 215–18.
[3] Newdegate to Stanley, 19 September 1849. Derby Mss, 148/1.

not at all prepared', Stanley reassured Newdegate, 'to give up the principle of Import Duties versus Direct Taxation.'[1] After canvassing opinion at a Birmingham dinner on 27 September, Newdegate told Disraeli that 'the land tax is not likely to be at all popular, and is thought at variance with the relief to the owners and occupiers of . . . landed property'.[2] Six weeks later Beresford reported that all the leading men in the party objected to Disraeli's scheme: 'there is a general feeling that a recurrence to Protection is absolutely necessary and, I am sure, as I have ever held to it, that we should work that feeling to the utmost extent'.[3]

It was for that purpose that the five-month-old National Association for the Protection of British Industry and Capital held an organisational meeting on 15 October. The association was headed by George Frederick Young, well known for his extensive shipyards in Limehouse, but an upstart in politics who was to be elected to the Commons for the first time in 1852. He had one quality which endeared him to hard-pressed farmers in the autumn of 1849; a fire-in-the-belly devotion to the Corn Laws and an outraged sense of the wrong which had been done to the landed interest. In May, the Earl of Stanhope had advised him to hold public meetings to petition the Crown for a dissolution of parliament, with a view to returning a majority pledged to the restoration of the Corn Laws.[4] In the following October, the Reigate Protection Society sent circulars to landowners throughout England soliciting their opinion on Stanhope's suggestion. There were 153 favourable replies, 7 doubtful, and 3 opposed. At its meeting of 15 October, Young's association condemned partial relief measures, adopted the Reigate plan, and passed a resolution expressing confidence in Disraeli's leadership but regretting its inability to support his sinking fund proposal.[5]

Disraeli, with his sure sense of English constitutional practice and political behaviour, considered Young's agitation to be

---

[1] Stanley to Newdegate, 25 September 1849 (copy). *ibid.* 178/1.
[2] Newdegate to Disraeli, 28 September 1849. Hughenden Mss, B/III/10.
[3] Beresford to Disraeli, 9 November 1849. *ibid.* B/III/53.
[4] Stanhope to Young, 24 and 29 May, 3 June, 1849. Young Mss, Add. Mss 46712/13, packet 15.
[5] *Illustrated London News*, 20 October 1849.

puerile, and expressed his dissatisfaction with it in a printed letter to Young. He had already, under pressure from Stanley, modified his proposals in a speech at Castle Hedingham on 5 October, in which he had abandoned the land tax revaluation and advocated supplying the sinking fund by a small *ad valorem* duty on imports. That the Protectionist party should demand more than that struck him as folly. Disraeli's letter to Young is the most complete statement of his position in the years 1849–52.

The present Parliament, freely and recently elected by the people, has betrayed no trust confided to it, and nothing, therefore, can justify your addressing the Crown for its dissolution but overwhelming evidence that the constituencies are passionately desirous to record a decided opinion upon the new commercial system, which at the last, and late, General Election they declined to do. No evidence of this kind has reached me. My judgment is, that in this moment, in case of a dissolution, the Protectionist party would not command a majority, and I am quite sure that if the result were, what some might consider, more favourable, and we were encumbered with a *bare* majority in favour of Protection, it would be a great calamity for this country. Addresses to the Crown for a dissolution of Parliament...are constitutional weapons to be had recourse to only in those great public emergencies, which, fortunately, occur rarely in the history of this country; and the political party, that attempts to raise this armour of Ajax in vain, only affords a terrible proof of its national impotence.

The political situation appears to be this: unless the agricultural constituencies (county and borough) are prevented from running amuck against the financial system of this country, which, out of suffering and sheer spite and vexation, it is not unnatural they should do, it is all over with England as a great monarchy; and it must become not only, in its imitation of the United States, a second-rate Republic, but a second-rate and manufacturing Republic. The agricultural constituencies, therefore, must at this moment be taught that there is no hope for them in the repeal of taxes, and that in a juster distribution of the burthens of the State, by a sinking fund supplied by import duties, they may obtain considerable, and lay the foundation of sufficient, relief. In this manner, the Country party might be reconstructed on two great popular principles – the diminution of public burthens and the maintenance of public credit; and its interests would be associated with the sympathies of the country.[1]

[1] Monypenny and Buckle, iii, 221–2.

Disraeli had not previously been so outspokenly in favour of abandoning protection. It is well to remember that at this time he thought of the colonies as a millstone around Great Britain's neck and that in 1852 his budget plans were to be destroyed by the Crown's insistence on a large military estimate. Left to himself, Disraeli would have embraced the liberal policy of increased direct taxation and retrenchment in government expenditure. In that way the 'country party' could, without being trapped in reaction, survive as the guardian of the aristocratic constitution. But Stanley believed that the party could continue, and so retain that preservative function, only by acknowledging the protectionist agitation in the agricultural constituencies. A return to protection might be impossible; but Stanley saw no reason openly to state that it was so. He considered Disraeli's letter to Young 'more unfortunate than his Aylesbury speech'[1] and gave his objections to Disraeli in detail.

I confess that what gives me most uneasiness about your letter is the indication which I fear I see in it, of your not only considering a return to Protection hopeless, but of your wishing to impress on our friends the conviction that it is so. Events alone can show whether at any time, and if so within what time, a return to that principle may be practicable: but of this I am firmly convinced, that the public mind is beginning to be impressed with the conviction that Free Trade has proved a delusion; and at the point at which we now stand, our clear policy is to seek to encourage this conviction. Our hold on the public mind is our adherence to the principles for which we have contended; and I think we commit a great error, and insure the loss of nine-tenths of the support we have, if we abandon the cause as hopeless, before our friends are prepared so to consider it.[2]

Disraeli remained sceptical of the popularity of protectionist platitudes, but he had lost the battle and came back into line on 31 October in a speech at Aylesbury affirming his adherence to the Corn Laws. Even his faithful colleague, Lord John Manners, had deserted him: 'as our party organisation is tolerably complete and at work under the symbol of Protection, it seems to me highly inexpedient...to change our flag'.[3] Disraeli's brief tru-

1 Stanley to Granby, 24 October 1849 (copy). Derby Mss, 178/1.
2 Monypenny and Buckle, iii, 223–6.
3 Manners to Disraeli, 24 October 1850. Hughenden Mss, B/XX/M/68.

ancy had produced a stiffening of the ranks. 'My opinion is that we shall never do any good by temporising,' commented the Duke of Newcastle. 'We are against free trade, we are in favour of protection. If we are, why dissemble in the slightest degree? Let us be rightly and clearly understood.'[1] That sentiment was echoed in a fresh spate of Protectionist pamphlets. '*Let the Tory be a Tory,*' thundered one of them. '*Let the Protectionist be a Protectionist.* Let there be no more trimming – no more compromise – no more of that *demoralising dishonesty*, that *political turpitude*, designated "PEELISM".'[2] Bentinck was not the only Strafford in the Protectionist party. With the lot of them Disraeli's shrewd political sense carried no weight.

As the financial pressure on the farmers grew more acute in 1850, Disraeli's moderation was drowned in a tide of protectionist meetings, at which the party's leading spokesmen, Granby, Newdegate, Manners, and Christopher, received the cheers of the farmers for preaching an undiluted protectionist text.[3] At each of these meetings the farmers demanded either the immediate imposition of an 8s. duty on corn or the dissolution of parliament. Stanley, though aware that a dissolution could not be granted, was content to keep up the agriculturalists' morale in this fashion. On 11 May 1850, he told a protectionist deputation to 'agitate the country from one end to the other'.[4]

In the House of Commons Disraeli was pursuing a different line. Eager to harry a divided Whig government, he had begun his annual motions for an inquiry into agricultural distress and for the reduction of burdens on land (by throwing the various charges on to the consolidated fund) in 1849. In August of the same year, Joseph Henley, a prospective member of a Protectionist cabinet, had startled the party by tabling a motion in the Commons to reduce civil servants' salaries by 10 per cent, as a means of lowering taxation and keeping down expenditure.

[1] Newcastle to Disraeli, 21 October 1849. *ibid.* B/III/34a.

[2] Pro Ecclesia Dei, *Our Duty and Our Encouragement: an Address to the Protectionist Constituency of these Realms* (London, 1850), 7.

[3] See reports in the *Illustrated London News*, 27 October; 8, 22, and 29 December 1849; 5, 12, 19, and 26 January; 4 April; and 11 and 18 May 1850.

[4] *Illustrated London News*, 18 May 1850.

Henley argued that the reduced cost of living under free trade made such reductions desirable. His motion was thus interpreted as a sign that the Protectionists were prepared to come to terms with free trade. Disraeli's deviation two months later spread uncertainty about the real aims of the Protectionist party, an uncertainty which was never dispelled and which hindered the growth of public confidence in the party.

One or two points need to be made about the revival of the Protectionist agitation in 1849 and 1850. In the first place, by rejecting Disraeli's compromise, Stanley missed a second, albeit not very sound, opportunity to throw off protection. The views of the majority of the party left him, perhaps, little choice. And yet it is evident that he sided with them against Disraeli. It is improbable that anyone in the party could successfully have challenged him had he decided to support Disraeli. That Stanley should have clung to the signs of a protectionist reaction is not surprising. The collapse of Chartism, the division within the Radical movement, and the impotence of Young Ireland meant that a cry of 'resistance to democracy' was almost meaningless. The Catholic issue was for the moment lying dormant. Deprived of a Protestant, anti-democratic programme, Stanley relied on the Corn Laws as the distinctive mark of his party. As a distinctive mark Disraeli's protection and water would not do. Nor was it easy for a party which had castigated Peel as a traitor and a defiler of political integrity to taint itself with Peel's sin. In 1846 Peel had argued that circumstances made the repeal of the Corn Laws expedient. Disraeli had never objected to that argument. His argument with Peel was the constitutional one. But most of the Protectionists had replied to Peel that protection was an enduring principle, a necessary prop in the maintenance of the aristocratic constitution. For two years they had been kept up to the mark by Lord George Bentinck. In 1849 they were not in the mood to be tricked by an *arriviste* Jew.

The mood of the party in the years 1849 to 1851 was based on the delusion that there was a genuine reaction against free trade in the country. Isaac Butt's prophecy of a Protectionist upsurge in Ireland was falsified by events. On 17 January 1850, a meeting of landlords in Dublin passed resolutions calling for corn duties and the dissolution of parliament,[1] but four days earlier, tenant farmers in Castletown-rock, county Cork, resolved

that the present cry for Protection is got up for selfish purposes, firstly to divert the minds of the people from the just demand for tenant right and reasonable rents; and secondly, to enable the Conservatives to get into the representation of the country, to oust the popular party, and to check the march of enlightened legislation; and hence we denounce the Protectionist meetings as a mockery, a delusion and a snare.[2]

Although many Protectionists remained convinced of their growing popularity in Ireland in 1850–1, the rapid spread of Tenant Protection Societies drew away potential supporters of the party.[3] Sharman Crawford wanted an amendment to the government's reply to the throne speech in 1850 calling for protection, but the Protectionist movement in Ireland was a landlord agitation which sought increased rents and reduced poor-rates. The wave of evictions in 1848–9 lent urgency to the tenant farmers' demands for reduced rents and security of tenure. The Protectionist revival in Ireland was delusive because it was largely landlord-inspired. In England it was so because it occurred in those places which were already represented by Protectionists in parliament. The Protectionist party was buoyed by the rare instance of a Protectionist gain in the towns, such as the by-election victories at Reading and Kidderminster, but a danger lurked even there. A repetition of similar successes might force Cobden to leave his campaign for free trade in land and take up suffrage extension in earnest, as he hinted at a public meeting in Leeds in December 1849.

We are told by these protectionist scribes that there is a reaction, because there have been two or three elections for places which have returned protectionists...I tell them that the decision of such places as Reading and Kidderminster will not have a feather's weight in the scale...Let them see a member returned for any one of the metropolitan districts, Edinburgh, Birmingham, Manchester, Liverpool, Leicester, Derby, Nottingham, Leeds, West Riding, Halifax, Bradford, Huddersfield...where the constituencies are free and beyond corruption and coercion.[4]

---

[1] *Ibid.* 26 January 1850.   [2] *Ibid.* 19 January 1850.
[3] See J. H. Whyte, *The Independent Irish Party, 1850–9* (Oxford, 1958), 4–13.
[4] Bright and Rogers, *Speeches by Cobden*, i, 415–16.

As for the predicted ninety seats which the Protectionists were to win in Ireland, Cobden remarked that such dreams were possible only because the representation of Ireland was 'a mockery and a fraud'.

The remedy which the political economists and the free traders prescribed for agricultural ills was 'high farming', the contemporary term for the improved methods of farming which Norfolk had long before made famous.[1] The central feature of high farming was the change from a system of rotation which left one strip of land to lie fallow each year to the four-course rotation, under which 'cash' or 'white' crops were not grown in successive years, but the land refertilised by green crops, especially the turnip, or by grasses, which were used for sheep-folding or cattle-grazing. The effect of these changes was a reduced emphasis on arable farming, a particular argument for high farming in years of low wheat prices. Machinery played an important, but secondary, role in the agricultural revolution. Besides the change to crop rotation, the new agriculture was marked by the use of artificial fertilisers, chiefly marl, lime, and manure, drainage works, and the rehabilitation of farm buildings and roads.[2]

In his tour of the counties in 1850–1, James Caird, the agricultural writer for *The Times*, found much to censure in the condition of English farming.[3] Buildings were frequently in a state of ramshackle neglect and drainage schemes incompletely carried out or not begun. By 1850 crop rotation had become widespread, but in the distressed conditions of the early post-repeal years, many farmers found it necessary to cultivate as many cash crops as possible. 'We know that we are not farming,' an Oxfordshire tenant told Caird; 'we are only taking out of the land what we can get from it at the least cost, as we don't know how long we may remain in possession and have no security for what we might be disposed to invest in improved cultivation.'[4] It was not only

---

[1] See N. Riches, *The Agricultural Revolution in Norfolk* (North Carolina, 1937).
[2] For a study of these developments, see J. D. Chambers and G. E. Mingay, *The Agricultural Revolution, 1750–1880* (London, 1966) and D. B. Griggs, *The Agricultural Revolution in South Lincolnshire* (Cambridge, 1966).
[3] J. Caird, *English Agriculture in 1850–51* (London, 1852).
[4] *Ibid.* 26.

in Ireland that insecurity of tenure and the uncertainty of adequate compensation for improvements prevented tenant farmers from modernising agriculture. The 1847–8 select committee on agricultural customs recommended the universal introduction of tenant right, a custom by which, in England, the incoming tenant compensated the outgoing farmer for permanent improvements which had been made on the farm. The custom had no legal force and prevailed in only a few counties. Caird's remedy was not tenant right but long leases, which in 1850 were available only on the largest farms.

The free traders accused the landowners of refusing to introduce long leases or tenant right in order to protect their political influence. That security of tenure might allow the tenant farmer to form independent political opinions undoubtedly worried the gentry, but the landowners' attitude was as much conditioned by fluctuations in prices. When long leases were granted, at a fixed rent, inflated prices seldom produced higher rents, but depressed prices almost always forced the landlord to concede abatements in rent.[1] In Surrey, Sussex, and Kent, where tenant compensation was the most liberal, the custom was subjected to fraudulent abuses. It was almost impossible to determine, after a crop had been harvested, how much fertiliser a farmer had used, or of what quality, or how recently.[2]

High farming was an immensely costly business and profitable only in the very long run. Rich aristocrats, like the Duke of Portland, the Duke of Bedford, and the Earl of Derby, could invest heavily enough to make improvements comprehensive and thus worthwhile;[3] few landowners could afford the £100,000 investment which made the Duke of Northumberland's estate a model of systematic management and improved farming.[4] The Duke of Wellington congratulated himself for his scientific farming, but he knew that 'few other gentlemen are able by their circumstances to devote the income of their land to its

---

[1] Chambers and Mingay, *Agricultural Revolution*, 165.

[2] *Report of the Select Committee on Agricultural Customs*, 1847–8, 430–7.

[3] For a description of the Portland and Derby estates, see Caird, *English Agriculture*, 199 and 266.

[4] F. M. L. Thompson, *English Landed Society in the Nineteenth Century* (London, 1963), 169.

improvement'.[1] A conscientious, but less rich, landowner, Sir James Graham, spent about £3,575 annually on improvements and was able to raise his rents by only £3,500 from 1818 to 1845.[2] No businessman would tolerate such a small return after three decades of risk, effort, and loss. The agent on the Marquis of Ailesbury's Wiltshire estates advised the Marquis in 1842 that his exhausted soil required 'a considerable period of improved management and comparative repose' and that he could nor therefore expect 'any immediate improvement in income'. Ailesbury knew that already from the experience of his Yorkshire estates, where, despite a 10 per cent rise in rents coincident with extensive improvements, in cropping, ploughing, and drainage, his annual income dropped by about £2,000.[3]

It is not surprising that in the sharp crisis of 1849–52 the gentry and farmers should ignore the political climate and counter the advice to farm high with a demand for the Corn Laws, nor that they should be more strident in that demand than the great landowners. As in 1844–6, it was the bottom of the agricultural pyramid which kept the landlords from wavering on protection.[4] In November 1849, Redesdale found that the landlords were 'beginning to think the advice to lay out their money, not to get any direct return for it, but only *in the hope* of keeping matters from getting worse, is rather absurd'.[5] Early in 1851, when corn prices fell to 36s., William Ferrand asked a meeting of farmers whether there were 'ever such madness for men professing themselves to be sane – to recommend you to farm high when they know that you cannot produce your corn except at a ruinous sacrifice?'[6] The Protectionist press and pamphleteers took up the campaign against high farming. One such pamphlet was Bulwer

[1] Earl of Stanhope, *Notes of Conversations with the Duke of Wellington, 1831–1851* (London, 1888), 159–60.

[2] D. Spring, 'A Great Agricultural Estate: Netherby Under Sir James Graham, 1820–1845', *Agricultural History* (April 1955), 73.

[3] F. M. L. Thompson, 'Engilsh Landownership: the Ailesbury Trust, 1832–56', *Economic History Review* (1958), 130–1.

[4] Stanley to E. Yorke, 17 April 1849 (copy): 'I think...the farmers are right in seeking the restoration of protection; and I hope the Landlords, and I believe the Country, ere long, will go with them' (Derby Mss, 178/1).

[5] Redesdale to Stanley, 1 November 1849. Derby Mss, 149/6.

[6] *Illustrated London News*, 1 February 1851.

Lytton's *Letters to John Bull*, written in 1851, and containing this passage, addressed to the political economists.

'Farm high' you say, 'Farm high!' And there ends all of your philosophy of relief. To farm high means to keep plenty of stock, and buy plenty of artificial manure. In other words, increase your gross expenditure in order to increase your net income – adventure your capital in the hope of a return. Excellent advice...But allow, at least, that two things are necessary to induce even men so obtuse as, in your superior wit, you deem the poor farmer, to follow your recommendation. First, you must not diminish the capital; and secondly, you must allow the speculator a reasonable hope that the return is likely to follow the expenditure...And I appeal to any farmer, if it be not true that, in cultivating his land, he is now sacrificing his capital.[1]

As the Protectionists had argued in 1846, protected corn was the prerequisite of high farming.

The party's single-minded devotion to the Corn Laws was disturbing to Disraeli. While his colleagues were making loud noises in the country, he was pricking Whig complacency with lesser schemes for the relief of agriculture. On 8 March 1849, he introduced resolutions in the Commons calling attention to the distress and requesting the equalisation of taxation on real and other property. In the financial year ending on Ladyday 1848, £12,000,000 in taxes had been levied on landed property, in the form of poor rates, highway rates, church rates, county rates, and the locally assessed land taxes. Disraeli's remedy implied either a general addition to the income tax or an increase in the schedules not touching real property. The Peelites objected to either change, and the resolution was defeated by 282 votes to 191.

The resolutions provided the first major debate in which Disraeli acted as the leader of his party in the Commons and he came out of it with an enhanced reputation. When the debate was over Russell described Disraeli as 'a much abler and less passionate leader than Lord George Bentinck'.[2] Stanley, who was

---

[1] E. Bulwer Lytton, *Letters to John Bull, Esq., on Affairs Connected with his Landed Property and the Persons Who Live Thereon* (London, 1851), 59.

[2] Russell to Queen Victoria, 11 March 1849. Benson and Esher, ii, 256.

still looking for a *pont d'or* which the Peelites might cross over, did not object to Disraeli's motions, especially since Disraeli was careful to make face-saving nods towards the Corn Laws. After Disraeli's speech on 8 March, Henry Greville noticed a marked change in Disraeli's parliamentary manner: 'nothing could be more eloquent and, what is more rare in his speeches, more temperate and concilatory. It consequently produced more solid effect than his more jeering and *smart* effusions.'[1] Disraeli's advance depended on the demonstration of superior ability, and Beresford has left an engaging picture of Disraeli in the autumn of 1849, setting about to become a great parliamentarian and to ingratiate himself with his party. The scene is Hughenden during the parliamentary recess:

He is living here very quietly and *working* very hard. He is reading up all the Blue Books of the past Session...He attributes Peel's great power and effect in the House to having always had Blue Books by heart, and having thereby the appearance of a fund of general knowledge greater than he really possessed...He certainly has great powers and not the least among them is the great command he has evidently over himself and his own feelings and passions. He acts and speaks with the greatest cordiality and shews the most complete confidence to me; certainly times are rather altered within one year in that respect. I am sure that you will be gratified to hear that he speaks most highly to me of your Son's great knowledge, application, and talent.[2]

Stanley was by now forced to cooperate with Disraeli 'cordially and without reserve',[3] although it was not until June 1850, that the salutation of his letters changed from 'My dear Sir' to 'Dear Disraeli'.

Disraeli's 1850 motion was less comprehensive than that of 1849. It asked only for the equalisation of the poor rate and was lost by the narrow margin of 273 votes to 252. The Protectionists were overjoyed by their largest muster ever, but the great reduction in the government's majority from the previous year was the result of 23 Peelites, including Gladstone, voting with Disraeli, and was therefore misleading. Goulburn, who with

[1] Viscountess Enfield, *Diary of Henry Greville*, i, 325.
[2] Beresford to Stanley, 30 September 1849. Derby Mss, 149/2.
[3] Disraeli to Newcastle, 23 February 1849. Newcastle Mss, NeC/5476.

Gladstone was thought to be the most Conservative Peelite, voted with Peel and Graham against Disraeli. And Gladstone supported the resolution because he believed that a committee of inquiry would either prove the notion that the land suffered from special tax burdens fallacious or recommend that relief be granted the farmers. If the latter, the ground would be cut from under the feet of those who were demanding the restoration of the Corn Laws.[1] Peelite support for Disraeli's resolution was therefore not a sign that the Peelites had moved closer to the Protectionists.

The 1850 session revealed, nevertheless, how shaky the government's foundations had become. No longer able to rely on a solid Peelite buttress, Russell's government was in constant danger of being defeated on a colonial question. Ever since the Canada Rebellion Losses Bill of 1849, when more than half the Peelites had voted with the Protectionists against the government, the administration of the colonies had been the subject of harsh criticism. In the Lords, the government survived on the Rebellion Losses Bill by only three votes, and that with the aid of proxies. In 1850, after the close division on Disraeli's agricultural resolution, Russell postponed the introduction of a bill for Australian self-government rather than risk defeat on it. A month later, the government escaped defeat on a motion to re-call troops from South Africa only because the Peelites felt constrained by the fact that it was Peel who had negotiated the treaty which had placed the troops there. George Cornewall Lewis expected that the government would be put in a minority by a Radical–Protectionist combination on a colonial question,[2] and Disraeli was criticised for raising agricultural motions instead of attacking the government all out on colonial matters.[3] But the defeat of the government on a colonial question would not have lent authority to the incoming government. Much of the dissatisfaction was not with policy but with the brusque, high-handed manner of the colonial secretary, Lord Grey. And the Radicals and Protectionists criticised the government from opposite sides of the fence: the Radicals wanted the government to

---

[1] 21 February 1850. *Hansard*, 3rd Series, cvii, 1204–14.
[2] Lewis to Head, 27 November 1849. Lewis, *Letters of Lewis*, 215–18.
[3] Hardwicke to Disraeli, 2 April 1850. Hughenden Mss, B/XXI/H/180.

cede self-government to the colonies more quickly, whereas the Protectionists were alarmed by Grey's seeming willingness to dismember the Empire.[1] When Disraeli hinted to Stanley that the party might catch power by allying itself with the Colonial Government Society – a Radical organisation established to secure Gibbon Wakefield's aims of responsible government and independence for the colonies – he received a sharp rebuff from his leader.[2]

Disraeli was, in these years, restlessly seeking any kind of combination which might place the Protectionists in power. Frustrated in his attempts to let down protection or to beat the government with Radical support, he began to sound out the Whigs on the possibility of junction. The notion was not so silly as it had been when he first took it up in 1844. Not only were many of the Whigs disappointed by the meagre compensation which the growers had received in 1846, but some of them were worried about the growing influence of the urban Liberals in their party. The advanced free trader, Earl Fitzwilliam, preferred in 1847 to share the representation of the West Riding with a Protectionist rather than an urban, Dissenter-backed Liberal. At the general election he was unable to prevent the return of Cobden, but when Lord Morpeth went to the Lords in 1848, Fitzwilliam cooperated with the Protectionist candidate, no Whig stood, and the Protectionist defeated the Radical candidate in a straight fight. Alarmed by Radical demands for pledges and suffrage extension, Fitzwilliam decided that 'the time is coming for a union of moderate men of both parties for the common safety'. The time was still forty years away. By 1852 the Liberal–Radicals had a clear majority without the Whigs on the register, and self-interest dictated a reconciliation between Whigs and Radicals in the riding.[3] If the view of one Leeds Whig accurately reflected the view of Whiggery as a whole, then a Whig–Protectionist coalition was never in the cards.

[1] See Grey's eloquent defence of the government's policy in Earl Grey, *The Colonial Policy of Lord John Russell's Administration* (London, 1853).

[2] Disraeli to Stanley, 17 December 1849; Stanley to Disraeli, 28 December 1849. Monypenny and Buckle, iii, 233–6.

[3] F. M. L. Thompson, 'Whigs and Liberals in the West Riding, 1830–1860', *English Historical Review* (April 1959), 236–7.

I should be sorry to see the Whigs entirely merged in the Conservatives. I do not like party divisions to run by classes and not by principles: all the aristocracy and gentry on one side, the democracy and
town people on the other: or all church against all dissent. Our old
party organisation was far better.[1]

That was a statement of the long-established and fondly cherished
Whig conviction that their party *represented* the popular element
in politics. Not until political parties had become more class-
based, in the 1880s, did Whiggery consent to throw in its lot
with Conservatism. The Protectionist difficulties would have
been over if, in 1851 and 1852, they had been able to detach
Palmerston and his conservative followers from the Liberal party.

The Protectionists were, at any rate, finding it difficult to put
their own house in order. John Tyrell attacked Stanley in the
Essex Herald for his stubborn attachment to the Corn Laws, and
Henley, who denied the existence of agricultural distress, continued to embarrass the party by recommending a reduction in
civil servants' salaries. Whipping was made almost impossible
by the lack of communication between Herries and Disraeli.
When Cobden introduced a motion in April 1850, for the reduction of government expenditure to the level of 1835, the Protectionists countered with an amendment to repeal the window tax.
Beresford got the Protectionists up for the division only to discover at the last moment that Herries and Newdegate were
opposed to the amendment. A full vote was thus lost and the
government defeated the amendment by three votes. Throughout 1850 Disraeli urged Herries to meet with him to discuss
party arrangements, but Herries would not yield. As the 1851
session approached, Disraeli lost his patience and wrote to Herries a sharp note: 'I wish I could induce you to such an act of
patriotism as to pay me a visit. I am quite alone, and think together we might prepare some measure for counsel.'[2] Herries'
withdrawal from the tripartite leadership was unfortunate, since
there were Protectionists who would follow him but who had
not yet got used to receiving instructions from Disraeli. Able

[1] *Ibid.* 237.
[2] Disraeli to Herries, 3 November 1850. Herries Mss, NRA/80.

debaters were still sadly wanting in the Commons,[1] and Beresford had a hard time mustering the country gentlemen. On the eve of Lord Granby's motion for a fixed duty on corn in July 1849, Beresford received notes from two Protectionists who had left town that day, 'one from that brute (physically and mentally, I mean) Sir W. Wynn, to whom I wrote strongly last night to urge his attendance. He is gone down today for the great and noble object of seeing his Hounds'.[2] Once the squires were at Westminster, it was not easy to keep them there. The postponement of the government's Irish Regulation Bill in February 1850, was a 'desperate blow' to Beresford, 'for having asked every man to come up from the country and no division, they will be furious and we cannot get them again'.[3]

Constituency organisation was just as haphazard. Beresford could not be expected to run affairs efficiently on his own, but Stanley remained complacently ignorant of the need for a larger electoral staff. 'Politics are in a very low state,' Phillips wrote to Disraeli in 1849. 'If Beresford did not send Trail down into the country every three months or so to do nothing and then to turn in his report, the cause of Protection would be at a standstill... There never was such mismanagement or rather there never has been anything but such mismanagement.'[4] Bungling cost the Protectionist party a seat at the Aylesbury by-election in April 1851, when William Ferrand the shop-worn, cantankerous Young Englander from Yorkshire was brought in after an unsuccessful search for a local candidate. Situated in the centre of Disraeli's county, Buckinghamshire, it was a seat which the Protectionists ought to have won. 'Where have we a chance of a Protectionist candidate', Stanley moaned, 'if not in a small town in the heart of an Agricultural County?'[5]

The party's relations with the press deteriorated. Since 1833, the *Morning Post* had been run in the agricultural interest by its

[1] Disraeli to his sister, 16 March 1849: 'If we only had half a dozen men in the Commons for Cabinet Ministers, and thirty or forty more capable of taking the inferior places, one might do, but, like India, there is a terrible want of officers' (R. Disraeli, *Beaconsfield's Correspondence*, 221–2).

[2] Beresford to Disraeli, 6 July 1849. Hughenden Mss, B/XX/Bd/18.

[3] Beresford to Disraeli, 28 February 1850. *ibid*. B/XX/Bd/27.

[4] Phillips to Disraeli, 6 September 1849. *ibid*. B/XXI/P/224.

[5] Stanley to Beresford, 2 December 1850 (copy). Derby Mss, 179/1.

editor and part-proprietor, C. Eastland Michele. In 1842, when the other owners were in favour of supporting the free-trade movement, Michele raised a mortgage of £25,000 to buy them out and keep the paper a protectionist organ. In 1847, Michele had to pay off the mortgage. A member of the staff who had close connexions with the Duke of Portland appealed to the Duke for money. But, despite Bentinck's intercession, the appeal was unsuccessful. And although the paper had shown substantial profits for thirty-five years, neither the Duke of Richmond nor Charles Newdegate could be persuaded to raise a subscription from among the Protectionists. Lord John Manners explained the Protectionists' indifference by the lack of regard which the country party had always shown for literature and the press.[1] In December 1849, the *Post* passed into the hands of the mortgager, a Lancashire businessman T. B. Crampton, who appointed Peter Borthwick editor.[2] Borthwick had been an opponent of Peel, but he was a protectionist only because of a connexion with the Jamaica lobby,[3] and the paper soon became Palmerstonian in its sympathies. After two months under Borthwick, William Johnston, a leader-writer of protectionist sympathies, was forced to leave the paper.[4] The loss of the *Post* was all the more unfortunate because Beresford had lost his influence with the *Morning Herald*,[5] and the Peelites had bought the *Morning Chronicle*, hitherto Palmerstonian, in February 1848.[6] In 1847 the Peelites had no national newspaper; by 1850 they had two of the most influential, in addition to the editorial support of *The Times*. In 1852, when his minority government badly needed press support, but instead found itself attacked in *The Times* and subjected to Sidney Herbert's abuse in the *Morning Chronicle*, Stanley came too late to 'admit, more than I ever did, the possible powers of the press in a crisis'.[7]

[1] Manners to Disraeli, 15 November 1848. Hughenden Mss, B/XX/M/35.
[2] Lucas, *Glenesk and the 'Morning Post'*, 29–40. See also W. Hindle, *The Morning Post, 1772–1937: Portrait of a Newspaper* (London, 1937), 177 ff.
[3] Stanley to Beresford, 11 November 1849 (copy). Derby Mss, 178/2.
[4] Johnston to Disraeli, 18 February 1850. Hughenden Mss, B/XXI/J/112.
[5] Beresford to Disraeli, March 1849. *ibid.* B/XX/Bd/9.
[6] Carlisle, *Correspondence of Abraham Hayward*, i, 124–5.
[7] Derby to Disraeli, 1852. Hughenden Mss, B/XX/S/105.

In the three years between the elections of 1847 and the close of the 1850 session the Protectionists had not been able to find a clear policy to present to the country. There had been no consistent point of attack on the Whig government. The organisation of the party was in a shambles and its leadership distracted. For all their difficulties, the Whigs appeared to be safe from a Protectionist challenge. In August 1850, Stanley wrote to Croker of his despair for the future of the country party in English politics.

All the tendency of our legislation and of our proceedings in Parliament is towards the lowering of the weight, in the social scale, of the proprietors of the soil; and while they, and those dependent upon them, are gradually sinking under the new pressure of their old burthens, the apparent success of the Free Trade policy, as exhibited by the state of the revenue and the amount of our foreign trade, furnishes a plausible argument in its favour, and blinds the eyes of the country to the real dangers we are incurring. The next election must be the turning point of our destiny; but who shall say what we may witness before that time? If the country has by that time seen its danger, *and felt it to be danger*, then there is some hope of a change for the better; but if this, or any Free Trade, Government *then* acquire a majority, the game is up, and I firmly believe we shall be in rapid progress towards a republic in name as well as in reality...and in everything the lowest and shortest-sighted utilitarianism will be the policy of England...I have never before taken so gloomy a view of our position; and to make matters worse, I see few, if any, young men coming forward or taking an interest in public affairs imbued with *Conservative* principles and ready to stand by and with 'their order'.

...[as for] the *gentlemen* of the country...apathy is fast destroying them. But desertions and defeats have at once reduced their means and depressed their spirits; and they neither can, nor will, make the pecuniary sacrifices and exertions which might yet place them at the head of a powerful party.[1]

[1] Stanley to Croker, 18 August 1850. Jennings, *Croker*, iii, 219–21.

7

1851

THE YEAR 1851 opened in England with the metropolis in preparation for its orgy of self-satisfaction in that spring and summer, the Great Exhibition. The monumental glass and iron Crystal Palace was a splendid, triumphant symbol of England's manufacturing prowess and technical skill. Disraeli understood the inevitability of social change. 'The age of ruins is past', says Sidonia. 'Have you seen Manchester?' But Stanley had not been reconciled to the changing order. His despondency at the end of 1850 was not caused merely by the weakness and disintegration of the Protectionist party, but by his awareness that the very structure of aristocratic government and society was being undermined by industrial growth. For Stanley, economic improvement was not necessarily a sign of progress; it was simply blinding the country to the 'real dangers' of political and social decline. Since 1846, Stanley had looked to a reunion of Peel's party as the way to keep the country from taking a downward path. Four years had gone by and not a single Peelite of stature had joined the Protectionists. Yet there was ground for continuing hope in the failure of Russell to lure any of the Peelites into his government. And in 1849 and 1850, several of the leading Peelites, including Gladstone, had frequently voted against the government. The Peelites could scarcely any longer be called a party and must soon choose to join either the Whigs or the Protectionists. Which way they would decide was one of the two great questions in political circles at the beginning of 1851. The other was whether Russell and Palmerston could continue much longer to sit in the same government. 'It is clear', Lord Redesdale wrote to Stanley, 'that no party as it now stands is by itself capable of carrying on the Government. The Whigs lean on the Radicals and Peelites – we cannot beat the Government except by the assistance of the Peelites.' The fate of the Protectionist

165

party lay in hands other than its own: the Protectionists could gain power only by 'a general smash of parties'.[1]

The disintegration of the combination of groups which maintained Russell in office began in 1850. Two events in that year, the Don Pacifico affair and the Papal Aggression trauma, broke the political calm which had followed the repeal struggle and kicked the Peelite and Irish props out from under the Whig government.

In June 1850, Palmerston won his famous victory in defence of his use of English naval strength to support the somewhat dubious claims of Don Pacifico, a Portuguese-born British subject, for damages after a Greek mob had ransacked his house. Palmerston's victory was far greater in the country than the majority of 46 by which the Commons approved his action indicated. Stanley had forced the debate in the Commons by getting the Lords to pass a motion of censure on Palmerston for his high-handedness. Aberdeen believed Stanley to be ready to form a government and interpreted the motion of censure as an earnest attempt to throw out the government.[2] Princess Lieven, the wife of the Russian ambassador, wrote that Stanley's speech was 'un évènement européen'.[3] But the hatred which European courts bore Palmerston was in direct inverse proportion to the acclaim which he received from liberal patriots in England for his manly defence of the liberty and security of the English subject. It would have been unpropitious to embark upon a Tory government by virtue of having condemned the foreign secretary who was suddenly the most popular politician in the country. Stanley seems not to have wanted to defeat the government. He did not instruct Disraeli to follow up the success of his motion in the Lords by introducing a similar motion in the Commons. It was left to the government to retrieve the situation by having the Radical, Arthur Roebuck, introduce a motion defending the government's foreign policy. Disraeli did not even speak on the motion until Russell pricked him by pointing out

[1] Redesdale to Stanley, 13 January 1851. Derby Mss, 149/6.
[2] Aberdeen to Princess Lieven, 11 June 1850. Parry, *Correspondence of Aberdeen and Lieven*, ii, 488–9.
[3] Princess Lieven to Aberdeen, 20 June 1850. *ibid*. ii, 493.

the inconsistency of his silence with Stanley's attack in the Lords.

Stanley's attack on Palmerston achieved its purpose. The Peelites were obliged to oppose the government on what amounted to a test of confidence. Graham, Gladstone, Herbert, and Aberdeen all denounced Palmerston's chauvinism in unequivocal language. Even Peel recorded a rare vote against the government. By making it impossible for Russell to yield to the request of Albert and the Queen that he remove Palmerston from the foreign office, Stanley had blocked the entry of the Peelites into the cabinet.

Peel's death, four days after the Don Pacifico division, was thought by some further to weaken the ties holding the Peelites to the Whigs. 'Upon Gladstone', Cornewall Lewis wrote, 'it will have the effect of removing a weight from a spring – he will come forward and take more part in discussion. The general opinion is that Gladstone will renounce his free-trade opinions, and become leader of the Protectionists.'[1] Gladstone was an unrepentant free trader, but long before Peel's death he had decided that a Protectionist term of office was 'not only a safe experiment (after 1848) but a vital necessity',[2] since the experience of office would prove to the Protectionists that the Corn Laws could not be restored. Then, once the food issue were removed from politics, there might be a Conservative reunion. Gladstone was critical of Peel's unwavering support of the Whigs because that hindered the growth of sympathy between Peelites and Protectionists. Aberdeen, too, had complained to Peel in April 1850, of Peel's indiscriminate support of everything the government did.[3] The free-trade issue apart, the House of Commons in 1850 was nearly equally divided between Liberals and Conservatives and the Peelites were becoming dissatisfied with a system which kept this from being reflected in divisions. After the vote on Disraeli's agricultural distress motion in February, John Young sent to Peel a division list marking the 35 Peelites who had opposed the government and the 28 who had supported it.

---

[1] Lewis to Head, 11 July, 1850. Lewis, *Letters of Lewis*, 224–7.
[2] Morley, *Gladstone*, i, 373.
[3] Aberdeen to Peel, 4 April 1850. Peel Mss, Add. Mss 40455, ff. 491–2.

On looking over it, you will see the thirty-five and twenty-eight are mostly men of considerable local influence, good fortune and high character. They form an important body, and will cast the balance to whichever party they may eventually join. They will stand by Free Trade; they are the men who carried the repeal of the Corn and Navigation Laws, and will steadily maintain that policy. But they have no sympathies with and no confidence in the present Government. They are with you, not with Lord Russell... they will not make sacrifices, and risk their seats night after night, and year after year, for those whom they cannot help regarding as political opponents.[1]

Young recognised the Peelites' difficulty of remaining an independent party without the leadership of Peel, but he saw no way out of it. At the beginning of 1850, he advised Gladstone not to cooperate with Stanley, himself a man not to be feared, but led astray by rash and violent followers who would pursue a thoroughly reactionary policy, especially in Ireland, where they would attempt to revive the Orange ascendancy. The restoration of Peel and Graham to power raised the equally fearsome prospect of the disestablishment of the Irish Church.

These appear to me the dangers either of Peel's return, or Lord Stanley's accession to office. The advantages would be a firmer general Government, a better colonial administration, and a less anxious and meddling foreign office – for I do not suppose that either would attempt to form a Government without having Lord Aberdeen for foreign minister... If the Protectionists were less unreasonable, and Lord Stanley would concur, the country certainly and perhaps we, the existing parliament, would afford materials and strength for a conservative party nearly as strong as Peel's once was. But it is union alone that could make such a force, and disunion and irreconcilable hostility are all that the Protectionists ever breathe.[2]

High feeling still ran between the two sections of the party, as an attempt to oust the Peelites from the committee of the Carlton Club in March revealed. But on the other hand, no leading Peelite had resigned from the club. And although Gladstone turned a cold shoulder to Protectionist feelers after his vote for Disraeli's

[1] Young to Peel, 22 February 1850. Parker, *Peel*, iii, 532–3.
[2] Young to Gladstone, 15 [January] 1850. Gladstone Mss, Add. Mss 44237, ff. 188–91.

February motion – since 'it did not appear to me that up to the present time the Protectionists had been properly an opposition, except with respect to questions of free trade' – he assured John Tyrell, the Protectionist envoy on this occasion, that he would not 'obstruct Lord Stanley's coming in for obstruction's sake'.[1]

By the spring of 1850, Aberdeen was in regular communication with Stanley about the government's Irish legislation and was referring to the government as 'them' and the Conservative peers as 'we'. He wrote of this new cordiality to Princess Lieven in March.

You will be glad to hear that there are appearances of some approximation between Stanley and Peel's friends. I should be very happy to contribute to this, if possible; but the difficulty is still great. The disposition on both sides is now good; and if we could only contrive to settle the original and sole cause of difference, a concert might speedily be established.

I think the opinions and views of the Duke of Wellington are a good deal changed. For the first time, I have seen him really indignant against the Government, in consequence of the Greek affair [Don Pacifico]. This must be taken as a fact of considerable importance.[2]

On 25 February, Russell introduced a bill to extend the Irish franchise to all occupiers of land rated to the Poor Law at £8 and to freeholders of land rated at £5. The bill seemed to offer a test of the sincerity of Gladstone's good will towards the Protectionists. The Protectionists concentrated most of their fire on the first proposal. The second did not restore the Irish electorate even to the size which it had been before the 40s. freeholder was disfranchised in 1829 as part of the Catholic Emancipation Act. The first proposal was far more radical. The 1832 Irish Reform Act, for which Stanley had been the responsible minister, had made the occupation franchise dependent on a long lease. In 1844 an abortive bill of Peel's government had proposed a £30 occupation franchise with or without lease. Stanley had supported that bill because of the high valuation.

---

[1] Gladstone memorandum of 27 February 1850. *ibid.* 44777, ff. 309–12.

[2] Aberdeen to Princess Lieven, 18 March 1850. Parry, *Correspondence of Aberdeen and Lieven*, ii, 421–2.

He was alarmed by Russell's bill which insisted on neither permanency of tenure nor profit above rent. In the English and Scottish franchises the amount of profit required increased as the length of tenure demanded diminished.[1]

Tory opposition to an extension of the Irish franchise traditionally issued from the fear that the forces of Irish nationalism would be strengthened, the Protestant Irish vote swamped, and the Union overthrown. The renewed political activity of the Catholic priesthood in the 1840s lent fresh urgency to the fear. In 1849, the Protectionists had opposed the government's scheme to change the Irish poor rate from a local to a national charge, arguing that it was 'a most preposterous idea to ask Protestant and industrious Ulster to pay for the poverty and improvidence of Catholic Munster'.[2] At the beginning of 1850, Stanley came to the defence of the Orange ascendancy when he castigated the government for relieving the Earl of Roden of his place on the Commission of the Peace for County Down, after Roden, the Grand Master of the Orange Lodge and Lord-Lieutenant of the county, had permitted an armed procession of 1,500 Protestants to march to his estate on the previous 12 July. On their return the Protestant marchers scuffled with some Ribbonmen, killing four and wounding thirty or forty. Stanley's defence of Roden tarnished his reputation for religious moderation.

Stanley's objection to extending the Irish franchise on the sole basis of rating was that that principle gave 'the whole preponderance to mere numbers over property, intelligence and independence, to Roman Catholic numbers over Protestant property'. He was, of course, being pushed by the extreme opinions of his followers. 'However little I may like to use this argument', he wrote to Aberdeen, 'I cannot overlook it.' Stanley would have liked to see the bill dropped altogether, since it had excited little interest in either England or Ireland.

If it be carried, I think it impossible that the Protestant Church in Ireland – I doubt whether the Union with Ireland – can be maintained; and a body of Representatives will be returned from Ireland of such a

[1] See Stanley to Aberdeen, 16 May 1850. Aberdeen Mss, Add. Mss 43072, ff. 146–54.
[2] Beresford to Stanley, undated. Derby Mss, 149/2.

description, and under such influence, that I firmly believe the last chance for the preservation of the Monarchy would lie in the repeal of the Union.[1]

But so great a reduction in the Irish constituency had taken place because of the impoverishment of the tenant farmers that the Peelites could not consent to oppose 'a bill which professes to remedy an evil universally admitted'.[2] Gladstone turned down Beresford's suggestion that he lead an outright opposition to the bill in the Commons,[3] and the bill passed, with the support of 19 Peelites and the abstention of the rest, by a majority of 254 to 186.

Aberdeen immediately started negotiations with Stanley about the possibility of an amendment to the bill in the Lords. There was a broad disposition among the Peelites to accept an amendment raising the franchise from £8 to £12. Graham had made a forthright declaration in the Commons of his preference for the higher valuation, and Gladstone and Goulburn had voted against £8 in committee. The Protectionists wanted the valuation raised to £15. When Aberdeen suggested that the Lords not divide on second reading and that both wings of the party combine in committee to raise the qualification to £12, Stanley, though he preferred £15, agreed to vote for the middle figure.[4] As Aberdeen pointed out, a £15 amendment would not gain Peelite support when it was sent to the Commons, whereas a £12 amendment was assured of success.[5] Stanley, however, was unable to restrain his followers. In July the Lords accepted the Earl of Desart's £15 amendment by a vote of 72 to 50. In the Commons a £12 amendment was passed and when it came up to the Lords, the Peelite peers abandoned the Protectionists and the bill was passed.

There were some Peelites who believed that their party ought

---

[1] Stanley to Aberdeen, 16 May 1850. Aberdeen Mss, Add. Mss 43072, ff. 146–54.

[2] Aberdeen to Stanley, 12 May 1850. Derby Mss, 135/7.

[3] Beresford to Gladstone, 19 April and 8 May 1850. Gladstone Mss, Add. Mss 44369, ff. 160–1, 186–7.

[4] Stanley to Aberdeen, 16 May 1850. Aberdeen Mss, Add. Mss 43072, ff. 146–54.

[5] Aberdeen to Stanley, 20 May 1850. Derby Mss, 135/7.

to have accepted the £15 amendment. Frederick Thesiger, a Peelite of marked anti-Catholic sensibilities who was moved by the franchise bill to write to Stanley for the first time, was 'struck with astonishment and almost with despair at the indifference and apathy with which this serious inroad upon the Constitution is regarded' and dismayed to see 'those to whom we should naturally look for guidance and support upon this critical occasion weigh, not the merits of the question, but its probable influence upon the continuance of the ministry'.[1] The Duke of Argyll also believed that it was the desire to keep the Whigs in which prevented the Peelites from accepting £15, and regretted that 'the fear of contributing to a mere Protectionist defeat of the Government is paralysing all the usual functions of opposition'.[2] But the Peelites had sound reasons for not going beyond £12. There was a difference between an increase in the electorate of 144,000 and 172,000, especially since the original bill would have increased it by 264,000. The £12 franchise did no more than bring the Irish vote into line with that established for England in 1832. If they were still Conservatives, the Peelites were not about to become reactionaries to prove it.

There were, moreover, the practical consequences of reunion to be considered. 'Measures, not men' argued Thesiger and Argyll. But if not Russell and free trade, what measures and which men? Until one or other of the Protectionists and the Peelites recanted on the tariff issue, combination to defeat the government was irresponsible mischief, since no basis existed on which to construct a new administration. All that had been achieved by five months' discussion was an increased cordiality between Stanley and Aberdeen and a demonstration of the earnestness with which each of them desired reunion.

On 29 September 1850, a papal brief proclaiming the restoration of the Catholic hierarchy in England, deposed since the Elizabethan settlement, sent Protestant temperatures soaring to a level they had not reached since the Gordon riots in 1780. On 7 October, Cardinal Wiseman, by then the week-old 'Archbishop

---

[1] Thesiger to Stanley, 7 March 1850. *ibid.* 152/8.
[2] Argyll to Aberdeen, 11 June 1850. Aberdeen Mss, Add. Mss 43199, ff. 1–4.

of Westminster', fanned the no-popery flames with his inaugural pastoral, which included the words, 'so that for the present, and till such time as the Holy See shall think fit otherwise to provide, we shall govern and continue to govern' the twelve sees created by the papal brief. English Protestants, frightened by the steady trickle of converts to Rome since Newman had crossed over in 1845, were in no mood to listen to Bishop Ullathorne's reasoned plea that Wiseman was speaking of spiritual governance only.[1] On 8 October *The Times* voiced the nation's hostility to 'papal aggression'. Guy Fawkes was scarcely to be seen on that 5 November, forgotten in the midst of what Lord Ashley called 'a storm over the whole ocean...a national sentiment, a rising of the land!'[2] Anglican and Nonconformist, Tory and Whig, joined together as English Protestants to denounce the innovation at meetings across the country. Russell had little choice but to announce the government's intention to resist an assault on the Reformation in a letter to the Bishop of Durham on 4 November.

Three weeks before the meeting of the 1851 session of parliament, Lord Redesdale sent an appraisal of the situation to Stanley.

The Government has a shell in the cabinet in the shape of this Popish affair ready to explode and blow them to pieces at any moment. If they are allowed to put the match out and make this shell harmless, they take in the new allies I have alluded to [those Peelites who were 'for taking a *very* liberal line'] and have a new lease with (very imperfectly) repaired premises. What we have to take care of is that the shell shall explode, and this requires careful management. We must not commit ourselves to any movement, or to any definite policy on this question... But while we keep ourselves clear we must hold the government tight to Lord John's letter. If we do this there must be a rumpus ...our line is to declare that we accept Lord John's letter as expressing the opinion and indicating the policy of the Government... and consequently await patiently the measures they intend to propose. This will put them in an awkward position among themselves, with their radical and popish allies... without embarrassing us in any way.[3]

---

[1] See the bishop's letter to *The Times*, 23 October 1850.
[2] Quoted in T. C. Edwards, 'Papal Agression: 1851', *History Today* (December 1951), 42–9.
[3] Redesdale to Stanley, 19 January 1851. Derby Mss, 149/6.

Stanley had already written to Lord Malmesbury that 'we should rather follow the stream, which is running quite strong enough, than attempt to take a lead of our own'.[1] Disraeli took Sir Robert Inglis under his wing 'to prevent his placing himself at the head of the low Church party',[2] and although Beresford stoked the Protestant embers in the country and Croker thundered against the Catholic Emancipation act in the *Quarterly Review*,[3] there was no resistance in the party to Stanley's decision not to press the government.

Parliament reassembled on 4 February. On 7 February the bill to forbid the assumption of territorial titles by the Catholic clergy was introduced. After a debate lasting four nights, prolonged by Irish and Radical opposition, the bill received a first reading of 395 votes to 63 on 14 February. Eight days later, having defeated a Protectionist motion for the relief of agricultural distress by only 13 votes and having suffered the indignity of seeing a Radical motion for the equalisation of the county and borough franchises pass a small House by 100 votes to 52, Russell and his government resigned. In the long run the papal aggression affair may have hurt the Protectionists by allowing – the ultra-Protestants to let off steam. Greville felt that had the Ecclesiastical Titles Bill not been passed, 'the effect would be to leave the question unsettled and to render a terrific No-Popery agitation the principal ingredient of a general election'.[4] In the short run the affair was disastrous for the Whigs. The Ecclesiastical Titles Bill undermined Russell's position. Twenty Irish Liberals voted with the Protectionists on Disraeli's agricultural distress motion.[5] At a great Radical meeting in Manchester on 23 January, all the speakers, including Cobden and Milner Gibson, announced their anger with a parliament which continued to squander public time and money on corn and Catholics.[6] Deeply disappointed by Russell's pandering to religious bigotry, and frustrated by his inability to tie the cabinet to fran-

---

1 Stanley to Malmesbury, 2 December 1850. Malmesbury, *Memoirs*, i, 267.
2 Disraeli to Stanley, 18 December 1850. Derby Mss, 145/1.
3 *Quarterly Review* (December 1850), 248.
4 Greville, iii, 400.
5 Whyte, *Independent Irish Party*, 22.
6 *Illustrated London News*, 1 February 1851.

chise reform and the repeal of taxes on knowledge, the Radicals turned out in force to support Locke King's motion for franchise equalisation, despite Russell's promise to bring in a bill of his own. Unable to carry on without Irish and Radical assistance, the government resigned.

So began a brief but involved ministerial crisis. 'In short', the Queen wrote, 'there *never* was *such* a *complicated* state of affairs.'[1] It appeared so to the royal couple partly because, ever since 1846, they had been eager to see the Peelites back in office, and the negotiations to form a new government revolved around the Peelites. 'Such was the confusion of the Ministerial movements, and political promenades', *Punch* commented when it was all over, 'that everybody went to call upon everybody.'[2] The confusion was chiefly in the minds of the Peelites. In outline the crisis is simple enough. On Russell's advice the Queen sent for Stanley on 23 February. Stanley told her that he could form a government only with the promise of a dissolution or junction with the Peelites, and advised the Queen to seek a Whig–Peelite government. On 24 February, the Queen informed Stanley that Russell was unable to come to an agreement with the Peelites, and on the following day, Stanley began his search for a government. Since the Queen would not promise him a dissolution, nor the Peelites join him, Stanley resigned the commission two days later, and the old Whig cabinet returned intact.

At the end of 1850, Disraeli had foreseen no immediate end to the fragmentation of political parties until large issues should again separate men into right and left.[3] In 1851 there were no such issues. The Peelites claimed that the Ecclesiastical Titles Bill was the bar to coalition with the Whigs,[4] which of course it was, but it is evident that they were not yet ready to cut the umbilical cord to the Conservative party, papal aggression or no papal aggression. Aberdeen deluded himself into thinking that he

---

[1] Queen Victoria to the King of the Belgians, 4 March 1851. Benson and Esher, ii, 380.

[2] *Punch*, 8 March 1851.

[3] Disraeli to Londonderry, undated. The Marchioness of Londonderry (ed.), *Letters from Benjamin Disraeli to Frances Anne, Marchioness of Londonderry, 1837–61* (London, 1938), 99.

[4] Prince Albert memorandum of 25 February 1851. Benson and Esher, ii, 361.

might have become prime minister but for his vote against the Ecclesiastical Titles Bill,[1] yet even before he saw Russell he wrote to Princess Lieven that he saw no tendency towards a Whig–Peelite coalition, and after hearing Russell's invitation to join him, he wrote to her that 'you will readily believe that I was not sorry to have such a reason for declining to do so, as was afforded me by the relation in which I stand to the Popery question'.[2] Graham made a deliberate appraisal of his incompatibility with the Whigs, that he could accept neither Palmerston nor a new reform bill.[3] Coalition would be fatal to exclusive Whiggery, but unless a Peelite were offered the leadership of a new government, Russell's proposals were, in the words of the Duke of Argyll, 'very like an invitation to join his crew from the captain of a sinking ship'.[4]

When Russell informed the Queen of his failure to woo the Peelites, she sent once more for Stanley. Again she refused Stanley's request for a dissolution, remembering her error in accepting Melbourne's advice to dissolve in 1841. Nor would the Peelites serve under Stanley. When the news of Russell's resignation reached the Duke of Newcastle (Lord Lincoln until January 1851), he wrote immediately to Graham advising no cooperation with Stanley on any terms. Newcastle thought independence the only honourable role for the Peelites.

I would make any sacrifice which would really serve the Queen and the country at this critical moment, but the Coalition would deprive us of all usefulness and leave the Queen eventually with no sincere friends to fall back upon.

Self-denial and a generous abnegation of all considerations but honour and patriotism are the great and distinguished duties which now devolve upon us.[5]

Graham, who was the most explicit in his rejection of the Whigs, was also farthest from the Protectionists. He told the Queen that

[1] Aberdeen to Arthur Gordon, undated. Lady Frances Balfour, *The Life of George, Fourth Earl of Aberdeen* (London, 1922), ii, 164.
[2] Aberdeen to Princess Lieven, 27 February 1851. Parry, *Correspondence of Aberdeen and Lieven*, ii, 549–50.
[3] Prince Albert memorandum of 23 February 1851. Benson and Esher, ii, 356.
[4] Dowager Duchess of Argyll, *Argyll Memoirs*, i, 432.
[5] Newcastle to Graham, 23 February 1851. Parker, *Graham*, ii, 129.

on the three great questions of his career, Catholic emancipation, reform, and the repeal of the Corn Laws, he had voted with
the Whigs, and that he looked to a closing of the ranks against
protection.[1]

On 26 February Stanley saw Gladstone and told him that
everything depended on his decision.[2] Gladstone heard Stanley
propose a duty of 5s. or 6s. on corn 'pretty much in silence but
with an intense sense of relief; feeling that if he had put protection in abeyance, I might have had a most difficult question to
decide, whereas now I had no question at all'. Nor did Aberdeen.
He did not 'pretend to understand the question of free trade, but
it was a point of honour with him not to abandon it, and now,
since Sir R. Peel's death, a matter of piety'.[3]

On 27 February, the Protectionists met at Stanley's London
residence to decide whether to form a purely Protectionist
government. Malmesbury wrote to Disraeli on the eve of the
meeting.

The question is an immense one, but it is restricted to one calculation.
1st, assuming, that we are defeated tomorrow by confessing ourselves
intellectually incapable of forming a government, 2nd, assuming, that
having formed one we propose our policy – financial – that we dissolve
– that we are beaten – that we go out. Which of the two defeats is
most humiliating and detrimental to *Stanley* personally, to *us* as a
Party?[4]

Malmesbury believed the former, but the party came to the
opposite conclusion. At the meeting at Stanley's house only
Malmesbury and Disraeli evinced any eagerness to take the high
risk. Disraeli has left an amusing account of the meeting.[5]
Henry Corry 'had not absolutely fainted, but had turned very
pale when the proposition was made to him of becoming a leading member of a Protectionist government'. Henley 'sat on a
chair against the dining-room wall, leaning with both his hands
on an ashen staff, and with the countenance of an ill-conditioned

---

[1] Prince Albert memorandum of 23 February 1851. Benson and Esher, ii, 356.
[2] Gladstone's account of this meeting is given in Morley, *Gladstone*, i, 406–7.
[3] Prince Albert memorandum of 23 February 1851. Benson and Esher, ii, 356.
[4] Malmesbury to Disraeli, 26 February 1851. Hughenden Mss, B/XX/Hs/8.
[5] Monypenny and Buckle, iii, 291–5.

Poor Law Guardian censured for some act of harshness. His black eyebrows, which met, deeply knit; his crabbed countenance doubly morose; but no thought in the face, only ill-temper, perplexity and perhaps astonishment'. Herries, who rushed in exclaiming 'What's all this?', 'was garrulous, and foresaw only difficulties'. Henley refused the Home Office and Herries the Exchequer. Stanley had a private conversation with Disraeli and announced that his attempt to form a government was at an end.

Beresford frantically rushed forward and took Lord Derby[1] aside, and said there were several men he knew waiting at the Carlton expecting to be sent for, and implored Lord Derby to reconsider his course. Lord Derby inquired impatiently, 'Who was at the Carlton?' Beresford said, 'Deedes'.

'Pshaw!' exclaimed Lord D. 'These are not names I can put before the Queen. Well, my Lords and gentlemen, I am obliged to you for your kind attendance here today; but the thing is finished. Excuse my leaving you, but I must write to the Queen at once.'

The meeting broke up with a good-humoured parting shot from a disappointed Lord Malmesbury: 'The best thing the Country party can do is go into the country. There is not a woman in London who will not laugh at us.'

Stanley made no overtures to Palmerston. There is no indication that he would have liked to, and after introducing a motion of censure against Palmerston just eight months before he was not in a position to do so. But, in a prescient note on the crisis, Peter Borthwick wrote that 'you may rely on this, that there is no combination of parties that can stand without Palmerston'.[2]

In the Lords, on 28 February, Stanley explained his failure to form a government on the embarrassing ground that his party 'though it no doubt comprises men of talent and intellect, yet contains within itself, I will not say no single individual, but hardly more than one individual of political experience and versed in political business'.[3] That was why the Peelites were so important to the Protectionist party. There were, nevertheless,

[1] Disraeli wrote the memorandum in the 1860s.
[2] Lucas, *Glenesk and the 'Morning Post'*, 72.
[3] *Hansard*, 3rd Series, cxiv, 1008. The unnamed individual was Herries.

other reasons for what Malmesbury called 'Stanley's failure of nerve'.[1] The Protectionists did not wish to become responsible for carrying out Russell's anti-papal policy. They had not contributed to the defeat of the Whig government and hence they felt no obligation to form one themselves. Since theirs would be a minority government, in order to command public support it needed to be acknowledged as the only possible government. In short, the conditions which made office inescapable in 1852 were absent in 1851.

Without a dissolution, Stanley could have held power only by renouncing protection, a course which would have broken up the party. The *Illustrated London News* congratulated Stanley on his discretion in words which pin-pointed the dilemma which lay at the very heart of the Protectionist party.

Lord Stanley is believed to be too wise a man to undertake a responsibility which would place him in a far more serious dilemma, publicly and privately, than ever beset any statesman of our time. He would either have explicitly to abandon protection and to maintain the free-trade policy, on which the country has set its heart, or he would have to re-impose a duty on corn. In the first place he would make so great a personal sacrifice as Sir Robert Peel made, without reaping the glory of the achievement, or gaining the gratitude of the country. He would be accounted a worse traitor to his party than that lamented statesman... In the second, and more improbable case, he would convulse the country.[2]

If those were the alternatives, how was Stanley ever to come into office? *The Times* lamented the absence of an 'Opposition convertible into a Government', an absence which left the country to suffer 'the negligence and imperfections of a Ministry as long as it acts... and the absolute paralysis of the State when it can act no longer'.[3]

There was one possible way out of the stalemate. To abandon protection while in opposition would bear less odium than to do so in order to come into office. Disraeli was eager to seize the

[1] Malmesbury, *Memoirs*, i, 278–9.
[2] *Illustrated London News*, 1 March 1851.
[3] G.H.L.Le May, 'The Ministerial Crisis of 1851', *History Today* (June 1951), 57.

opportunity which the failure to form a government afforded of letting down protection. He argued that a Protectionist government had been shown to be impossible: 'every man of experience and influence, however slight, had declined to act under Lord Derby unless the principle of protection were unequivocally renounced'.[1] But to follow Disraeli's suggestion was to forfeit the chance of a Protectionist victory at the polls. Russell had returned to power, as Greville wrote, 'damaged, weak, and unpopular'.[2] The Queen could not a second time refuse Stanley a dissolution if Russell should again be forced to resign. Stanley, who for four years had based his strategy on the hope of Conservative reunion, now turned his gaze towards the next election. The Peelites were becoming unfathomable, and by their stubborn and increasingly ineffectual independence were weakening their hold on the public mind. On 28 February Stanley announced in the Lords that his party stood for a 5s. duty on corn. Anything less would have thrown the party into disarray. Corn prices had not yet risen above 38s.; a 5s. duty would still leave the price of corn lower than Peel's 'reasonable price' of 44s. to 48s.

Gladstone and Greville both believed that Stanley would have let free trade be had it not been for pressure from his followers and a concern for personal consistency. Greville thought that Stanley was 'sick to death of his position as leader of the Protectionists'.[3] In the spring of 1851, however, Stanley was in better spirits than at any time since 1846. Far from interpreting his failure to form a government as evidence of the bankruptcy of protectionism, Stanley looked forward with excitement to an early entry into office. On 2 March Lord John Manners encouraged George Frederick Young to rally the country for the coming elections, starting with the next day's meeting of Young's National Association.

I have just left Lord Stanley and have his permission to say that you will be warranted in speaking the language of hope to the Delegates tomorrow. All in his opinion will depend upon the General Elections, which he thinks near at hand, as parties are so evenly balanced that no

[1] Monypenny and Buckle, iii, 296.   [2] Greville, iii, 389.   [3] *Ibid*. iii, 386–7.

Government can long command a majority in the present House of Commons.

Had it been July he would have run the risk of forming an Administration; but with a hostile majority to face, all the business of the Session to transact...he felt he should be damaging the cause and injuring the country if he persevered...

Animate the delegates therefore to action in their respective localities, and bid them select for candidates men of practical ability.[1]

Lord John Russell returned to office committed to a reform bill. Stanley looked upon the next elections as a struggle between conservatism and the forces of democracy. The mark of his new enthusiasm for politics was that for the first time he accepted the necessity of exploiting anti-Catholic feeling in the constituencies as a means of outbidding Liberalism. He expressed his new pugnacity in a letter to Croker on 22 March.

There is at the moment an utter break-up of all parties, except the Protectionists, who are, notwithstanding their recent disappointment, gradually consolidating themselves....

If I can consolidate with them the now awakened spirit of Protestantism, and at the same time keep the latter within reasonable bounds, I can go to the country with a strong war-cry, with which, indeed, *The Times* furnished me the other day, 'Protestantism, Protection, and down with the Income Tax'. But let our watchwords be what they may, the real struggle, the real battle of the Constitution which has to be fought is whether the preponderance, in the legislative power, is to rest with the land and those connected with it, or with the manufacturing interests of the country. If the former, the Throne is safe; if the latter, in my deliberate judgment, it is gone. How are we then to bring the masses of the electors to the support of the former rather than the latter alternative?

In my mind, among all its evils and all its dangers, the evocation of the Protestant spirit, which has been aroused, is not without its use. Even the most Radical towns...are so furiously anti-Papal, that that feeling will neutralise the cheap bread cry.[2]

As Lord Lonsdale noted with great pleasure, Stanley had 'recast his parts' and was 'ready for anything'.[3] For the first time since

[1] Manners to Young, 2 March 1851. Young Mss, Add. Mss 46712/3, packet 18.
[2] Stanley to Croker, 22 March 1851. Jennings, *Croker*, iii, 235–7.
[3] Lonsdale to Croker, 23 March 1851. *ibid.* iii, 239–40.

1846, Stanley wanted to defeat the government. If he could get the Whigs out before the end of the session they would not be able to dissolve on the issue of parliamentary reform. Instead, he would be able to dissolve as prime minister and might then be able to stem 'with temper and moderation...the Democratic tide which has been flowing of late with formidable rapidity'.[1]

On 2 April, Stanley gave a dinner at the Merchant Tailors' Hall for all the Protectionist peers and commoners. He delivered a speech which was splendidly calculated to unite the party and leave the doubters, like Disraeli and Henley, to wailing and gnashing of teeth. He began with a reference to the late ministerial crisis.

I come before you...not flushed with victory...I come before you after a temporary failure which I know must have inflicted on many of those whom I now address, not only disappointment on personal, but disappointment on public grounds...I must take [this meeting] as a... most distinguished mark of your continued adherence, together with me, to those principles which, even in the moments of greatest despondency, we have continued to cherish, and of the final triumph of which I am now as sanguine as ever.

Warming to his audience, Stanley repudiated his previous ban on anti-Peelite attacks and recalled to the party that twelve years before they had heard

the soundest lessons of Conservative policy – (cheers) – the soundest doctrines of attachment to our Protestant institutions and our Protestant constitution – and the most able vindication of the Protectionist policy, from the lips of the late Sir Robert Peel – (cheers).

He then denounced the 'unwarrantable' papal aggression and ended with a tribute to George Bentinck, without whose efforts, he said, the party would not have been in the proud and confident position in which it now found itself.

It is owing to his energy and courage in the first instance that this great party arose from its alarm and apprehension, and grew by no small degrees, but mainly by a steadfast yet temperate maintenance of its own principles of policy, to that position in which it is now placed,

---

[1] Stanley to Croker, 14 March 1851. *ibid*. iii, 231–3.

and in which, by the admission even of its opponents, it forms a minority dangerous at least to the ministers of the day.[1]

Aberdeen was pained to see Stanley place himself 'at the head of the party of bigotry and intolerance in this country',[2] and indeed the speech bore all the marks of a deliberate break with the Peelites. They were no longer quite the force they had been and Stanley had decided that, for the moment at least, they were not worth conciliating. They had not supported Disraeli's agricultural distress motion in February, and after the ministerial crisis, Malmesbury came to the conclusion that the Peelites would eventually join the Whigs.[3]

Malmesbury and Beresford had all along been trying to distract Stanley from his fixation with the Peelites. At last they appeared to have been successful. A tone of bitterness and disgust began to pervade Stanley's references to the Peelites. 'We have a majority in our hands, in Parliament and in the Country,' he wrote to Lord Lyndhurst, 'and a Government delivered over to us by their own weakness, but we cannot make use of it, because men essential to the formation of a Cabinet, and who can do nothing of themselves, will not yield to their own conviction of the ruin resulting from a course which they have been deceived into taking'.[4] Having given up on the Peelites, Stanley fell back on Protestant bigotry. Aristocratic ascendancy had somehow to be maintained.

The Protectionist party was well qualified to conduct a Protestant offensive. Forty-five of its members were also members of the National Club, with whom Stanley had now decided to cooperate. When Russell came back into office he dropped all but the preamble and the first clause from the Ecclesiastical Titles Bill. Stanley, who in February had told the Queen that he hoped the bill could be obviated by a mere parliamentary declaration of principle and the appointment of a committee to inquire into the

---

[1] *The Speech of the Right Honourable Lord Stanley at Merchant Tailors' Hall on Wednesday, April 2, 1851* (London, 1851).

[2] Aberdeen to Princess Lieven, 3 April 1851. Parry, *Correspondence of Aberdeen and Lieven*, ii, 566.

[3] Malmesbury to Stanley, undated. Derby Mss, 144/1.

[4] Stanley to Malmesbury, 15 February 1851 (copy). *ibid.* 179/1.

status of English Catholicism,[1] gave full rein to Frederick The-siger, a Peelite who returned to the Protectionists over the religious issue, to re-introduce all the penal clauses into the bill. In that form what proved to be an unenforceable act was passed.

On 11 April Disraeli introduced a resolution in the Commons calling upon the government to accept the principle that any readjustment of taxation must include the reduction of the charges upon land. The Protectionists failed by only 13 votes – one fewer than in February – to defeat the government. But the display of strength was deceptive. In the minority were 28 Irish 'Catholics' and 5 Whig protectionists, men who would be in the opposition to a Stanley government. Russell's majority in the Commons, on the basis of that division, was not 13 but 79. There was thus much ground to be made up in an election.

In the first week of May, Stanley felt that the government would not last the session, and he had made up his mind 'at all hazards' to form a government when the Whigs fell.[2] Joseph Hume's motion to limit the income tax to one year instead of three had been carried against the government by a vote of 244 to 230, causing Greville to remark that 'there seems no doubt that Protection has raised many adherents of late, and that in the event of a dissolution most of the counties and agricultural boroughs will return Protectionists'.[3] But Stanley's hopes that the elections would take place that summer under his premier-ship were dashed on the rocks of Protectionist disunion and mismanagement. On 10 May, Urquhart's motion charging the government with having encouraged the papal aggression was beaten by 79 votes, when the 45 members of the National Club voted with the government, according to Malmesbury 'from their foolish dislike of Disraeli and Mr. Beresford'.[4] Had those Protectionists voted with the rest of the party the government would have been in a minority of over 40. Stanley was distressed by the want of communication between the leaders in the Commons and the backbenchers. It was apparently not understood by

[1] Prince Albert memorandum of 25 February 1851. Benson and Esher, ii, 356.
[2] Stanley to Lyndhurst, 5 May 1851. Lyndhurst Mss, ff. 129–30.
[3] Greville, iii, 406.
[4] Malmesbury, *Memoirs*, i, 284.

the members of the National Club that Urquhart's motion was not intended to deflect the course of the Ecclesiastical Titles Bill through the Commons. 'In the absence of such an understanding', Stanley wrote, 'I am not surprised at the result, however I may regret that an opportunity was lost of striking a party blow, which may not recur this session.[1] On 5 June, Thomas Baring's motion to prohibit the adulteration of coffee by chicory was lost by 5 votes when several Protectionists voted with the government. Two days later, Walpole introduced a motion to stiffen the wording of the preamble to the Ecclesiastical Titles Bill, which was defeated because the Protectionist backbenchers did not know what was up and left early. That 'bungle', as Stanley called it, revealed 'a want of power, among our leaders in the H. of Commons, of controlling and conducting a debate, which has deprived them of authority and confidence'.[2]

None of these matters was sufficient by itself to bring down the government, but Russell had resigned on a minor question in February, and a series of regular defeats at the hands of an obstructionist opposition might have forced his hand again. What consequences the postponement of the elections until the summer of 1852 had for the Protectionists is guesswork. But it may at least be noted that by then agricultural prices were at last starting to rise again, and that in 1851 the conversion of some prominent men, Gladstone's friend James Hope and Archdeacon Manning among them, in addition to the almost daily spotlight on the Ecclesiastical Titles Bill, sustained the anti-Catholic fever at a pitch higher than a year later. Then too, the disagreement between Stanley and Disraeli over the Corn Law issue was much more concealed in 1851 than it was in 1852.

George Cornewall Lewis summed up a session which was barren of legislation except for the Ecclesiastical Titles Bill.

Of the three parties, the Government was on the whole the *least* damaged by the session. The Peelites made themselves unpopular by their line on the Anti-Papal Bill. As they had not, as a party, distinguished themselves by any particular love of religious equality, their conduct was referred partly to a love of Catholicism, partly to faction.

---

[1] Stanley to Freshfield, 21 June 1851 (copy). Derby Mss, 179/1.
[2] Stanley to Croker, 7 June 1851 (copy). *ibid.*

The Protectionists were weakened by various blunders...also by their ambiguous language on the subject of Protection...My belief is, that if they come in, they would only temporize.[1]

In the autumn of 1851, the division in the party over commercial policy came once more into the open. At Aylesbury on 17 September and at Salt Hill on 7 October, Disraeli gave his opinion that a return to protection would require 'an almost universal feeling in the country' in its favour and that, especially since the 1851 harvest was a good one, the question was therefore not one of practical politics.[2] Since June, Edward Stanley, now the heir to the Derby Earldom, to which Stanley had succeeded in June, had been preaching the line that the working classes were enjoying unprecedented prosperity under free trade.[3] In Oxfordshire, Henley advised the farmers not to listen to the false prophets who promised them a return to protection.[4] All this was gall and wormwood to Lord Granby who resigned his position as one of the three Commons' leaders because he felt himself placed in a false position. He did not deny that Disraeli's schemes might afford relief to the landed interest, but '2 systems are before the world – England has to choose between them'.[5] Disraeli's position, of course, was that England had already chosen. Herries did not resign his share in the leadership, but he assured Granby that he would not be led by anyone 'out of the straight path' of protection.[6] The cracks in Protectionist unity which had been papered over in 1849 were once more exposed.

At the end of 1851, the Protectionists appeared to be no closer to power than they had been at the beginning of the year. Then an event long delayed, but pregnant with possibilities for the future, crashed upon the political world. After two years of haggling with the Court, Russell, under fire for Palmerston's hasty and imprudent, though unofficial, recognition of Louis

[1] Lewis to Head, 1 September 1851. Lewis, *Letters of Lewis*, 239–43.
[2] Monypenny and Buckle, iii, 309–10.
[3] W.B. Ferrand to Disraeli, 8 June 1851. Hughenden Mss, B/XXI/F/126.
[4] Beresford to Derby, undated. Derby Mss, 149/3.
[5] Granby to Derby, 13 September 1851. *ibid*. 150/314.
[6] Herries to Granby, October 1851 (draft). Herries Mss, NRA/80.

Napoleon's *coup d'état*, dismissed his foreign secretary on 19 December. 'The long postponement of this wise and necessary decision', Graham wrote to Aberdeen, 'has been most unfortunate. The state of parties and of affairs would have been widely different if it had been taken earlier.'[1] In September, Graham's chief reason for turning down Russell's offer of a place in the government had been his dislike for Palmerston's bellicose foreign policy.[2] Palmerston's removal smoothed the path to Whig–Peelite junction, but if Peter Borthwick were right in saying that no combination could stand without Palmerston, was there any longer good reason to join the Whigs?

Palmerston's fall held, therefore, a mixed significance for the Protectionists. Although the Peelites might now be lost for ever, there was perhaps a brighter prize to be won. Palmerston was known to be firmly opposed to a second reform bill; he had threatened to resign rather than acquiesce in one in 1850–1. The Protectionists may have made too much of Palmerston's opposition to total repeal in 1846, but he was, at least, not bound by considerations of personal consistency to a permanent adherence to free trade. On domestic matters, Palmerston was an unimaginative conservative who could feel quite at home in the Protectionist party. If, on the other hand, he remained outside the party, he was a constant threat to Derby because he appealed to the same body of moderate opinion as Derby did, but was a much more popular figure. Like Derby, he wished to attract the support of those 'fair, calm, sensible persons who have something to lose, who have no intention of losing it, who hate change, who love improvements, who *will* be ruled in a manner they understand'.[3] If, moreover, Palmerston could be persuaded to take the lead in the Commons, then the continuing difficulty of Disraeli's standing with many Protectionists could be overcome.

Palmerston's dismissal meant that Russell had either to gain Peelite accessions to his government or fall. Unofficial soundings of the Peelites in January 1852, revealed that Russell could expect no help from that quarter. Russell was thus left in too

[1] Graham to Aberdeen, 25 December 1851. Parker, *Graham*, ii, 143.
[2] *Ibid*. ii, 144.
[3] *The Economist* on the death of Palmerston, 28 October 1865.

precarious a position to carry reform and income-tax proposals through the Commons, and the end of what turned out to be the last purely Whig government was at hand. It came on a minor point of what had become a major issue. Russell introduced a bill to establish a regular, local militia, and on 20 February Palmerston's amendment to make it a national force passed by 135 votes to 126. On the next day the Whig ministers resigned.

8

OFFICE AND DEFEAT

THE FALL of the Whig government was caused, not by an important national event, nor by a noticeable shift in public opinion, but by the disintegration of the liberal elements inside the House of Commons. There were no signs of a wave of popular enthusiasm for the Protectionist party or its policy. In the Commons the party remained a minority. For Derby, nevertheless, the situation was significantly different from that created by Russell's resignation a year earlier. This time he could not refuse the Queen's commission to form a government. The vote on the Militia Bill was a far more decisive defeat for the Whigs than the one on the Radical reform bill, and without Palmerston the Whigs could not carry on. In 1851, Derby had advised the Queen to look to him only as a last resort because the necessity for a new government had not been shown. In 1852 that necessity was obvious.

Derby received the news of the government's resignation at Badminton, in a letter from Disraeli urging him to form a strong government by bringing in Palmerston as leader in the House of Commons.[1] Two months earlier Disraeli had ridiculed the idea that Palmerston might join the Protectionists, but now he thought that since Palmerston had been responsible for the defeat of the government and had placed himself in an isolated position, he might be induced to work with Derby. Disraeli's willingness to sacrifice his own ambition deeply impressed Derby.

Whatever may be the issue of the present crisis, or the details of the arrangements consequent upon it, I shall never forget the generous self-sacrifice offered by the note which I received by Mackenzie at Badminton this morning. While I am sure that every instance of the kind tends to raise the character of public men generally, I am equally convinced that each case, even if the offer be accepted, must ultimately

[1] Disraeli to Derby, 20 February 1852. Monypenny and Buckle, iii, 342.

redound to the credit and advantage of the man who makes it from public motives.[1]

Disraeli's repeated offers to stand down in order to make way for a Peelite or Palmerston, unless interpreted as calculated insincerity, provide a corrective to the view that Disraeli was motivated solely by the desire to get to the top of the greasy pole.

At the beginning of 1852, politicians of all shades, except the Manchester Radicals, were held by fears of the military ambitions of the Emperor Louis Napoleon. When Derby saw the Queen on 22 February, he told her that in view of the uncertainty about the Emperor's intentions an immediate dissolution was inadvisable, and that in order to strengthen his following in the Commons he wished her permission to negotiate with Palmerston. The Queen, though downcast by the prospect of Palmerston's early return to office, granted it.[2] Derby offered Palmerston the Exchequer and the lead in the Commons, but was turned down. Palmerston told Derby that he could not accept the offer to join a government which would make protection an 'open question': he had always been in favour of a small fixed duty on corn, had fought for that compromise in 1846, 'but it was too late to think of such things in 1852'.[3] To his brother, Palmerston gave a more deep-seated explanation of his decision, that he would better serve his own interests by remaining available to the Whigs.

After having acted for twenty-two years with the Whigs, and after having gained by, and while acting with, them any little political reputation I may have acquired, it would not answer nor be at all agreeable to me to go slap over to the opposite camp, and this merely on account of a freak of John Russell's which the whole Whig party regretted and condemned...and though I should be conscious that I am wanting in many of the requisite qualifications for the post of Prime Minister, yet I think, on the whole, my deficiencies are not greater than those of Derby and John Russell, or of any other person who at present could be chosen for such a duty.[4]

[1] Derby to Disraeli, 21 February 1852. *ibid*. iii, 342–3.
[2] Prince Albert memorandum of 22 February 1852. Benson and Esher, ii, 449.
[3] Monypenny and Buckle, iii, 344.
[4] Palmerston to W. Temple, 30 April 1852. Ashley, *Palmerston*, i, 336–41.

Palmerston's decision left Derby to construct a cabinet from among those persons whose ability he had, in 1851, contrasted so unfavourably with that of the Peelites. The only members of the new government who had previous cabinet experience were Derby himself, Herries, who took the board of trade, and Lord Lonsdale, who became lord president of the council. None of the others was a privy councillor, a circumstance which allowed Disraeli to describe their receiving the seals of office in *Endymion* as 'a spectacle never seen before and which in all probability will never be seen again'. Malmesbury recorded in his memoirs that, but for the accident that in 1844 he had published the diplomatic journal and correspondence of his grandfather, he 'should have been so great a novice in political business as were most of my colleagues'.[1] Disraeli became the chancellor of the exchequer, Malmesbury was given the foreign office, Spencer Walpole the home office, and Sir John Pakington the colonial office. The new ministry quickly became known as the 'who, who' ministry, after the near-deaf Duke of Wellington asked that question as the name of each new appointment was read in the House of Lords.

Disraeli's appointment raised the most criticism. The *Edinburgh Review*, which affected to see in Disraeli only 'meretricious glitter, overwhelming presumption, open disregard of principle, innate vulgarity... and utter absence of earnestness and truth', called his high appointment 'one of the most startling domestic events that have occurred in our time'.[2] Perhaps no man ever reached so high a place in parliament without having won the confidence of his colleagues. As Herbert Paul wrote, 'it is easier to assume that he was a man of genius than to account for him without the assumption'.[3] It was thought remarkable to combine the chancellorship of the exchequer with the leadership in the Commons. Since 1830 only Lord Althorp had combined the two jobs. But Herries had refused the exchequer in 1851, and Thomas Baring refused it in 1852. After them, Disraeli was the logical choice, and his appointment may be seen as a mark of the

[1] Malmesbury, *Memoirs*, i, 41.
[2] *Edinburgh Review* (January 1853), 421.
[3] H. Paul, *A History of Modern England* (London, 1904), i, 246.

increased importance of the office, previously considered to be departmentally inferior to the office of first lord of the treasury. It is, nevertheless, somewhat mystifying that, by placing Henley at the board of trade, Derby chose to give to the most outspoken free traders in the party the two critical financial and commercial posts.

Otherwise, the cabinet was composed of staunch protectionists, including in the persons of Derby, Salisbury, and Lonsdale, three of the country's richest landowners. G. F. Young declined the offer of the vice-presidency of the board of trade because of poor health. His cohort, Robert Christopher, was made chancellor of the Duchy of Lancaster, a non-cabinet position, and when Delane suggested to Disraeli that he be ignored as the crotchety Duke of Buckingham had been by Peel, Disraeli replied that 'it was very well to deal with one Duke of Buckingham, but in our Cabinet we have six Dukes of Buckingham'.[1] The cabinet was also exclusively Protestant, because, as Derby explained, there were no Roman Catholic supporters of the Protectionist party.[2]

Inexperienced and narrowly based as the government was, predictions that it would last for only a few weeks ignored a number of factors which held out the prospect of a longer life. The Liberal opposition was enfeebled by its division into Palmerston and Russell factions, the former including a handful of chauvinistic Radicals and those conservative Whigs, like Lord Lansdowne, for whom Russell's reform opinions were too advanced. Palmerston showed his friendliness towards the new government by placing himself at Malmesbury's service and by rebuffing Russell's attempt at reconciliation early in March. The Irish Radicals, while not expecting any plums from the Protectionists, would not vote them out merely to put Russell back in power. Only the Manchester men and the Grey–Russell Whigs favoured outright opposition from the start.

The success or failure of the government hung, of course, on the attitude of the Peelites. No longer an organised body with

[1] Gladstone memorandum of 12 March 1852. Gladstone Mss, Add. Mss 44778, ff. 1–4.
[2] Derby to Lambert, 25 March 1852 (copy). Derby Mss, 180/1.

an acknowledged leader, they yet possessed the ability, rare in English history, with its persistent tendency towards a two-party system, of deciding which major party should hold office. There had been some Peelite defections to the Protectionists, a process reflected in the shrinking Whig majorities of 1850 and 1851. But there is no evidence that the defectors were receiving the whip from either major party. C. H. Stuart cautions us against ascribing to the Peelites weight as a third party which was not theirs,[1] but their weight was that of forty to fifty men who had not yet made up their mind. Being unorganised, their behaviour was difficult to predict. Clarendon called them 'a little band of conceited colonels without general officers and no rank and file',[2] and Gladstone knew that they must soon join one party or the other or else earn 'Burke's description of the independent gentlemen as those on whom nobody can depend'.[3]

After their refusal to join him in 1851, Derby did not approach the Peelites when forming his government, but at the beginning of 1852 it still seemed probable that most of them would rejoin the Protectionists once the Corn Laws passed out of politics. Graham was certainly strongly inclined towards the Whigs, but in March he divorced himself from the Peelites by espousing the extension of the franchise in a speech at Carlisle. Gladstone informed him that party connexion between them was at an end.[4] Graham's antecedents were Whig and, now that Peel was gone, he felt uneasy among the Conservatives. It was easier for him to return to the Whig cradle than it was for most of the Peelites to set upon a Liberal career. Aberdeen looked to a future junction with the Whigs, but Gladstone, Herbert, Newcastle, and Goulburn still dreamed of a Conservative reunion.[5]

[1] C. H. Stuart, 'The Formation of the Coalition Cabinet of 1852', *Transactions of the Royal Historical Society*, 5th Series (1954), 48.

[2] Clarendon to Cornewall Lewis, 10 November 1851. Maxwell, *Clarendon*, i, 328.

[3] Stuart, 'Coalition Cabinet', *op. cit.* 49.

[4] Gladstone to Graham, 27 March 1852 (copy). Gladstone Mss, Add. Mss 44163, ff. 55–6.

[5] Gladstone memoranda of 25, 26, 27, and 28 February and 12 March 1852. Gladstone Mss, Add. Mss 44778, ff. 1–20; Redesdale to Derby, 6 February 1852: 'I think it right to mention to you a conversation which Nelson reported to me he had with Newcastle...the Duke told him that he and his friends had refused the

The fear of democracy and of French military ambition might draw the Conservatives defensively together.[1] Malmesbury could not understand why the Peelites would not serve in any ministry, since they were unable to govern by themselves,[2] but the explanation was simple: they were Conservatives, but free traders, free traders, but not Liberals. The Peelites wanted, as Herbert told Malmesbury in 1850, the 'unfortunate delusion that Protection could be restored' cleared away so that the Conservatives could cooperate 'on social and political matters which are far more important to the vitality of this country'.[3] In March 1852, Herbert still saw 'the materials, both in men and in measures, for a sound and practical Government, if the men do not get so bespattered in this transition from Protection to Free Trade opinions' and was 'for giving them every facility and every bridge to cross over without a taunt or reproach'.[4] Gladstone too, suspicious of the attitude that party ties were of little importance in maintaining confidence in the House of Commons, was loath to dissolve his connexion with the Conservatives.[5] In February 1852, then, the main body of the Peelites was disposed to give the Protectionist government a fair trial.

On 27 February, Lord Campbell met Derby in the robing room just before Derby was to make his first ministerial statement in the Lords and wished him joy. Derby replied that he was 'much

---

offers of the Whigs and had hoped that this being known matters might be smoothed for a reconciliation of the various members of the old conservative policy, but that he feared your speech on the point of protection had been too strong' (Derby Mss, 149/6).

[1] George Hope, a Peelite who had remained close to Derby after 1846, wrote to him on 12 December 1851: 'The accomplishment of a military revolution in France and the near approach of what Mr. Bright calls a parliamentary one in this country, wake one up to look about, with what light one has, however little it may be, to see what our position is...whether...the Conservative party is to remain divided not only about some things, but about all, and because it cannot agree about everything, is to agree about nothing' (Derby Mss, 134/1).

[2] Malmesbury, *Memoirs*, i, 278.

[3] *Ibid.* i, 257.

[4] Herbert to Gladstone, 30 March 1852. Stanmore, *Herbert*, i, 150; Herbert to his wife, 22 March 1852. *ibid.* i, 148.

[5] Morley, *Gladstone*, i, 405.

more to be pitied than congratulated'.[1] To defend protection in 1852 was an unenviable task. Derby was forced to do so because, as he told Malmesbury, 'to take office as a Protectionist and then spontaneously to abandon the principle of Protection would involve a degree of baseness from the imputations of which I would have hoped that my antecedents (to borrow a French expression) might have relieved me'.[2] In the Lords Derby denounced Russell's proposals to lower the franchise to £5 in the towns and £20 in the counties: incalculable injury was done to the monarchy and to the 'real and true liberties' of the country by constantly 'unsettling everything and settling nothing'. He then proceeded to give a full-blooded defence of protection as a principle, but announced that the government would not tamper with the existing commercial system until the electorate had been given a chance to express its opinion on the matter.[3] Thus was initiated the awkward, muddled course of declaring for protection in principle without carrying it out in practice. *The Economist* warned Derby that the country would protest against 'so unstatesmanlike a proceeding'.[4]

Two weeks later Derby laid down in the Lords the basis on which the Protectionists would appeal to the country at the elections, which he promised to call before the 1853 session.

Will you Protectionists and Free Traders, all you who desire the advantages of all the interests of the country, place your confidence in, and give your support to, a government which, in the hour of peril, did not hesitate to take the post of danger when the helmsman left the helm? Will you support a government which is exerting itself to protect the country against any hostile attack, to maintain the peace of the world, to maintain and uphold the Protestant institutions of the country... to supply some barrier against the current of that continually increasing and encroaching democratic influence in this nation, which is bent on throwing the whole power and authority of government nominally into the hands of the masses, but practically and really into those of demagogues and republicans... a Government which is

---

[1] The Hon. Mrs Hardcastle, *The Life of John, Lord Campbell* (London, 1881), ii, 303.

[2] Malmesbury, *Memoirs*, i, 299.

[3] *Hansard*, 3rd Series, cxix, 871–906.

[4] *The Economist*, 28 February 1852.

determined to resist that noxious and dangerous influence and to preserve inviolate the prerogatives of the Crown, the rights of your Lordships' house, and the liberties of a freely elected and freely represented House of Commons?[1]

That was a bland statement to serve as a party manifesto, but Derby had given up hope for a Protectionist majority and was appealing for a Conservative one. Privately he had confided to the Queen that protection was beaten; publicly 'he could not with honour or credit abandon that Measure unless the country had given its decision against it'.[2]

Disraeli's conscience was less tender. In April he presented a provisional budget, not really a budget at all, but a statement of his financial principles. The Queen wanted the £2,000,000 surplus left untouched in case of foreign difficulties, and changes in the taxation system had to be postponed until the report of the 1851 committee on the income tax had been received. Nevertheless, Disraeli took the opportunity to counteract what he considered to be the imprudently rigid protectionism of Derby's ministerial statement of 27 February.[3] His theme was that the gradual elimination of customs duties and excise taxes over the previous decade left direct taxation as the only means of raising the revenue, and the implication that he considered protection to be obsolete was strengthened by his quoting figures to show that, thanks to increased imports, the treasury had not suffered from the reduction of duties on timber, coffee, and sugar. The consequence was that direct taxation must be embraced wholeheartedly. 'The government of the country deem it their duty to denounce as most pernicious to all classes of this country the systematic reduction of indirect taxation, while at the same time you levy direct taxes from a very limited class.' Disraeli enunciated two principles of direct taxation: that it should be as nearly universal in its incidence as indirect taxation, and that it should be assessed at different rates on permanent and temporary incomes.

That was stern stuff for a party which for a generation and

---

[1] 15 March 1852. *Hansard*, 3rd Series, cxix, 1010.
[2] Prince Albert memorandum of 22 March 1852. Benson and Esher, ii, 465–6.
[3] For Disraeli's speech see *Hansard*, 3rd Series, cxxi, 9–36.

more had fulminated against the income tax and which had accepted it from Peel in 1842 only on the understanding that it was to be a temporary expedient. Palmerston found Disraeli's argument 'excellent, well-arranged, clear and well-delivered',[1] but Derby, who from his seat in the gallery heard someone call the speech 'the eulogy of Peel by Disraeli', was disconsolate, and wrote chastisingly to Disraeli.

On the whole I cannot but say that I should have listened with far more pleasure to your statement had I been able to shut my eyes and persuade myself that I was listening to Charles Wood congratulating the country on the eminent success of his financial policy and encouraging the country to persevere in and extend it, exaggerating its advantages and passing lightly over its injurious consequences.[2]

Disraeli had placed the party in an embarrassment from which it would be difficult to escape. If the Protectionists became converts to free trade, they would be 'justly stigmatised as imposters who have obtained office under false pretences'; but not to do so after Disraeli's speech was humiliating. Eight days after Disraeli's financial statement, Derby tried to mend the fences by speaking veiledly of 'mutual concessions and mutual compromises', at a Mansion House banquet.[3] But the damage could not be repaired. When Lord John Russell reviewed the session on the eve of the elections, he charged the government with going to the country without a policy, since Disraeli had found 'a critic, a commentator and an adversary' in Lord Derby.[4]

It was, indeed, a Janus Protectionist party which fought the elections of the summer of 1852. While most of the Protectionists held by their principles, the two cabinet ministers responsible for commercial policy, Disraeli and Henley, stated in the election addresses that there was no chance of the country's going back on free trade. Derby had said almost as much in the House of Lords. Late in May he reported to the Queen that accounts from the country had revealed so strong a feeling against a small fixed duty that 'in the Debate last night he felt himself called upon

---

[1] Palmerston to W. Temple, 30 April 1852. Ashley, *Palmerston*, i, 336–41.
[2] Monypenny and Buckle, iii, 366.
[3] *Ibid.* iii, 367.
[4] 14 June 1852. *Hansard*, 3rd Series, cxxii, 636.

publicly to state, that while his opinions remained unaltered, he had no expectation that a majority would be returned at the General Election which would warrant his proposing it'.[1] The result was that there was no way of knowing whether the return of a Protectionist meant the return to Protection. In the 1852 elections, Derby's reputation suffered, not from giving the electorate a clear policy of a small duty on corn, but from giving it no policy at all. He placed himself in the ridiculous position of asking the country to supply the policy.

Of course, as a peer, Derby was prevented by constitutional tradition from interfering directly in the elections. There was still no national party programme to which to tie candidates. And it is clear that Derby did not want Conservatism to be dragged down by protection. But his equivocation meant that there was no way to interpret the implication of a Conservative majority for future tariff policy, which Derby claimed was the significance of the elections, and it earned him the contempt of his opponents. The gravest charge against Derby, made by the *Edinburgh Review*, was that he had reduced the elections to a mere contest for place.

An abstract entity was formed called Derbyism; and the persons initiated into the mysteries and hidden doctrines to it were called Derbyites...Lord Derby, with a gracious smile, says to the country: 'Pray have the kindness to give me a policy!' The agricultural and Protectionist constituencies make him a low bow and say: 'We place unlimited confidence in your Lordship's administration.' This operation may prove the good breeding and excellent manners of the English people, but we do not perceive...that Protectionist electors have given their confidence to any set of principles or for any other purpose than that of keeping a given set of men in office.[2]

Derby had made the resistance to democratic republicanism and Church disestablishment part of his 'programme', but in the settled atmosphere of 1852 such a promise carried little weight.

In these circumstances the elections excited no more interest than they had in 1847. Only 212 of the 374 constituencies were

---

[1] Derby to Queen Victoria, 25 May 1852 (copy). Derby Mss, 180/2.
[2] *Edinburgh Review* (October 1852), 530.

contested, mostly the boroughs; even in the boroughs the turn-out was consistently lower than 50 per cent. Derby's prediction that the government would receive a majority, though not for protection, proved fanciful, but a precise calculation of party standings after the elections is impossible. For one thing, who were Peelites and where they should be placed were almost in-soluble questions. Gladstone, Young, and Bonham pored over lists and corresponded at length in late July and August, but were unable to agree how large the Peelite group was or who comprised it. Bonham gave Gladstone a 'generally accurate' figure for the elections of 313 declared opponents of the govern-ment and 288 Derbyites; in addition there were 50 Peelites, of varying degrees of hostility to the government, but on none of whom Derby could rely.[1] Young was more pessimistic. He divided the free-trade Conservatives into 31 Peelites and 28 Derbyites, and added that only 20 of the former would follow Gladstone, Herbert, and Newcastle if they joined the Whigs.[2] Little more can be said than that the Peelites were little affected by the elections and remained about 40 strong. That was enough to deprive Derby of a dependable Conservative majority.

Before the elections, Young reckoned the Protectionists at about 280.[3] After the elections, Derby estimated the number to be 310, a more realistic estimate than Disraeli's 330.[4] The *Illus-trated London News* diffidently divided the Commons into 312 ministerialists, 325 opponents of the government, and 18 doubt-fuls, but added that since issues had not been prominent at the elections the figures were no real guide to the temper of the new House.[5] Their figures and Derby's included the Peelites among the ministerialists. As before the elections, then, every-thing depended upon the Peelites.

The government had failed to gain a majority and the obvious reason why was that there was no reason why they should have. They maintained their hold on the English and Welsh counties,

---

[1] Bonham to Gladstone [29 July 1852], Gladstone. Mss, Add. Mss 44110, ff. 230–1.

[2] Young to Gladstone, 10 August 1852. *ibid*. 44237, ff. 211–14.

[3] Young to Gladstone, 6 May 1852. *ibid*. 44232, ff. 203–4.

[4] 16 December 1852. *Hansard*, 3rd Series, cxxiii, 1699; Greville, iii, 459.

[5] *Illustrated London News*, 6 November 1852.

but made only slight gains in the towns. The Conservatives won 145 borough seats to the opposition's 234. The Protectionist failure may in part be attributed to the inefficiency of the party's electoral machinery and in part to the irrelevance of an anti-democratic appeal. Derby's association of his party with the defence of the constitution, though sincere, was a weak attempt to divert attention from the tariff issue. Russell had done nothing since January 1852 to encourage Radicalism and Radicalism by itself was too weak to achieve anything. Inside the Commons it was divided into colonial, financial, and franchise reformers, and outside it was almost non-existent. Working-class energies were beginning to be devoted to the organisation of trade unions and the establishment of educational associations. Bonham's analysis of the election returns did not distinguish between Whigs and Radicals because the distinction was too fine. No one suspected the Whigs of democratic zeal; Russell's reform proposals were treated with an easy tolerance by his colleagues. Aberdeen remarked that an anti-democratic cry might have been effectual in France 'but we have nothing here to fear in this respect',[1] and the *Edinburgh Review* mocked the Protectionists for offering themselves as 'a safeguard against unreal dangers'.[2]

Many Protectionists considered Protestant fears of popery to be their strongest card, but the evidence for anti-Catholic influence on the results is inconclusive. In May the Protectionist member for Warwickshire, Spooner, demanded an inquiry into the Maynooth grant, and Walpole's reply suggested that the government might be willing to conduct such an inquiry. But at the elections, ministerial candidates in Ireland canvassed in defence of the Maynooth grant.[3] George Cornewall Lewis attributed his defeat in Herefordshire to the joint action of Protectionist bribery and false rumours circulated by the Anglican clergy that he had turned Roman Catholic, but for four years his free-trade opinions had been attacked by the farmers in his constituency and he told Greville privately that he was beaten on the commercial

[1] Aberdeen to Princess Lieven, 31 May 1852. Parry, *Correspondence of Aberdeen and Lieven*, ii, 627–8.

[2] *Edinburgh Review* (April 1852), 586.

[3] See 'The Government and the Elections', *Fraser's Magazine* (July 1852), 112–26.

issue.[1] In Middlesex, the Radical, Bernal Osborne, withstood both the Marlborough fortune and placards put out by the evangelical party calling him the 'Leader of the Pope's Brass Band' to defeat the Protectionist Lord Blandford. While the Protectionists concentrated on Osborne's liberal religious record, Osborne reminded the electors of the real issue.

Don't believe what has been told you by the old Tory gang, who, being short of a cry at the present election, have dug out of its grave...the old ghost of the 'No Popery' cry. It is not the Pope; it is bread, it is tea, it is sugar – it is your beef that is in question.[2]

In Scotland, where neither the Church of England nor the Protectionist party could claim a monopoly of anti-Maynooth sentiment, the Protectionists won only 16 of the 30 county seats and none of the boroughs.

The Protectionist party was unable to compensate for its intellectual effeteness with a smooth-running organisation. Information about the party's electoral machinery is slight, although the very poverty of references to it in the Disraeli and Derby Papers is evidence of its own. Not until the fall of the government opened up the prospect of a long spell in opposition did Malmesbury, Disraeli, and Stanley set about re-organising the party, at Malmesbury's urging.

I cannot refrain from urging on you [he wrote to Disraeli in January 1853], before we begin a new lease of Opposition, the absolute necessity of reforming our personnel and getting matters into an administrative form...Had you twice the talent and eloquence you possess, you could do nothing...It is better to fail in orators to back you by words than in men to back you by votes. *We lost the Elections from bad management* and are out in consequence.[3]

One of the first steps was to replace Beresford and Newdegate as party whips, but, although Beresford was sufficiently out of touch to forecast the election of 339 Derbyites in 1852 as a conservative estimate,[4] he was not so much to blame for the dismal state

---

[1] Lewis, *Addresses and Speeches*, 58–61; Greville, iii, 463–4.
[2] Bagenal, *Life of Osborne*, 126–31.
[3] Malmesbury to Disraeli, 12 January 1853. Hughenden Mss, B/XX/Hs/29.
[4] Beresford to Disraeli, undated. *ibid.* B/XX/Bd/87.

of affairs as his enemies claimed. Beresford's appeals to Derby to improve the organisation of the party in the country had for five years gone unanswered, and Beresford was so far removed from Disraeli by political opinion that relations between the two men were never cordial. Organisation, at any rate, can never be divorced from policy. When Beresford complained to Derby of the great want of good Protectionist candidates, he condemned his own narrow and unfashionable politics. In the summer of 1852, Lord Henry Lennox reported to Disraeli that four young Conservative journalists had refused to write for the *Herald*, because they could not participate in the anti-Catholic campaign. 'It is too annoying to lose promising, young stuff for so absurd and bigoted a piece of folly.'[1] It was primarily because of his religious views that Beresford was removed by Disraeli in 1853.

In one respect the end of Beresford's rule came too late. His corrupt conduct at the elections shocked the Peelites and contributed to their decision not to make their peace with the Protectionists. *The Economist* believed that there was 'more truckling, more corruption, more fanaticism and more debauchery, than on any previous occasion' at the 1852 elections.[2] Cardwell, the only leading Peelite to lose his seat, was beaten at Liverpool by the combination of Protectionist money, intimidation, and exploitation of the religious issue. 'The Peel party', a Liverpool Protectionist wrote to Disraeli, 'generally headless and broken, were evidently prepared to fall into your ranks and I regret much to find that unnecessary hostility in election matters, chiefly, it would seem, owing to Major Beresford, should have created a bitterness which it will require tact to get over.'[3] Graham was appalled by Beresford's methods and thought that they must prove to the Peelites that junction with Derby was impossible.[4] Aberdeen and Newcastle put all thought of Conservative reunion behind them. Newcastle told Aberdeen that he could not join Derby without a sense of moral and political degradation.[5]

---

[1] Lennox to Disraeli, 7 August 1852. *ibid*. B/XX/Lx/8.
[2] *The Economist*, 7 August 1852.
[3] G. Mathew to Disraeli, 6 September 1852. Hughenden Mss, B/XXI/M/26.
[4] Graham to Bonham, 18 July 1852. Peel Mss, Add. Mss 40616, ff. 342–5.
[5] Newcastle to Aberdeen, 2 August 1852. Aberdeen Mss, Add. Mss 43197, f. 11.

The alienation of the Peelites was the more critical for the government because it was disappointed of the large gains which, a year earlier, it had expected to make in Ireland. Lord Naas, the Irish secretary, had predicted a Protectionist gain of 7 to 9 seats, owing to the eclipse of Russell's reputation in Ireland.[1] In the event the Protectionists won 10 new seats and lost 6 for a net gain of 4, leaving the party standing in Ireland at 53 Derbyites and 62 opposition members, of whom only 8 were Whigs and Peelites. The new Independent Irish party controlled the striking total of 50 seats.[2] In Ireland the Protectionists were richer and better organised than elsewhere,[3] and the results were a great disappointment.

In May Lord Eglinton, the lord lieutenant of Ireland, reported that Ireland was so quiet that he had little to do and that the Irish would soon forget how to shoot one another.[4] Then, on 15 June, the government's untimely proclamation reminding the Catholics that it was against the law for them publicly to exercise their religion or to wear the habits of their order broke the calm. Rioting began all over Ireland. On the Sunday of 27 June the Catholics in Stockport held their annual procession of school children, and on the following Tuesday the town was the scene of bitter rioting between Catholics and Protestants. Although twenty-four Irish labourers' houses were sacked and two Catholic chapels wrecked, in one the tabernacle broken open and the sacred hosts spilled, the government undertook no prosecutions.[5]

Lord Glengall claimed that in Mallow, Corhil, and Waterford, the constituencies which he knew about, Protectionist hopes of victory were frustrated by the proclamation and the Stockport riot.[6] The historian of the Independent Irish party estimates that those events cost the Protectionists at least 7 seats.[7] The point is near indisputable for Waterford, Clare, Carlow county, and

[1] Naas to Derby, July 1852. Derby Mss, 155/1.
[2] These are Naas' figures and correspond to John Young's (Young to Gladstone, 27 July 1852. Gladstone Mss, Add. Mss 44237, ff. 207–8).
[3] See Whyte, *Independent Irish Party*, 54–7.
[4] Eglinton to Derby, 12 May 1852. Derby Mss, 148/2.
[5] Whyte, *Independent Irish Party*, 59.
[6] Glengall to Derby, 16 July 1852. Derby Mss, 120/2.
[7] Whyte, *Independent Irish Party*, 61.

Carlow town, which the Protectionists lost by 33, 2, 14, and 12 votes. But it would be misleading to assume that events at the last moment deprived the Protectionists of the full fruits of a vigorous revival in Ireland. There was no such revival. The election of 1852 found English parties at their lowest ebb in Ireland at any time between 1829 and 1880. By 1850 neither party had links with Irish Radicalism such as had tied O'Connell to Lord Melbourne's government in the late 1830s. By vying for the Protestant vote in England, the Whigs and the Protectionists spurred the growth of the Independent Irish party, which was organised to return only candidates who would pledge themselves to support neither English party until tenant right and the disestablishment of the Irish Church were accepted. By the spring of 1852, before the proclamation and the riots, the Tenant Right League and the Catholic Defence Association had joined the economic and religious grievances in order to fight a united campaign on the basis of 'independence'.[1]

The Protectionists reaped no harvest from the Irish Catholics' disillusionment with Russell. In October 1851, in consequence of the passing of the Ecclesiastical Titles bill, the Catholic Defence Association had been founded with the express purpose of preventing Whig returns at the elections. Lord Glengall tried to interest Derby in a proposition put to him by the leaders of the Association, Sadleir and Keogh, that they cooperate with the Protectionists against Whig candidates, but Derby made the obvious point that the Protectionist party could not meet the views of the Association without forfeiting Protestant support in England.[2] However gingerly Protectionist candidates in Ireland treated the Maynooth issue, Derby gave Irish Catholics little incentive to vote for them. No Catholics served in his government and only one received a place in the Irish administration, a marked retrogression from the days of Peel and Russell. Catholic crown prosecutors on the Leinster and Connaught circuits were replaced by Protestants. And during the months before the elections a committee was sitting to determine whether to add to the

[1] *Ibid.* 31–8.
[2] Glengall to Derby, 17 October 1851, and 9 January 1852. Derby Mss, 120/2; Derby to Glengall, 19 October 1851 (copy). *ibid.* 179/1.

Irish executive's authority a new crime bill. It is thus not surprising that clerical intervention and intimidation, on behalf of the Irish Independent party, reached its peak in the 1852 elections and that it was so successful.

When the new parliament assembled in November, the Protectionists were in no stronger a position than they had been after the elections of 1847. The slow trickle of Peelite backbenchers into their ranks had increased their numbers slightly, but the Peelites who counted were now lost and the government had forfeited any bargaining power which they might have had with the Irish Radicals. The only important question facing the new parliament was whether the government could get its budget accepted, and for that the Protectionists could count only on the continuation of the dissensions within the opposition.

Throughout July, August, and September, a mountain of correspondence piled up as the Whigs and Peelites sought a basis for a suitable government to replace Lord Derby's. Two main difficulties had to be overcome. The first was that Lord John Russell clung to his claim to lead the coalition despite the fact that he had lost the confidence of the Irish, the Radicals, and Palmerston. The trouble was that many of the Whigs felt bound by loyalty to Russell, even although his services had become a liability to them. 'His talents are beyond dispute,' Palmerston wrote, 'but the infirmity of his judgment seems undeniable. At the same time there he is, at all events leader *par droit de naissance*, even though his title by *conquête* has been somewhat shaken'.[1] The second difficulty was the reluctance of Herbert and Gladstone to enter upon outright opposition to the government. 'The key to my position', Gladstone wrote many years later, 'was that my opinions went one way, my lingering sympathies the other.'[2] Herbert held that the government must be seen to have destroyed itself, and that combination of the opposition elements must therefore await Disraeli's budget. The summer-long negotiations ended in a much closer relationship between

---

[1] Palmerston to W. Temple, 23 May 1852. Ashley, *Palmerston*, i, 341–3.
[2] Morley, *Gladstone*, i, 417.

the Whigs and the Peelites and in the reluctant submission of Russell to Aberdeen's claim on the leadership of a Whig–Peelite coalition. There was not to be any official cooperation between the two groups against the government, so that Russell's comment that 'little is to be made of all this, except that we all agree in defending the Free Trade policy'[1] was, in the narrow view, true. The Peelites rejected the suggestion of a vote of confidence in Derby's government at the beginning of the autumn session. Yet for the first time since the upheaval of 1846 the road was clear to the formation of a coalition, supported by a majority in a House divided, not into Whigs, Radicals, Peelites, Conservatives, and Protectionists, but into left and right.

When the session began in November, Derby announced that, although his opinions were unchanged, he was bound to accept 'the deliberate expression' of the electorate against the restoration of protection.[2] Amid all the difficulties which he had to face in framing his budget, Disraeli was at least able to prepare a free-trade one. The task was still formidable. Disraeli had no practical experience of financial matters and the House of Commons contained a phalanx of financial experts, or, at any rate, men like Goulburn, Gladstone, Graham, Francis Baring, and Charles Wood who so considered themselves. In February, Disraeli had protested to Derby that he was ignorant of finance, and Derby had told him not to worry: 'You know as much as Mr. Canning did. They give you the figures.'[3] Presenting a budget in November made matters all the worse. The civil service had to estimate the revenue and expenditure four months before the end of the fiscal year. Malmesbury and Lord Henry Lennox had on that account tried to dissuade Disraeli from bringing down the budget before the usual time, but neither the Whigs nor the Peelites would consent to delay.

Disraeli knew that he could not expect Peelite support. Gladstone maintained that he awaited the budget with an open mind, but in July he had told Aberdeen that he could not accept Disraeli, whose opinions were 'quackish', as chancellor of the

<hr>

[1] Russell to Lansdowne, 28 August 1852. Walpole, *Russell*, ii, 159.
[2] *Hansard*, 3rd Series, cxxiii, 52.
[3] Monypenny and Buckle, iii, 344.

exchequer.[1] In a desperate attempt to save the government, Disraeli turned to the Irish party. In September, 48 Irish members had pledged themselves to 'independence' until tenant right was granted and the Ecclesiastical Titles bill repealed. Then on 22 November the government introduced four bills for Ireland, one of which provided for compensation for agricultural improvements, including those already effected. No English party had gone so far before. And when, on 7 December, three days before the debate on the budget was to begin, the Irish introduced their own bill to legalise the free sale of land, Disraeli agreed to send both bills to a select committee. Walpole had talks with Sergeant Shee, who had introduced the Irish members' bill, and Disraeli negotiated with George Moore, the member for Mayo. The result was an agreement that the Irish Independent Party would support the budget on the understanding that the government would accept a decision of the select committee in favour of the Irish members' land bill.[2]

Disraeli, however, had gone behind his party's back. According to Delane's account of the affair to Greville, when Naas and Napier, secretary and under-secretary for Ireland, heard of the deal, they 'came in great fury to Dis. and Walpole' with threats of resignation.[3] On 10 December Derby silenced the possibility of a revolt within the party by announcing in the Lords that he would not accept the Irish party's bill even if the select committee recommended its adoption.[4] After his budget was defeated, Disraeli claimed that he had been 'thwarted' by Derby,[5] but it is probable that at the last moment the Irish would have voted against a budget which extended the income tax to Ireland.

Disraeli's greatest handicap was that he was prevented from framing a budget, as he wished to do, on the basis of a commercial

[1] Gladstone to Aberdeen, 30 July 1852 (copy). Gladstone Mss, Add. Mss 44088, ff. 133–7. Russell was also pre-determined against the budget: 'I cannot imagine', he wrote to Graham on 19 July, 'it can be otherwise than the greatest delusion, or such a disturbance of our whole financial system that it must be blown out of water' (Parker, *Graham*, ii. 166).

[2] Whyte, *Independent Irish Party*, 95.

[3] C. C. F. Greville (ed. H. Reeve), *A Journal of the Reign of Queen Victoria from 1852 to 1860* (London, 1887), i, 33.

[4] *Hansard*, 3rd Series, cxxiii, 1206–7.

[5] Greville, *Journal from 1852 to 1860*, i, 32.

treaty with France. He wanted to rest British foreign policy on a thorough understanding with France, based on a reciprocal trading agreement by which France would reduce her duties on linen, cotton, and iron, and England hers on French brandies and silk. Had such a treaty accompanied a free-trade budget, the Radicals might have found the policy irresistible. There were, however, two snags. The board of trade pointed out that reductions conceded to France would be claimed by Portugal, Spain, and Sicily, and that four treaties could not be negotiated by December.[1] More important were the prevalent fears of Louis Napoleon's military ambitions. The Queen and Prince Albert forced Disraeli to allow for increased defence expenditures of £230,000 to support 2,000 artillery men, 1,000 cavalry, and 5,000 seamen.[2] In the first week of October, before the royal demands had been made, Disraeli told his sister that he was in good heart. Three days before he presented the budget, he could 'hardly see how the Budget can live in so stormy a sea' and felt wretched at having been 'called upon to change all my dispositions'.[3] In 1860 the plaudits for arranging a commercial treaty with France went to Gladstone and Cobden.

The final details of the budget were agreed upon by the cabinet on 2 December, and on the following night Disraeli presented it to a full House.[4] He began by saying that his budget was intended to establish the country's financial system 'upon principles more adapted to the requirements of the times, and especially to the industry of a country pre-eminent for its capacity for labour', and that he therefore wished to have it considered as a whole, not as a collection of isolated, self-arguing units. That was the signal for a radical budget.

The heart of the budget consisted of resolutions dealing with (1) the malt tax, hops tax, and tea duty, (2) the property and income tax, and (3) the house tax. Disraeli entered a free-trade plea for a reduction in the malt tax: 'we should best enable the

---

[1] Monypenny and Buckle, iii, 396–7.
[2] See Queen Victoria to Derby, 23 October 1852. Benson and Esher, ii, 481; see also Malmesbury's diary of the October and November cabinet meetings (Malmesbury, *Memoirs*, i, 360–72).
[3] Monypenny and Buckle, iii, 404, 425–6.
[4] For Disraeli's speech see *Hansard*, 3rd Series, cxxiii, 836–908.

people to engage in that competition to which they are for ever destined by cheapening as much as possible that which sustains their lives'. The tax was to be reduced by one half, not so much for the benefit of the malt grower, although properly dealt with – Disraeli must have longed to tell the House that the tax would have been repealed but for the increased defence expenditure – the reduction would give some relief to the agricultural interest, as for the benefit of the consumer. The duty on tea, 'the principal solace of every cottage in the kingdom', was to be reduced over a six-year period from 2s. 2¼d. in the pound to 1s., and the tax on hops from 2d. in the pound to 1d.

These reductions entailed a loss in revenue of £3,700,000, made in the confidence that the revenue of the country 'shall mainly depend on the consuming power of the people'. That was an almost Keynsian concept, far in advance of orthodox financial thinking. Disraeli returned to his theme of the previous April, that direct taxation should be levied almost as universally as indirect taxation. He challenged the free traders to accept the consequences of the prosperity of the middle and working classes which they had been so triumphantly proclaiming. 'We deem it our duty to denounce as most pernicious to all classes of this country the systematic reduction of indirect taxation, while at the same time you levy your direct taxes from a very limited class.' In 1842 a duty on spirits and a stamp duty had been levied on Ireland in place of an income tax, but the first had since been rescinded and the second brought in only £16,000. The income tax was therefore to be extended to Ireland. In England some exemptions were retained, but the exemption level on industrial incomes was lowered from £150 to £100 and on property incomes from £100 to £50. For farmers the exemption level was raised. Their profits were to be taken as one-third of their rents instead of as one-half. Finally, in fulfilment of his second principle, that the income tax should acknowledge the difference between permanent and precarious incomes, Disraeli proposed to tax the first (landed and funded property) at the rate of 7d. in the pound and the second (profits from farming, trade, and the professions) at 5¼d.

The alterations in the income-tax structure would have little immediate effect on the revenue. But the remission of indirect taxes transformed a surplus of £1,600,000 into a deficit of £2,100,000, and to supply that deficit Disraeli proposed to double the house tax. Parliament had for a long time accepted the principle of a house tax, and since its introduction the window tax, the tax on bricks, glass, and timber, and, most grievous of all, the tax on corn had been reduced or repealed. It was therefore not a hardship for the existing formula by which houses and shops valued at £20 paid a tax of 9d. and 6d. in the pound to be changed so that houses and shops valued at £10 should pay 1s. 6d. and 1s.

As soon as Disraeli sat down, Derby wrote to the Queen.

Mr. Disraeli spoke for about five hours, with no apparent effort, with perfect self-possession, and with hardly an exception to the fixed attention with which the House listened to the exposition of views of your Majesty's servants. It was altogether a most masterly performance, and he kept alive the attention of the House with the greatest ability.[1]

George Hamilton wrote to Disraeli's wife that 'a more surprising effort has never been made and he has been greatly cheered'.[2] But, as Gladstone wrote, though 'his proposals dazzled for a day', the opposition had a week to discover that they made up 'a scheme of illusory compensation and dislocated experiments'.[3]

Lord Lyndhurst made a perceptive comment on the budget in a letter to Disraeli's wife. 'I cannot refuse myself the pleasure of congratulating you on Disraeli's great success, and on the skilful and brilliant manner in which he turned the weapons of the Free-Traders and Radicals against themselves, pounding them in their own mortar.'[4] But Lyndhurst was a Tory. Macaulay said almost the same thing, but with a Whig twist. 'The plan was nothing but taking money out of the pockets of the people in towns and putting it into the pockets of growers of malt. I greatly doubt whether he will be able to carry it.'[5] Although the reduction in

---

[1] Derby to Queen Victoria, 3 December 1852. Benson and Esher, ii, 493.
[2] Monypenny and Buckle, iii, 433.
[3] Morley, *Gladstone*, i, 434.
[4] Monypenny and Buckle, iii, 434–5.
[5] G. O. Trevelyan, *Life and Letters of Lord Macaulay* (London, 1883), ii, 579.

the malt tax was generally regarded as an illusory benefit to the farmers, held out to them as an appeasement, and although the budget provided for no reductions in the local charges on landed property, the opposition considered that the landed interest had been given an unduly favoured place in Disraeli's scheme. Charles Wood argued that, if Disraeli were really concerned to help the consumer, he should have reduced the timber duty, not the malt tax.[1] Cobden called the distinction between funded and other property for income tax purposes 'the odious principle of compensation' in disguise. He did 'not recognise any right on the part of the representatives of the agricultural districts, or any claim arising out of free trade, which entitles them to levy a tax on some particular kind of property in the towns in order to relieve certain kinds of property in the country'. The house tax merely added to the burden to be placed on the urban taxpayer, and the towns, 'those centres from which radiate the light and intelligence of the country', would not submit to such treatment.[2] In Gladstone's view the most damning aspect of the budget was that the brunt of the new taxation would fall on one class within the towns, on those people whose income was between £50 and £100 and who owned houses of the value of £10 to £20.[3]

The budget was lost, however, not principally because it set country against town. By extending the income tax to Ireland, Disraeli abandoned any chance of Irish support. More important, by undertaking a radical reconstruction of the whole structure of English taxation, he offended those Peelites who believed that it was impossible to improve upon the financial principles of their late master. Gladstone wrote in horror to his wife that Disraeli's was 'the least conservative budget I have ever known'.[4]

The distinction between the rates on funded and other property was held to be a breach of faith with the public creditor, a violation of the principle that all income must be taxed equally in justice to the contract on which the fundholder lends his money. Goulburn argued that funded property, thought to be the most secure, was to become precariously dependent on the will of a

[1] *Hansard*, 3rd Series, cxxiii, 1297.   [2] *Ibid*. cxxiii, 318–21.
[3] *Ibid*. cxxiii, 1370.
[4] Morley, *Gladstone*, i, 437.

minister.[1] Disraeli was also ridiculed for having to supply a deficit by new taxation, when the deficit was his own creation. That was, of course, a pedantic way of looking at the budget. Disraeli was not juggling a few figures around in order to maintain a surplus, but, as he said, establishing the financial system upon new principles. The Peelites would have none of it. Previous governments, Goulburn lectured Disraeli, had 'proceeded on the sound basis of having first secured by a skilful management of the receipts and expenditure of the country a large available balance, out of which they could afford to make reductions'.[2] In the final speech on the sixth night of the debate, Gladstone delivered a eulogy of Peel's financial policy, from which Disraeli had departed by not reducing the duties on raw materials (timber) and on articles of food (cheese and butter) and by not maintaining a surplus. It was the surplus which really mattered and which had controlled all of Peel's operations.[3]

Even if the opposition had been satisfied with the manner in which the surplus was contrived, it was still a very small surplus for a country worried about the possibility of war with France. For the Peelites, a reduction in the malt tax was not worth endangering the country's defences. Goulburn criticised Disraeli for abolishing the Public Loans Commission and then placing the estimated £400,000 in repayments in the revenue to provide a surplus, instead of using the money towards paying off the national debt. Disraeli's reply, a veiled plea for planned deficit budgeting, made little impression on the defenders of financial orthodoxy.

The public credit of the nation is in danger! I doubt whether such mere personal imputations and wide assertions are quite justifiable. He says the public credit is in danger. Well, I don't think it is. I think public credit never was in a better position. I never remember any period in the history of this country when her resources were, I may say, daily, so visibly increasing.[4]

[1] *Hansard*, 3rd Series, cxxiii, 1298. It is interesting to note that *The Times* supported Disraeli on this matter. In 1851 the paper had criticised Charles Wood for failing to distinguish between the two kinds of property. 'Any system which treats a permanent and a transitory income as identical for fiscal purposes is an act of public dishonesty of the grossest kind' (*The Times*, 18 February 1851).

[2] *Hansard*, 3rd Series, cxxiii, 1404.

[3] *Ibid*. cxxiii, 1681.   [4] *Ibid*. cxxiii, 1660.

The opposition of the Peelites left only one hope for the government, the Radicals. In desperation Disraeli went to see Bright on 15 December, the day before the division on the budget was to take place. He was, perhaps, encouraged by Bright's silence in the debate and by three friendly letters which Bright had written to him in the last week of November. Releasing all his frustrations to Bright, Disraeli spoke of 'that *infernal question*, the question of Protection' and of 'those *damned defences*', said that he would not have touched the malt tax except that something had to be offered the farmers, promised that 'if he could get a vote, a majority of *one* only, his honour would be saved and he would give up House Tax and Malt, and remodel his scheme, and, for final bait, pictured the day when he, Bright, and Cobden might all sit in the same government.[1] So dearly did Disraeli love place. It was an artful display, but Bright was not taken in, and Derby, who got wind of Disraeli's intriguing, gave the fledgling cabinet minister a severe reprimand.

We may buy off a hostile vote before Christmas; but how shall we stand afterwards? We have abandoned the principle of Protection in deference to the voice of the country; we always said that we would do so. We prepared our Budget, of which one main element was the reduction of the malt tax as the *only* relief granted to the land, and that granted because it was only incidentally a relief to them, accompanying advantages, in the spirit of Free Trade policy, to the consumers …We have staked our existence on our Budget *as a whole* – we have asked for a decision of Parliament…can we with credit accept a departure from it…You had better be defeated honestly in a fairly-fought field than escape under a cloud, to encounter aggravated defeat with alienated friends and sneering opponents…if we are to be a Government, we must be so by our own friends, and in spite of all combinations, and not by purchasing a short-lived existence upon the forbearance of the Radical party.[2]

Those principles which had determined Derby's conduct in 1845–6 sustained him in defeat in 1852. Derby was willing to call the cabinet together to discuss whether they should resign or

---

[1] Walling, *Diaries of Bright*, 128–30.
[2] Monypenny and Buckle, iii, 440–1.

rctrcat from the budget if they were beaten, but Disraeli saw that that was unnecessary.

I do not think there is any necessity to call a Cabinet, for, I am sure, everyone must agree with you on the subject.

Your letter has removed the only dark spot in my political career, which was the fear, from something you once said to me, that retirement from office would be the term of your political life. Personally, I should then feel isolated; but, as it is, I would prefer being your colleague in opposition to being the colleague of any other man as Minister.[1]

The *Quarterly Review* accounted it a tactical error for Disraeli to stake the government on a vote on the budget as a whole. But Disraeli would not have agreed with Croker that his was 'as *common-place* a budget as ever was propounded'.[2] The budget was of a piece. Clause by clause voting would not have secured its passage through the Commons.

The drama of Disraeli's final appeal and Gladstone's impassioned rejoinder, on 16 December, may be relived in the pages of Buckle. Disraeli ended with his famous charge of coalition, in those days a severe term of abuse.

When parties are balanced – when a government cannot pass its measures – the highest principles of public life, the most important dogmas of politics degenerate into party questions... Well, direct taxation, although applied with wisdom, temperance, and prudence has become a party question... Yes! I know what I have to face. I have to face a coalition. The combination may be successful. A coalition before this has been successful. But coalitions, although successful, have always found this, that their triumph has been brief. This, too, I know, that England does not love coalitions.[3]

Unerring prophecy, but strange language from the man who had taught Peel the lesson that all political questions were party questions, and who, the day before, had been to see Bright.

Gladstone denied the accusation of a pre-arranged coalition. He was about to vote against the budget, not in order to come into office, but because he considered it 'the most subversive in

---

[1] *Ibid.* iii, 441–2.   [2] *Quarterly Review* (January 1853), 238.
[3] *Hansard*, 3rd Series, cxxiii, 1666.

its tendencies and ultimate effects that I have ever known submitted to this house'.[1] There was truth on both sides. All the elements for a coalition government were gathered. Disraeli's budget provided the coalition with an early and, by the principles of its members, justifiable entry into office. By a vote of 305 to 286, Derby's government was destroyed and the life of the Protectionist party ended.

[1] *Ibid.* cxxiii, 1669.

9

CONCLUSION

I F HISTORIANS were asked to name the greatest English prime minister of the nineteenth century, Peel would probably head the poll. His fame and high reputation have lasted from his death, from a contemporary's judgement 'that he touched the dry bones of the Tory party, giving thereto a new life and a better name, and if it might be, a wider and a wiser purpose'[1] to a more modern biographer's extravagant praise of the repeal of the Corn Laws as 'the greatest effort ever made to raise collectively the standard of life of the whole lower class'.[2] But Peel did not so much give the Conservative party a new life, as set some Conservatives on the road which led to the Liberal party. The incipient liberalism of the Peelites, as much as the personal distrusts which the split in 1846 engendered among Conservatives, prevented the reunion of the Conservative party. Derby and the Protectionists have won the obscurity of conservatives in a liberal age. The post-reform years were frustrating years for a Tory. John Henry Newman could take refuge in the Roman Catholic Church, but, as the failure of the Protectionist party showed, there was no comparable haven in politics. 'What an unhappy being a real Tory must be, at least in England,' Lady John Russell wrote early in 1846, 'battling so vainly against time and tide, and doomed to see the idols of his worship crumbled to dust one after another.'[3]

From 1829 to 1874 golden bows and arrows of desire were powerless to halt the advance of Liberal opinion and legislation. At the end of 1852 Toryism had reached its nadir. Many of the Protectionists who voted for Disraeli's budget were as displeased with it as their opponents. They had spent their political careers

[1] George Peel in Parker, *Peel*, iii, 561–2.
[2] Ramsay, *Peel*, 329.
[3] MacCarthy and Russell, *Lady John Russell*, 80.

fighting against direct taxation, and as recently as April 1851, had supported Herries' motion to limit the income tax to one year in the hope that it would thereafter be abandoned. Croker regretted, not that Derby went out, since the coalition was bent on his overthrow, but 'that he did not go out on some principle round which his friends and the country could have rallied'.[1] Croker's chagrin that the Protectionists had not been defeated on a point in 'sympathy with the feeling that was prominent at the late elections – the vindication and maintenance of the PRO-TESTANT CONSTITUTION'[2] was mere reaction. Immediately after the elections, Malmesbury wrote to Disraeli that the future of the party depended upon their bringing forth 'grand and good measures' by which the party could establish a firm basis of popular support in the country.[3] But Malmesbury gave no hint of what those measures might be. Finance was the question of the day, and many Protectionists believed that Conservatism had been dragged down with Disraeli's budget. 'Where it will all end,' Spencer Walpole wrote, 'Heaven only knows! I tremble for the future.'[4] The Earl of Hardwicke expressed the gloom which enshrouded the Conservative party in a letter to Croker at the end of December 1852.

I think the game is up as regards the Conservative party (so called). It is clear to me that the union of Whigs and Peelites, with the side-door open to the Radicals, leads to these consequences – that while our party will be thinned, so slow and moderate will be the democratic downward tendency, that as a party we shall be deprived of a link strong enough to hold us together.

It is, moreover, now so clear that the power and preponderance are in the hands of, and turn to, the trade, moneyed and manufacturing classes, that the land will be governed by them and obliged to submit to a state of things that will enhance the value of trade.[5]

Not until 1874 did the Conservative party control a majority

[1] Unaddressed letter, 11 February 1853. Jennings, *Croker*, iii, 263–6.
[2] *Quarterly Review* (December 1852), 274.
[3] Malmesbury to Disraeli, 24 September 1852. Hughenden Mss, B/XX/Hs/27.
[4] Walpole to Croker, 13 January 1853. Jennings, *Croker*, iii, 262–3.
[5] Hardwicke to Croker, 30 December 1852. *ibid.* iii, 260–1. See also Lord Lonsdale to Croker, 22 May 1853: 'Our men are deserting. We have no rallying point to keep our troops together. We are helpless as a party. Something may turn up, but this is a remote expectation' (*ibid.* iii, 267–8).

of the House of Commons. D.G.Barnes had no doubt who was responsible for this long exile in the wilderness.

As far as I know no one has ever seriously questioned Disraeli's judgment in hounding Peel out of the party in 1846; but it seems a good case could be made for the harm he did his party and his own career during the next generation. Protection was soon buried as an issue and there was really no reason why the Peelites...should have permanently remained out of the party...the principal reason seems to have been that the leaders never forgave Disraeli's conduct in 1846.[1]

It may be doubted that Disraeli hurt his own prospects. And it hardly needs saying that the Conservative party was broken because he and Bentinck chose to oppose the repeal of the Corn Laws in 1846. But it was not simply free trade which they opposed. Barnes begged the question of what choice Peel gave them. They could either have fallen back, as Wellington did, on the notion dear to the eighteenth century, that the first duty of loyal subjects was to support the government of the Crown. Or they could have accepted the fact that the stability of a government had come to rest, not on the Crown, but on party. Peel wavered between the two notions. Bentinck, who would not be sold, and Disraeli, who repeatedly warned Peel of the consequences of acting independently of party, did not. The bulk of the Protectionists may not have seen the issue so clearly as Disraeli did, but their instincts rightly found Peel's betrayal repugnant. Circumstances made a liberal trading policy desirable, but Peel acted secretly and precipitately. Government by party encourages political integrity only so long as politicians are made liable when they change their loyalties or break their promises, both to their party and to the electorate. In resisting Peel's 'national' plea in 1846, Disraeli and his followers served British democracy.

Of course, they paid for it. For seven years the satisfaction of their ambitions depended upon either a Protectionist reaction or a Conservative reunion. Neither came to pass, partly because they were contradictory ends, and the simultaneous pursuit of both prevented the bold and open prosecution of one or the other. Reunion was always a more realistic proposition than a return to

[1] D.G.Barnes, *A History of the English Corn Laws* (London, 1931), 280.

the Corn Laws, but for so long as the latter desire was publicly proclaimed as policy, the former was impossible. By the time that protection died in 1852, it was too late to reconstruct the old party. Successive offers from the Protectionists to the Peelites were rejected on specific grounds, one of which was, indeed, Disraeli, to whom Gladstone would go 'for the delight of the ear and the fancy' but never for conviction.[1] By 1852 specific points of contention were not so important as the effects of the passing of time. Seven years eroded old loyalties and gave the Peelites the freedom to make new friends and to cast their minds about the future direction of politics. The future was clouded – in 1852, Aberdeen could say without intention of wit or paradox that no government 'can be too liberal for me, provided it does not abandon its conservative character'[2] – and the Peelites entered a coalition government, not the Liberal party. The dream of Conservative reunion lingered until 1859. But the general tendency of affairs led the Peelites away from those who stood for nothing more than standing still.

I never heard you called a Peelite [Newcastle wrote to the Whig, Lord Granville, in 1853] but I have always perceived that if bygone nicknames are abandoned, there is no more difference of opinion between you and me than there must always be for any two men who think for themselves... *Peelism* – if I must still use the word – is really the most advanced form of Liberal opinion, cleared of that demagogic Liberalism which characterises the Liberalism of twenty years ago and, on the other hand, of that oligarchic tendency of the old Whigs, who, wishing to extend freedom, sought to do it by making use of the people, instead of identifying themselves and their own interests with the people.[3]

By 1852 Aberdeen and Newcastle had come to accept the need for franchise reform,[4] and in 1853 Gladstone introduced the succession tax, which was in Croker's view 'a more serious derangement of the old constitution than Catholic Emancipation or even

---

[1] Morley, *Gladstone*, i, 356.

[2] Aberdeen to Princess Lieven, 5 March 1852. Balfour, *Life of Aberdeen*, ii, 166.

[3] Newcastle to Granville, 18 April 1853. Lord Fitzmaurice, *The Life of Granville George Leveson Gower, Second Earl Granville* (London, 1905), i, 79–80.

[4] See Newcastle to Gladstone, 26 August 1852. Gladstone Mss, Add. Mss 44262, ff. 125–30.

the Reform Bill'.[1] That was a measure of how far the Peelites had travelled since 1846 while the Protectionists had been running as hard as they could to stay in the same place. 'I see few, if any, young men coming forward, or taking an interest in public affairs, imbued with Conservative principles and ready to stand by and with "their order"', Stanley wrote to Croker in 1850.[2] The Protectionists clung to the Corn Laws in their fear of leaving the familiar landed world which was crumbling around them. They became a party of one idea, and when that was taken from them they were left intellectually barren and emotionally defeated.

Only the most devout worshipper at the altar of success would argue that the failure to achieve an end discredits its pursuit. For the Conservative party, nevertheless, the Protectionist years were wasted ones, perhaps because the grasp was not worth the reach. The Conservative organisation and intellect were left to wither. Derby did little to stay the process. He was not the work-a-day politician that Peel and Gladstone were. The account of his reaction to the defeat of his government by one of his followers illustrates both his love of his country life and his detached approach to politics.

After resigning office in December, 1852, he ran down to Knowsley like a boy escaped from school. He immediately had recourse to his gun, and during a day's rabbit shooting gave vent to his feelings in the following characteristic manner. 'Ha!' he would cry, as a rabbit crossed the ride, 'there goes Gladstone; hope I haven't missed him. There do you see that big fellow? That is Graham. He'll be none the worse for a few pellets in his ribs', and so on through the rest. I once told this to his son, the fifteenth Earl, who laughed heartily at it. He said he had never heard the story, but that it was exactly like his father.[3]

Contemporaries seldom did justice to Derby's deep attachment to the landed class and, after he left the Whigs, to the Conservative party, although *The Times* admitted snidely that 'if devotion to one's order is principle, Lord Stanley is a high principled

[1] Croker to Herries, 31 July 1853. Herries Mss, NRA/67.
[2] Stanley to Croker, 18 August 1850. Jennings, *Croker*, iii, 221.
[3] T.E.Kebbel, *Lord Beaconsfield and Other Tory Memories* (London, 1907), 92. The story was told to Kebbel by Admiral Hornby.

man'.[1] There was nothing unorthodox about Greville's loaded question whether, in quitting Peel's cabinet in December 1845, Stanley's motive was 'ambition and power, or only sport and mischief'.[2] Derby was slow to make up his mind in 1846 because he could not decide which he ought to serve, the landed interest or the Conservative party. Once he was convinced that Peel was on the road to Liberalism, he saw that he might serve both by leading the Protectionists. It was not easy for him. All his antecedents had been with the liberal side of English politics, as a Whig and as a minister in Peel's government. It was he, after all, who had given enthusiastic backing to Peel's concessions to Ireland and had, indeed, drafted the abortive tenant compensation bill of 1845. It was he, too, who had introduced the Canada Corn Bill of 1843, and who had strongly supported the reduction of the sugar duties in 1844.

Yet by 1852 his new surroundings had made him the most articulate spokesman for the reactionary party. His party shifts earned him the opprobrium of contemporaries.

It is impossible to *admire* Peel [Abraham Hayward wrote] as a statesman or a man. But neither can I admire Stanley, who takes the lead with the Whigs in passing the Reform Bill, and actually brings in the Slavery Abolition Act, then joins Peel and votes for the new Tariff, then joins the Protectionists in railing at Peel... Whig, Peelite and Protectionist by turn, and the most violent of the violent in each. This is a little too much.[3]

It was not Derby, however, who changed, but those around him. Events in early Victorian England moved too quickly for him. Old-fashioned in his style of dress and in his oratory, he was somewhat out of place in the utilitarian post-1832 world. His letters are often models of reasoning upon general principles. He could cut through detail to general Conservative principles, but he never got up the details for himself, nor undertook a sustained parliamentary campaign. In part this explains the listlessness of the Protectionist opposition. Nor did Derby take much interest in electoral business. He told the Earl of Donoughmore before

---

1 *The Times*, 11 May 1847.

2 Greville, ii, 370.

3 Hayward to Lady Charleville, 18 November 1848. Carlisle, *Correspondence of Abraham Hayward*, i, 135.

the 1852 elections that he did not know how many tenants on his Tipperary estates had the vote, 'never having taken part in Election matters'.[1] His effectiveness as a party leader was further weakened by his detachment from his followers. He seldom visited the Carlton Club and gave dinners for the party only at Disraeli's and Malmesbury's insistence.

Relaxed, unambitious, aloof, Derby was nevertheless devoted to Conservative principles and faithful to the Conservative party. From 1846 to 1852 he had little room for manoeuvre. He understood the limitations placed upon him, not just that of being a peer when the *raison d'être* of his party was an issue which had to be joined almost exclusively in the House of Commons, but the far greater limitation which the want of men of ability and industry placed upon his freedom of action. For Derby there was always much more at stake than either power or the Corn Laws. There was the need to preserve a party capable of checking the democratic tide of the nineteenth century. He tried to steer a course between the two rocks on which the party might founder. One was that, if the views of the old guard were ignored, the party might be scattered to the winds. Derby was not going to repeat Peel's mistake.

Peel's great error has always been disregarding the opinion of his party, whenever it did not exactly square with his own; and I am confident that no man in these days can hope to lead a party who cannot make up his mind sometime to follow it.[2]

There is to be found, in great measure, the explanation for Derby's right turn, especially on Irish questions, after 1846. The danger from the other direction was not so great, but Derby was continually on guard against it. In 1867 Gathorne Hardy found Disraeli's greatest fault to be that 'he is always looking for what will suit others, rather than what is sound in itself'.[3] On several occasions between 1846 and 1852 Disraeli courted the Whigs, the colonial reformers, the Radicals, and the Irish, but never with the sanction of Derby. Conservatism in opposition was preferable to latitudinarianism in office.

[1] Derby to Donoughmore, 27 May 1852 (copy). Derby Mss, 180/1.
[2] Stanley to Bentinck, 27 October 1847 (copy). *ibid.* 177/2.
[3] Monypenny and Buckle, iv, 516.

BIBLIOGRAPHY

PRIMARY SOURCES

(A) *Manuscript Sources*

Aberdeen Mss (British Museum)
Brougham Mss (British Museum)
Croker Mss (British Museum)
Derby Mss (Knowsley, Lancashire)
Ellenborough Mss (Public Record Office)
Gladstone Mss (British Museum)
Goulburn Mss (Surrey County Record Office)
Graham Mss (Bodleian Library, Oxford)
Herries Mss (British Museum)
Hughenden Mss (Hughenden, High Wycombe)
Newcastle Mss (Nottingham University Library)
Peel Mss (British Museum)
Portland Mss (Nottingham University Library)

(B) *Government Publications*

Parliamentary Debates, *Hansard*, 3rd Series, 1841–52.
Parliamentary Papers:
    1837, xxxiii (75). First Report of Commission into Railway Communications in Ireland.
    1837–8, xxxv (1945). Second Report of Commission into Railways in Ireland.
    1845, xii (490). Report of Lords' Committee into Drainage of Estates.
    1845, xix (605). Report of Commission into Land Tenure in Ireland.
    1847–8, vii (461). Report of Select Committee on Agricultural Customs.

(c) *Newspapers and Contemporary Journals*

Annual Register	Morning Chronicle
British Protestant	Morning Herald
British Quarterly Review	Morning Post
Edinburgh Review	Standard
The Economist	The Times

Fraser's Magazine   Quarterly Review
Illustrated London News   Westminster Review
John Bull

(D) *Contemporary Pamphlets and Printed Speeches*

Agricola, *An Address to the People on the Subject of Free Trade.* London, 1850.

Alison, A., *Essays Political, Historical and Miscellaneous,* 3 vols. Edinburgh, 1850.

Almack, J., *Character, Motives, and Proceedings of the Anti-Corn Law Leaguers.* London, 1843.

Anglia, *England and Ireland, a Political Cartoon.* London, 1844.

The Government and the Irish Roman Catholic Members. London, 1851.

Anon., *How Much Would the Four-pound Loaf Be Lowered by the Repeal of the Corn Laws?* London, 1844.

Is the Strong Heart of England Broken? (undated).

The Ministry and the Session: a Review of the Legislation of 1852. London, 1852.

The Morality of Public Men: a Letter to the Earl of Derby. London, 1852.

The Political Crisis: Shufflers or Statesmen? London, 1852.

A Short Letter to the Earl of Derby on Present Prospects. London, 1852.

Things as They Are and Things as They Ought to Be: a Report of the Cambridgeshire Farmers' Association. London, 1843.

Tracts on Protection. London, 1850.

What Have the Whigs Done? London, 1841.

What Is To Be Done? or Past, Present, and Future. London, 1844.

Bankes, G., *Speeches at Agricultural Meetings of Sturminster and Blandford.* Dorchester, 1847.

Blackburn, J., *The Three Conferences Held by the Opponents of the Maynooth Endowment Bill in 1845.* London, 1845.

Facts and Observations Relating to the Popish College of Maynooth. London, 1845.

Britannicus, *Corn Laws Defended; or Agriculture Our First Interest.* London, 1844.

Bulwer Lytton, E., *Letters to John Bull Esq., on his Landed Property and the Persons Who Live Thereon.* London, 1851.

Cayley, E. S., *Reasons for the Formation of the Agricultural Protection Society.* London, 1844.

Colquhon, J. C., *The Effects of Sir Robert Peel's Administration.* London, 1847.

Day, G.G., *Defeat of the Anti-Corn Law League in Huntingdonshire.* London, 1843.

Speech at Huntingdon on Forming an Anti-League Association, 1844. London, 1844.

A Letter to Richard Cobden. London, 1844.

The Effects of Free Trade. London, 1851.

Drummond, H., *Government By the Queen and Attempted Government From the People.* London, 1842.

Everard, R., *The Effect of Free Trade on the Various Classes.* London, 1850.

Foe, D., *The Shortest Way with the Free Traders.* London, 1850.

Gladstone, W.E., *Remarks Upon Recent Commercial Legislation.* London, 1845.

Hill, J., *The Defeater Defeated: a Refutation of Mr Day's Pamphlet.* London, 1843.

Hubert, H.S.M., *To Protect Native Industry is a National Duty.* London, 1850.

Irish Catholic, *The Government of Lord Aberdeen and the Government of Lord Derby.* Dublin, 1853.

Leicestershire Farmer, *What Are You At? A Plain Question to the Earl of Derby.* London, 1852.

Lewis, G.C., *Addresses and Speeches Relative to the Election for the County of Hereford in 1852.* London, 1857.

Lincolnshire Landowner, *A Reply to the Anti-Corn Law League.* London, 1843.

Newdegate, C., *Letters to the Right Hon. H. Labouchere.* London, 1852.

Parliamentary Reporter, *Memoirs of the New Ministry.* London, 1852.

Peel, R., *Tamworth Election,: Speech of June 28, 1841.* London, 1841.

Speech at Tamworth, July 28, 1841. London, 1841.

Letter to the Electors of Tamworth. London, 1847.

Pro Ecclesia Dei, *Our Duty and Our Encouragement: an Address to the Protectionist Constituency of these Realms.* London, 1850.

Report of the Committee of the General Ship-Owners Society for the Year 1840. London, 1841.

Report of the Meeting for the Establishment of a Yorkshire Protective Society. London, 1844.

Rockingham Whig, *Derby or Democracy?* London, 1852.

Rolfe, J., *The Injustice of the Present Free-Trade Policy.* London, 1850.

Smith, Sir C.E., *The Romanism of Italy.* London, 1845.

Stanley, Lord, *Speech at Merchant Tailors' Hall on Wednesday, April 2, 1851.* London, 1851.

Vyvyan, Sir R., *Letter to his Constituents Upon the Commercial and Financial Policy of Sir Robert Peel's Administration.* London, 1842.

Warren, S., *The Queen or the Pope?* London, 1851.

Young, G. F., *Speech at Framlingham, Suffolk, January 9, 1851*. London, 1851.

    Free-Trade Fallacies Refuted. London, 1852.

SECONDARY SOURCES

Acland, A. H. D. (ed.), *Memoir and Letters of the Right Honourable Sir Thomas Acland*. London, 1902.

Acland, J., *The Imperial Poll Book, 1832–64*. Brighton, undated.

Alfred (S. Kydd), *The History of the Factory Movement*, 2 vols. London, 1857.

Allyn, E., *Lords Versus Commons: A Century of Conflict and Compromise, 1830–1930*. Philadelphia, 1931.

Anon., 'Notes on the Greville Memoirs', *English Historical Review*, January 1886, 105–37.

Argyll, Dowager Duchess of (ed.), *George Douglas, Eighth Duke of Argyll, Autobiography and Memoirs*, vol. 1. London, 1906.

Ashley, E., *The Life of Henry John Temple, Viscount Palmerston: 1846–1865*, 2 vols. London, 1877.

Ashworth, H., *Recollections of Richard Cobden and the Anti-Corn Law League*. London, 1876.

Ashworth, W., *An Economic History of England, 1870–1929*. London, 1960.

Aspinall, A. (ed.), *The Correspondence of Charles Arbuthnot*. London, 1941.

    Three Early Nineteenth Century Diaries. London, 1952.

Awdry, F., *A Country Gentleman of the Nineteenth Century, Being a Short Memoir of the Right Honourable Sir William Heathcote*. London, 1906.

Aydelotte, W. O., 'A Statistical Analysis of the Parliament of 1841: Some Problems of Method', *Bulletin of the Institute of Historical Research*, November 1954, 141–55.

    'The House of Commons in the 1840s', *History*, October 1954, 249–62.

Bagenal, P. H., *The Life of Ralph Bernal Osborne, M.P.* London, 1884.

Baines, E., *The Life of Edward Baines*. London, 1851.

Balfour, Lady Frances, *The Life of George, Fourth Earl of Aberdeen*. London, 1922.

Baring, F. H., 'Lord John Russell's Attempt to Form a Government in 1845', *English Historical Review*, April 1908, 317–23.

Barnes, D. G., *A History of the English Corn Laws, 1660–1846*. London, 1931.

Bassett, A. T. (ed.), *Gladstone to his Wife*. London, 1936.

Bell, H. C. F., *Lord Palmerston*, 2 vols. London, 1936.

Benson, A. C. and Viscount Esher (ed.), *The Letters of Queen Victoria*, vols. 1 and 2. London, 1907.

Black, R. D. C., 'The Classical Economists and the Irish Problem', *Oxford Economic Papers*, March 1953, 26–40.

Blake, R. N. W., *Disraeli*. London, 1966.

'The Fourteenth Earl of Derby', *History Today*, December 1955, 850–9.

'The Rise of Disraeli' in H. R. Trevor-Roper (ed.), *Essays in British History Presented to Sir Keith Feiling*. London, 1964, 219–46.

Brady, A., *William Huskisson and Liberal Reform*. London, 1928.

Briggs, A., *The Age of Improvement*, 2nd edition. London, 1960.

Chartist Studies. London, 1959.

'Middle-Class Consciousness in English Politics, 1780–1846', *Past and Present*, April 1956, 65–72.

Bright, J. and Thorold Rogers, J. E. (ed.), *Speeches on Questions of Public Policy by Richard Cobden*, vol. 1. London, 1870.

Brightfield, M. F., *John Wilson Croker*. Berkeley, California, 1940.

Broughton, Lord, *Recollections of a Long Life*, vols. 5 and 6. London, 1911.

Brown, L., *The Board of Trade and the Free-Trade Movement*. Oxford, 1958.

'The Board of Trade and the Tariff Problem', *English Historical Review*, July 1953, 394–421.

Burn, D. L., 'Canada and the Repeal of the Corn Laws', *Cambridge Historical Journal*, II, 3 (1928), 252–72.

Burn, W. L., 'Free Trade in Land: an Aspect of the Irish Question', *Transactions of the Royal Historical Society*, 4th Series, 1949, 61–74.

Cahill, G. A., 'Irish Catholicism and English Toryism', *Review of Politics*, January 1957, 62–76.

'The Protestant Association and the Anti-Maynooth Agitation of 1845', *Catholic Historical Review*, October 1957, 273–308.

Caird, J., *English Agriculture in 1850–51*. London, 1852.

Campbell, Lord, *Lives of Lord Lyndhurst and Lord Brougham*. London, 1869.

Carlisle, H. E. (ed.), *A Selection From the Correspondence of Abraham Hayward, Q.C.*, vol. 1. London, 1886.

Cecil, A., *Queen Victoria and Her Prime Ministers*. London, 1953.

Chadwick, O., *The Victorian Church: Part I, 1829–1860*. London, 1967.

Chambers, J. D., and Mingay, G. E. *The Agricultural Revolution, 1750–1880*. London, 1966.

Clapham, J.H., 'The Last Years of the Navigation Acts', *English Historical Review*, July and October 1910, 480–501 and 687–707.

Cockburn, H., *Journal of Henry Cockburn, Being a Continuation of the Memorials of his Time, 1831–54*, 2 vols. Edinburgh, 1874.

Collieu, E.G., 'Lord Brougham and the Conservatives' in Trevor-Roper, *Essays in British History*, 195–218.

Conacher, J.B., 'The British Party System Between the Reform Acts of 1832 and 1867', *Canadian Historical Association Report*, 1955, 69–78.

'Peel and the Peelites, 1846–50', *English Historical Review*, July 1958, 431–52.

'The Politics of the "Papal Agression" Crisis, 1850–51', *Canadian Catholic Historical Association Report*, 1959, 13–27.

Condon, M.D., 'The Irish Church and the Reform Ministries', *Journal of British Studies*, May 1964, 120–42.

Connell, K.H., 'The Potato in Ireland', *Past and Present*, November 1962, 57–79.

Cook, Sir E., *Delane of 'The Times'*. London, 1915.

Dalling, Lord (ed. E. Ashley), *The Life of Henry John Temple, Viscount Palmerston*, vol. 3. London, 1874.

Dasent, A.I., *John Thadeus Delane, Editor of 'The Times', His Life and Correspondence*, 2 vols. London, 1908.

Davis, H.W.C., *The Age of Grey and Peel*. Oxford, 1929.

Disraeli, B., *Lord George Bentinck: A Political Biography*. London, 1852.

Disraeli, R. (ed.), *Lord Beaconsfield's Correspondence with his Sister, 1832–1852*. London, 1886.

Dobson, W., *History of the Parliamentary Representation of Preston*. London, 1856.

Dod, C.R., *The Parliamentary Companion*. London, 1841 *et seq.*
Electoral Facts from 1832 to 1852. London, 1852.

Dreyer, F.A., 'The Whigs and the Political Crisis of 1845', *English Historical Review*, July 1965, 514–37.

Duffy, Sir C.G., *Young Ireland: A Fragment of Irish History*. London, 1880.

Duncombe, T.H., *The Life and Correspondence of Thomas Slingby Duncombe*, vol. 2. London, 1868.

Edwards, T.C., 'Papal Aggression: 1851', *History Today*, December 1951, 42–9.

Enfield, Viscountess (ed.), *Leaves from the Diary of Henry Greville*, vol. 1. London, 1883.

Erickson, A.B., *The Public Career of Sir James Graham*. Oxford, 1952.

BIBLIOGRAPHY

Edward T. Cardwell: *Peelite*, in *Transactions of the American Philosophical Society*, April 1959.

Ernle, Lord, *English Farming, Past and Present*, revised edition by Sir D. Hall. London, 1936.

Faber, R., *Beaconsfield and Bolingbroke*. London, 1961.

Fairlie, A., 'The Nineteenth-Century Law Reconsidered', *Economic History Review*, December 1965, 562–73.

Fay, C. R., *The Corn Laws and Social England*. Cambridge, 1932.

Feiling, Sir K. G., *The Second Tory Party, 1714–1832*. London, 1938.

Fitzmaurice, Lord E., *The Life of Granville George Leveson Gower, Second Earl Granville*, vol. 1. London, 1905.

Fletcher, G., *Parliamentary Portraits of the Present Period*. London, 1862.

Fraser, Sir W., *Disraeli and his Day*. London, 1891.

Fulford, R., *The Prince Consort*. London, 1949.

Gash, N., *Politics in the Age of Peel*. London, 1953.

    Reaction and Reconstruction in English Politics, 1832–52. Oxford, 1965.

    'Ashley and the Conservative Party in 1842', *English Historical Review*, October 1938, 679–81.

    'F. R. Bonham: Conservative "Political Secretary", 1832–47', *English Historical Review*, October 1948, 502–22.

    'Peel and the Party System, 1830–50', *Transactions of the Royal Historical Society*, 5th Series, 1950, 47–69.

Gathorne-Hardy, A. E. (ed.), *Gathorne Hardy, First Earl of Cranbrook, A Memoir*, vol. 1. London, 1910.

Gladstone, W. E., 'The History of 1852–60 and Greville's Latest Journals', *English Historical Review*, April 1887, 281–302.

Gooch, G. P. (ed.), *The Later Correspondence of Lord John Russell, 1840–1878*, vol. 1. London, 1925.

Greville, C. C. F. (ed. H. Reeve), *A Journal of the Reign of Queen Victoria from 1837 to 1852*, 3 vols. London, 1885.

    A Journal of the Reign of Queen Victoria from 1852 to 1860, vol. 1. London, 1887.

Grey, Earl, *The Colonial Policy of Lord John Russell's Administration*, 2 vols. London, 1853.

Grigg, D. B., *The Agricultural Revolution in South Lincolnshire*. Cambridge, 1966.

Guttsman, W. L., *The British Political Elite*. London, 1965.

Halévy, E. (trans. E. I. Watkin), *A History of the English People in the Nineteenth Century*, vols. 3 and 4. Benn edition, 1962.

Harris, W., *The History of the Radical Party in Parliament*. London, 1885.

Hearnshaw, F. J. C., *Conservatism in England*. London, 1933.

Henderson, W. O., 'Charles Pelham Villiers', *History*, February 1952, 146–57.

Herries, E., *Memoir of the Public Life of the Right Honourable John Charles Herries*, 2 vols. London, 1880.

Hexter, J. H., 'The Protestant Revival and the Catholic Question in England, 1778–1829', *Journal of Modern History*, September 1936, 297–319.

Hill, R. L., *Toryism and the People, 1832–46*. London, 1929.

Hirst, F. W., *Gladstone as Financier and Economist*. London, 1931.

Holland, B., *The Fall of Protection, 1840–50*. London, 1913.

Hovell, M., *The Chartist Movement*. London, 1925.

Hughes, J. R. T., *Fluctuations in Trade, Industry and Finance: a Study of British Economic Development, 1850–60*. Oxford, 1960.

Hutcheon, W., (ed.), *Whigs and Whiggism: Political Writings by Benjamin Disraeli*. London, 1913.

Irving, J., *Annals of Our Time*. London, 1869.

Jennings, L. J. (ed.), *The Correspondence and Diaries of the Late Right Honourable John Wilson Croker*, vols. 2 and 3. London, 1885.

Johnson, D. W. J., 'Sir James Graham and the Derby Dilly', *University of Birmingham Historical Journal*, January 1953, 66–80.

Jones, E. L., 'English Farming Before and During the Nineteenth Century', *Economic History Review*, August 1962, 145–52.

Jones, W. D., *Lord Derby and Victorian Conservatism*. Oxford, 1956.

Jones Parry, E. (ed.), *The Correspondence of Lord Aberdeen and Princess Lieven, 1832–1854*, 2 vols. London, 1939.

Kebbel, T. E., *Selected Speeches of the Right Honourable, the Earl of Beaconsfield*. London, 1882.
　History of Toryism from 1783 to 1881. London, 1886.
　Life of Lord Beaconsfield. London, 1888.
　The Life of the Earl of Derby. London, 1892.
　Lord Beaconsfield and Other Tory Memories. London, 1907.

Kelley, R., *The Transatlantic Persuasion: The Liberal–Democratic Mind in the Age of Gladstone*. New York, 1969.

Kemp, B., 'The General Election of 1841', *History*, June 1952, 146–57.
　'Reflections on the Repeal of the Corn Laws', *Victorian Studies*, March 1962, 189–204.

Kent, J., *The Racing Life of George Cavendish Bentinck, M.P., and Other Reminiscences*. London, 1892.
　Records and Reminiscences of Goodwood and the Dukes of Richmond. London, 1896.

Kitson Clark, G., *Peel and the Conservative Party*. London, 1929.
　The Making of Victorian England. London, 1962.

BIBLIOGRAPHY

An Expanding Society: Britain, 1830–1900. London, 1967.

'The Repeal of the Corn Laws and the Politics of the Forties', *Economic History Review*, August 1951, 1–13.

'The Electorate and the Repeal of the Corn Laws', *Transactions of the Royal Historical Society*, 5th Series, 1951, 109–26.

'Hunger and Politics in 1842', *Journal of Modern History*, December 1953, 355–74.

Lang, A., *Life, Letters and Diaries of Sir Stafford Northcote, First Earl of Iddlesleigh*, vol. 1. London, 1890.

Lawson-Tancred, M., 'The Anti-League and the Corn Law Crisis of 1846', *Historical Journal*, III, 2(1960), 162–83.

Leader, R. E., *Life and Letters of John Arthur Roebuck*. London, 1897.

Le May, G. H. L., 'The Ministerial Crisis of 1851', *History Today*, June 1951, 52–8.

Lever, T. (ed.), *The Letters of Lady Palmerston*. London, 1876.

Lewis, G. F. (ed.), *Letters of the Right Honourable Sir George Cornewall Lewis, Bart., to Various Friends*. London, 1870.

Londonderry, Marchioness of, *Letters from Benjamin Disraeli to Frances Anne, Marchioness of Londonderry, 1837–61*. London, 1938.

Lucas, R., *Lord Glenesk and 'The Morning Post'*. London, 1910.

MacCarthy, D. and Russell, A., *Lady John Russell, A Memoir*. London, 1910.

Maccoby, S., *English Radicalism, 1832–52*. London, 1935.

Magnus, Sir P., *Gladstone*, 2nd edition. London, 1963.

Malmesbury, Earl of, *Memoirs of an Ex-Minister*, vol. 1. London, 1884.

Martin, T., *A Life of Lord Lyndhurst*. London, 1883.

Martineau, H., *Letters From Ireland*. London, 1852.

Martineau, J., *The Life of Henry Pelham, Fifth Duke of Newcastle*. London, 1908.

Mask (pseud.), *Pencillings of Politicians*. London, 1839.

Maxwell, Sir H., *The Life and Letters of George William Frederick, Fourth Earl of Clarendon*, vol. 1. London, 1913.

Maynall, J., *The Annals of Yorkshire*, vol. 1. London, 1878.

McCalmont, F. H., *The Parliamentary Poll Book*. Nottingham, 1910.

McCord, N., *The Anti-Corn Law League*. London, 1958.

McDowell, R. B., *British Conservatism, 1832–1914*. London, 1959.

Milburn, J. B., *The Restored Hierarchy, 1850–1910*. London, 1911.

Molesworth, N. W., *The History of England from the Year 1830*, vols. 1 and 2. London, 1871–2.

Monypenny, W. F. and Buckle, G. E., *The Life of Benjamin Disraeli, Earl of Beaconsfield*, vols. 2 and 3. London, 1912 and 1914.

Moore, D. C., 'The Corn Laws and High Farming', *Economic History Review*, December 1965, 544–61.

Morley, J., *The Life of William Ewart Gladstone*, vol. 1. London, 1903. *The Life of Richard Cobden*, 2 vols. London, 1908.

Morrell, W. P., *British Colonial Policy in the Age of Peel and Russell*. Oxford, 1930.

Mosse, G. L., 'The Anti-League: 1844–46', *Economic History Review*, December 1947, 134–42.

Non-Elector, *Lord John Manners: A Political and Literary Sketch*. London, 1872.

Norman, E. R., *Anti-Catholicism in Victorian England*. London, 1968.

Nowlan, K. B., *The Politics of Repeal*. London, 1965. 'The Meaning of Repeal in Irish History', *Historical Studies*, IV, 1–17.

Office of *The Times*, *The History of The Times*, vols. 1 and 2. London, 1935 and 1939.

Orwin, C. S. and Whetham, E. H., *History of British Agriculture, 1846–1914*. London, 1964.

Parker, C. S., *Sir Robert Peel From his Private Papers*, vols. 2 and 3. London, 1899. *The Life and Letters of Sir James Graham*, 2 vols. London, 1907.

Paul, H., *A History of Modern England*, vol. 1. London, 1904.

Peel, G. (ed.), *The Private Papers of Sir Robert Peel*. London, 1920.

Penty, A. J., *Protection and the Social Problem*. London, 1926.

Petrie, Sir C., *The Carlton Club*. London, 1955.

Pollard, W., *The Stanleys of Knowsley*. Liverpool, 1868.

Raikes, H. (ed.), *Private Correspondence of Thomas Raikes with the Duke of Wellington and Other Distinguished Contemporaries*. London, 1861.

Raikes, T., *A Portion of the Journal Kept by Thomas Raikes, Esq., from 1831 to 1847*, vols. 3 and 4. London, 1857.

Ramsay, A. A. W., *Sir Robert Peel*. London, 1928.

Raymond, E. T., *Disraeli: The Alien Patriot*. London, 1925.

Read, D., *Cobden and Bright: A Victorian Political Partnership*. London, 1967.

Redford, A., *Labour Migration in England, 1800–50*. London, 1926.

Reid, T. W., *The Life, Letters and Friendships of Richard Monckton Milnes, First Lord Houghton*, 2 vols. London, 1862.

Riches, N., *The Agricultural Revolution in Norfolk*. North Carolina, 1937.

Richmond, Duke of, *Memoir of Charles Gordon Lennox, Fifth Duke of Richmond*. London, 1862.

Roberts, D., *Victorian Origins of the Welfare State*. New Haven, 1960.

BIBLIOGRAPHY

Rostow, W. W., *British Economy of the Nineteenth Century*. Oxford, 1948.

Russell, Lord John, *Recollections and Suggestions, 1813–73*. London, 1873.

St John-Stevas, N. (ed.), *Bagehot's Historical Essays*. New York, 1965.

Saintsbury, G., *The Earl of Derby*. London, 1892.

Schwabe, S., *Reminiscences of Richard Cobden*. London, 1895.

Smart, W., 'The Antecedents of the Corn Law of 1815', *English Historical Review*, July 1909, 470–89.

Smellie, K. B., *A Hundred Years of English Government*. London, 1950.

Southgate, D., *The Passing of the Whigs, 1832–1886*. London, 1962.

'*The Most English Minister...*': *The Policies and Politics of Palmerston*. London, 1966.

Spring, D., 'The English Landed Estate in the Age of Coal and Iron: 1830–1880', *Journal of Economic History*, Winter 1951, 3–24.

'Earl Fitzwilliam and the Corn Laws', *American Historical Review*, January 1954, 287–304.

'A Great Agricultural Estate: Netherby Under Sir James Graham, 1820–1845', *Agricultural History*, April 1955, 73–81.

'English Land Ownership in the Nineteenth Century: a Critical Note', *Economic History Review*, April 1957, 472–84.

Stanhope, Earl of and Cardwell, E. (ed.), *Memoirs by the Right Honourable Sir Robert Peel*, vol. 2. London, 1858.

Stanhope, Earl of, *Notes of Conversations with the Duke of Wellington, 1831–1851*. London, 1888.

Stanmore, Lord, *The Earl of Aberdeen*. London, 1893.

Sidney Herbert, Lord Herbert of Lea, vol. 1. London, 1906.

Stewart, R. M., 'The Ten Hours and Sugar Crises of 1844: Government and the House of Commons in the Age of Reform', *Historical Journal*, XII, 1(1969), 35–57.

Stuart, C. H., 'The Formation of the Coalition Cabinet of 1852', *Transactions of the Royal Historical Society*, 5th Series, 1954, 45–68.

Thomas, J. A., *The House of Commons, 1832–1901*. Cardiff, 1939.

'The House of Commons, 1832–67', *Economica*, April 1929, 49–61.

'The Repeal of the Corn Laws', *Economica*, April 1929, 53–60.

Thompson, F. M. L., *English Landed Society in the Nineteenth Century*. London, 1963.

'English Landownership: the Ailesbury Trust, 1832–56', *Economic History Review*, August 1958, 121–32.

'Whigs and Liberals in the West Riding, 1830–1860', *English Historical Review*, April 1959, 214–39.

Tilby, A. W., *Lord John Russell: A Study in Civil and Religious Liberty*. London, 1930.

Tollemache, L. A., *Talks with Mr Gladstone*. London, 1898.

Tooke, T. and Newmarch, W., *A History of Prices and of the State of Circulation from 1792 to 1856*, vols. 4, 5 and 6. London, 1928 edition.

Torrens, W. M. (ed.), *Memoirs of Viscount Melbourne*. London, 1890.

Trevelyan, G. O., *Life and Letters of Lord Macaulay*, 2 vols. London, 1883.

Walker-Smith, D., *The Protectionist Case in the 1840s*. Oxford, 1933.

Walling, R. A. J. (ed.), *The Diaries of John Bright*. London, 1930.

Walpole, S., *The Life of Lord John Russell*, 2 vols. London, 1889.

Ward, J. T., 'West Riding Landowners and the Corn Laws', *English Historical Review*, April 1966, 256–72.

Ward-Perkins, C. N., 'The Commercial Crisis of 1847', *Oxford Economic Papers*, 1950, 74–94.

Whibley, C., *Lord John Manners and his Friends*, 2 vols. London, 1925.

Whyte, J. H., *The Independent Irish Party, 1850–9*. Oxford, 1958.

'The Influence of the Catholic Clergy on Elections in Nineteenth-Century Ireland', *English Historical Review*, April 1960, 239–59.

Woodham-Smith, C., *The Great Hunger*. London ,1962.

Woodward, E. L., *The Age of Reform, 1815–70*. Oxford, 1938.

Young, G. M., *Victorian England: Portrait of an Age*, 2nd edition. London, 1953.

INDEX